Samuel Tilden

The Real 19th President

Elected by the People's Vote

Nikki Oldaker with John Bigelow

"When the People Rise the System Gets Cleansed"...
—Samuel Jones Tilden

Dedicated To All Future
Presidential Candidates...BEWARE!

Acknowledgments

I'd like to thank my dear sweet husband, Eric Oldaker, who worked endless hours honing characters traits I would have overlooked. To my mother-in-law, Mrs. Joyce B. Oldaker, who contributed her editing skills and time to assist me. A very special personal thank you to my closest friend, confidant and publicist, Norma A. Lee for always being there to encourage me to keep moving forward in life and to pursue my dreams and goals. A special thanks to all the National Arts Club Presidents for preserving Samuel Tilden's historical landmark Gramercy Park home. Last but not least to the Trustees of the New York Public Library for continuing to support Samuel Tilden's dream of a free public library for all.

Contents

Part One

Tilden

Chapter One—November 6, 1876—New York City 11

Chapter Two—November 7, 1876, Election Day 16

Chapter Three—Tilden is President Elect 19

Chapter Four—Hayes Admits Defeat 25

Chapter Five—Democrats Celebrate 28

Chapter Six—Conspiracy to Steal a Presidency 30

Chapter Seven—Day After Election 38

Chapter Eight—Which Candidate wins? 46

Chapter Nine—Fearing the Worse 59

Chapter Ten—Soldiers Ordered to Keep the Peace... 62

Chapter Eleven—Legal Electors 67

Chapter Twelve—Scandals and Assumptions 74

Chapter Thirteen—Certificates Are Opened 78

Chapter Fourteen—Negotiations Begin 83

Chapter Fifteen—Chance Meeting 87

Chapter Sixteen—Publishing the Case 91

Chapter Seventeen—Messages Galore 94

Chapter Eighteen—New Rules 97

Chapter Nineteen—Christmas Eve 1876   106

Chapter Twenty—The Special Commission Bill   116

Chapter Twenty-One—Special Commission Act Passes   122

Chapter Twenty-Two—A problem with the Independent Justice   128

Chapter Twenty-Three—A Republican Victory   134

Chapter Twenty-Four—Your Fraudulency—Old 7 to 8   141

Part Two

Samuel J. Tilden

Chapter One   153

Chapter Two   178

Chapter Three   198

Appendices

Draft of the Address Prepared for the Minority
of the Electoral Commission of 1877   252

Last Will and Testament   261

To the Mayor, Alderman, and Commonalty
of the City of New York   278

PART ONE

"Tilden"

Adapted from a screenplay by Nikki Oldaker

—based on a true story

November 6, 1876
New York City

The sign on the door indicates *Managing Editor* and the name above the sign is *John C. Reid*. It is Election Eve and the mood is tense for the two reform candidates running for President of the United States in the Centennial election. The Republicans are fearful, feeling that in this election the Democrats are going to win the White House from them. The National Headquarters for both the Republicans and Democrats are in New York City. As Reid looks through his office windows at the bustling city street below, he can almost feel the damp and bone chilling drizzle that is steadily falling from the overcast sky, a typical New England weather event New Yorkers are accustom to. He thinks to himself, *Damn Dirty Democrats are going to win the White House.* A majority of the city dwellers are home with their families hunkered down by their fireplaces while hundreds of others, that are loyal to both parties, parade around in the streets holding up campaign signs.

On this election eve, not one voter, the party leaders on either side or the candidates themselves, suspect that any newspaper editor has any reason or the influence to devise a scheme to hijack the election. However, this editor not only understands the power of the press, but also has every intention on using it. This newsman knows his paper has the credibility to pull it off and he is willing to put his reputation on the line to confuse the voting results. *After all,* he thinks to himself, *why be the managing editor of the* New York Times *if you can't wield some of that power and influence when it's important and necessary to do so?*

The Democratic Campaign Headquarters located at the Everett House on 4th and 17th streets is a short distance from the Republican Headquarters, situated in the 5th Avenue Hotel on 5th Avenue and 23rd streets. The Democratic nominee is New York Governor Samuel Jones Tilden. He is popular for his reform tactics and the takedown of Tammany Hall Boss William Tweed and the Mid West Canal Rings. The Republican candidate is Rutherford B. Hayes, also known for his reform tactics. He is currently Governor of Ohio, a Civil War veteran and hero to his party. Hayes and most of his supporters are fearful that they're going to lose control of the White House and be blamed for the corruption running rampant in the current Grant Administration. They are counting on keeping control in the Senate and have plans to win back control from the Democrats in the House.

The latest polls are showing Tilden slightly ahead by a comfortable margin. Many in the country are dismayed with politics after two terms of scandal within the Grant administration. The Democrats boast of having over half the country's population and are ready for change. They are convinced if Tilden wins, they will have it. At the present time, not one person realizes or even imagines that in a few days there will be protesting riots in the streets with bloodshed and anarchy. After all, the Civil War has just recently ended and the bloody violence with it. The country is in the midst of healing itself.

John C. Reid, as Managing Editor, continues to analyze and monitor the pre-election results for the *New York Times*. He spent time in the infamous Libby Prison Camp where an estimated 56,000 prisoners died of disease and malnutrition. As a vocal advocate for Negro equality during the Civil War he defended the rights of freedom for all men regardless of color. Reid doesn't like the Democrats and he likes Tilden even less. Though Tilden is against slavery and wants reforms in the South, something with which Reid is in total agreement, this does nothing to reduce his distaste for the Democratic candidate. Reid wants Hayes and the Republicans to run the country and no one or no thing is going to change his mind. *And I'm going to do everything I can to make it happen, even if it means committing … fraud,* he thinks to himself. With this final thought and this very last word, he pauses; the simple word "fraud" leaves a bad taste in his mouth. But just as suddenly his thoughts return to the Democrats and their candidate. Steeling himself and his resolve once more, he realizes he must remain focused. He knows what he must do and has spent a lot of time planning his scheme. He knows he needs the support of the Republican leaders to pull this off. He must convince the party leaders that the three states of Louisiana, South Carolina and Florida are key to taking the election from Tilden. As long as these three states remain under reconstruction and Republican control under the Grant administration, there's a good chance his plan to deceive will work. *Certainly the current President and his Republican Administration will support his efforts,* he thinks to himself. He also takes into account Tilden's a man of high integrity and ego and that he'll go along with a recount, just to prove to the populous that he has won the election fair and square. Reid's plan is flawless as far as he's concerned, the *Public Trust or Article II of the U.S. Constitution – clause 3 –* are just minor issues that can be dealt with swiftly and efficiently at a later time.

The Electors shall meet in their respective States, and vote by Ballot for two Persons, of whom one at least shall not be an Inhabitant of the same State with themselves. And they shall make a List of all the Persons voted for, and of the Number of Votes for each; which List they shall sign and certify, and transmit sealed to the Seat of the Government of the United States, directed to the President of the Senate. The President of the Senate shall in the Presence of the Senate and House of Representatives, open all the Certificates, and the Votes shall then be counted. The Person having the greatest Number of Votes shall be the President, if such Number be a Majority of the whole Number of Electors appointed; and if there be more than one who have such Majority, and have an equal Number of Votes, then the House of Representatives shall immediately chuse by Ballot one of them for President; and if no Person have a Majority, then from the five highest on the List the said House shall in like Manner chuse the President. But in chusing the President, the Votes shall be taken by States, the Representation from each State having one Vote; A quorum for this Purpose shall consist of a Member or Members from two thirds of the States, and a Majority of all the States shall be necessary to a Choice. In every Case, after the Choice of the President, the Person having the greatest Number of Votes of the Electors shall be the Vice President. But if there should remain two or more who have equal Votes, the Senate shall chuse from them by Ballot the Vice President.

Reid, now focused, is determined and ready to rock the boat of the American voting system and the people who put their faith in it. He's a writer and editor with great influence, and he knows how to challenge others. He has done it everyday for a living. He knows that the words in the U.S. Constitution are just words with great intent to create a system of justice for the people and written by good men. It is his conclusion that these words, just like the men from the past that wrote them, are flawed.

✦

Born February 9, 1814, Samuel Jones Tilden was a frail child and he spent many days during his childhood fighting off colds and fevers. During his on again off again recuperating periods, he would spend many hours reading his beloved collection of books. Since his childhood, Tilden was always exceptionally brainy and analyzing numbers came naturally to him. During his youth he was exposed to many of the leading political leaders of the day because of his father's connections to local, state and federal politicians. President Martin Van Buren was one of Samuel's favorites and a close friend of the Tilden family. Van Buren spent years during his own political career mentoring young Tilden as well as consulting with him about the issues of the day.

As he grew older, Samuel's education and life experiences in law, politics and economics groomed him for the Presidency. He appreciates his social life and values his privacy. He has become one of America's top notch corporate attorneys during the rail development across the nation and has represented the legal interests of many wealthy clients, while also investing in coal mines and such other like businesses. These clients have earned him millions, making him one of the wealthiest and most affluent attorneys in the country.

The things that Samuel holds most dear in his life is his family, intelligent conversation, beautiful women, riding and owning spirited horses. Art and rare book collections are his passions, as well as economics, law, writing government policies and political reforms. His skills in these areas, with his honesty, have earned him the public's trust and admiration. Tilden is considered by many of his peers to be the *greatest Democrat ever and master of all political strategy.* He greatly admires the talents and culture of artists, playwrights and actors for their contributions to the world. He often invites them to his home to mingle with political associates at social gatherings. He also includes many young people to attend his gatherings and introduces them to his business associates to start the young entrepreneurs off with sound business advice and seed money to launch their endeavors. Tilden believes strongly that the younger generations are the future of America and he advises them to watch over their and others rights as American citizens and to guard American ideals with jealous care.

Tilden is regarded as a hero by many for testifying for hours, at the now famous Boss Tweed Tammany Hall trial. He explained in detail, to the jury and all others present, how Tweed and his cronies pilfered and diverted up to $200M of taxpayer dollars from city and state coffers. It took two trials before Boss Tweed was convicted for forgery and grand larceny. Soon after, Tweed escaped prison and fled to Cuba – then later to Spain, to avoid being captured. Tilden was relentless in his efforts to locate Tweed. Eventually, he found him hiding in Spain and had him extradited back to New York to finish his prison sentence. Tweed once recaptured and returned to prison, complained, "I guess Tilden has killed me at last. I hope he is satisfied now." Boss Tweed and several of his Tammany Democrats created many political enemies for Tilden. They wanted revenge against him for his betrayal to their organization. John Kelly, the newly elected Tammany Boss, guaranteed Tilden that if he is nominated over their candidate, William Wheeler, for the Presidency, then the reformed Tammany Democrats will stand behind Tilden for President. Less than two years after being elected Governor of New York, Tilden, at age sixty-two, was nominated unanimously at the Democratic National Convention as their candidate for the 1876 Presidential election.

CHAPTER TWO

November 7, 1876, Election Day

It's cold, damp and pouring rain outside. About mid morning, Samuel, dressed in his best black suit with a red flower in the button-hole, casts his ballot near his home in Gramercy Park. While at the polls, he accepts some advanced congratulations and thanks people for their support. He makes no assumptions, at this time, whether he will win or not but he is pleased by his neighbor's care and devotion to his campaign. Once outside, he climbs into his carriage and asks his driver to take him to his campaign headquarters.

While quietly displeased with the nasty weather conditions under his breath, Samuel's coach driver works his way slowly through the crowd. He halts the carriage as close as he can to the entrance of the Everett House Campaign headquarters, in the midst of hundreds of well wishers. Tilden supporters have stood in the foul weather for hours just to get a glimpse of the man they believe is going to be the next President of the United States. Samuel, not wanting to disappoint anyone, steps out onto the street and works his way through the crowd, shaking hands and offering his gratitude for their support. When he finally makes it to the entrance to the building, he turns and waves again to the cheering crowd that is waving their hats and handkerchiefs. He enters the building in good spirits, but contemplates after experiencing the large crowd, that it might be a good idea to have someone with him when he goes out again, to get him through the assembly safely.

Once inside campaign headquarters, Samuel greets and extends his appreciation to the devoted campaign workers in the room who have worked night and day to help him get elected. Some are busy shuffling paperwork while others count voter returns on a large tally board, hanging on the wall at the far end of the room. Samuel walks toward the tote board and is quickly greeted by his nephew William and other campaign managers, John Bigelow, Mr. Dan Magone and Congressman Abram Hewitt. William suggests to his uncle," You looked like you were having a good time with the crowd out there." Not giving his uncle time to respond he adds, "People can get a little rambunctious. When you leave, I'll send two of our men with you." Samuel nods in agreement.

Colonel William T. Pelton, Tilden's nephew, lived in Samuel's home as a young boy when his mother Mary Tilden Pelton, Samuel's older sister, moved in to manage his home and household affairs at the Gramercy estate. As a young boy, William was very fond of his uncle and loved Tilden like a son would love his father. Samuel's influence on William led him into the arena of politics. After attaining the rank of Colonel in the Union Army, and upon his release from the military, Colonel Pelton became the manager and Secretary of the Democratic National Committee. Unbeknown to Samuel, Williams' involvement will cost him dearly in the days to come, including their close and trusting relationship.

John Bigelow, a man in his early sixties, is Tilden's closest confidant and neighbor at Gramercy. He is an American diplomat, writer, lawyer and, with William Cullen Bryant, part owner and editor of the *New York Evening Post*. He writes editorials enthusiastically supporting free trade and denouncing slavery, an issue he and Samuel strongly agree upon. In 1861 he traveled to Paris as consul general under the Lincoln Administration and in 1865-66 served as the U.S. minister to France. While in France, Bigelow was instrumental in generating support for the Union cause and discouraged Napoleon III from undertaking an imperial expedition to Mexico. Samuel treasures their friendship and John's advice.

Bigelow steps up beside William and announces to Samuel, "Bets are running one-hundred to eighty in your favor." Samuel, delighted by the news and numbers responds modestly, "Are they now? You can tell this already? It's hardly afternoon."

"We suspect a landslide," Dan Magone adds. Magone, another of Tilden's campaign managers, is the Chairman of the New York State Democratic Committee.

Congressman Abram Hewitt, Chairman of the National Democratic Committee as well as a businessman who has been recently elected to Congress, chimes in, "Telegrams are telling of victory every minute." Samuel stares at Hewitt for a moment with pause and Hewitt questions, "Do you doubt it?" Samuel not wanting to seem too confident smiles and turns back to the tote board, "I certainly do not doubt your expertise."

With both Dan Magone and Congressman Abram Hewitt, Samuel feels he has a winning team working on his behalf. He also knows he has an advantage over Hayes with both the Republican and Democratic National Campaign headquarters being located in New York City. It gives him more opportunity to micro-manage this campaign than it does Hayes, who resides in Ohio and can not easily access his managers.

CHAPTER THREE

Tilden is President Elect

A few hours later in front of the Tilden mansion at Gramercy Park, hundreds of spectators and supporters have congested the streets, holding and waving their campaign signs for Tilden. This is a much larger crowd than the one he had just experienced a few hours earlier in front of the Everett house. The people have gathered in the streets near the front and on both sides of the park, in front of his home. They want to be a part of history and to get a closer look at their next President when he arrives.

Standing in the bay windows in the front of the house, Mary Tilden Pelton watches the growing crowd with a few of her closest friends and other family members living at the Tilden estate. Mary is Samuels' older sister and William's mother. After becoming a wealthy attorney, Samuel invited his sister to move in with her son and his family so she could take charge of his household.

Sarah, a well-known New York Socialite and one of Mary's dearest friends, stands nearby with the others, waiting for Samuel's arrival. Each of these women is filled with just as much anticipation as the spectators outdoors. Mary, always her younger brother's protector becomes more concerned for Samuel's safety as she glances at the gathering crowd. With no open access through the mass of people to the streets beyond, she thinks to herself, *He'll have to walk through them, just to get into the house.*

Mr. Smith, Samuel's personal Secretary, is a quiet, shy man in his late forties. Along with his assistant, he is seated behind a desk in the Reading Room, busily receiving telegrams. The Reading Room is located just off the Living Room, where the smaller crowd of Tilden family and friends have gathered. Several butlers and housekeepers quietly go in and out of the dining area, setting up a lunch buffet. Mary, not moving from the window, remarks with some concern, "So many people... just standing in the rain."

One of the four Socialites responds with glee, "A little rain won't melt them Mary – They're here to see your brother. He'll make an admirable President. We're so happy for both of you."

Mary looks back from the window at the ladies and asks, "Would there be any interest amongst my nearest and dearest friends wanting to fill the position of First Lady?" One of the women blurts out, "I would of course." Another declares, "I want to be the first to dance with Samuel at the Inaugural Ball." Sarah, without skipping a beat, snobbishly quips, "After me you will."

Mary is amused by the friendly back biting between her friends and pushes back the window curtain a little further so she can see better. Good-naturedly she scolds, "Ladies – remember your manners. We are high society, after all." The ladies giggle and continue to peer out the window and enjoy the exhilaration of the crowd.

Outside in front of the mansion, hundreds of people continue to wave their hats and handkerchiefs, focusing on the arrival of Samuel's horse and carriage. It is quite an honor to stand in the rain so they can be the first to congratulate the next President of the United States. Many have heard by early rumors from newsmen that Samuel has already beaten Hayes by a large number of popular votes. The crowd, growing more enormous by the minute, does not seem to care that they could catch a cold with the damp rain falling steady from the overcast sky. Many of them believe that just like a wedding couple when getting married on a rainy day it's a sign of good luck for Samuel's election.

Working the horse and carriage carefully through the gathering crowd, Samuel's driver calls out, "Coming through. Make room for me to pass please! I have with me the next President of the United States!" Samuel, amused by the driver's remarks, calls out to him, "A bit premature don't you think?" The driver turns back to look at Samuel through the carriage window, "The Presidency is yours and they know it. It's an honor to drive you."

Inside the carriage and sitting opposite Samuel, are two good-sized men, former Civil War soldiers. William had earlier asked them to escort his uncle through the crowds safely and the men were honored to do so. Security was never an issue before this day for Samuel, but with all the people approaching him he figured it was a good idea just for today. He was hoping that once the excitement wore down, it would be something he wouldn't have to depend on again. More than anything, Samuel cherishes his privacy and enjoys his freedom to take walks and ride his horse down the streets of New York City.

Inside the mansion, Mary moves away from the window toward the buffet table to inspect the food. "He must be famished," she says to no one in particular. Sarah walks over to Mary, takes her by the hand and leads her toward the foyer and the front entrance. Sarah, energized by all the excitement, notes "The food looks just fine. Come, let's go outside – this is a once in a life time event and I don't want to miss one minute more." Smiling at her friend's obvious excitement, Mary follows Sarah's lead to the front entrance without argument. The other ladies excitedly agree and follow Mary and Sarah to the outside front porch. Cheers from the crowd fill the air as the women make their appearance. Sarah, Mary and the other women wave their handkerchiefs back at the crowd and wait with the others for Samuel to exit from his carriage, which has just pulled to a stop amongst the cheering crowd.

The door of the carriage opens and two guards are the first to step out onto the street. They quickly command the crowd," Step back please! Make room for Mr. Tilden!" With full confidence in his two burly escorts, Samuel steps out of the carriage onto the street. Hundreds of cheering spectators huddle around the candidate, waving their handkerchiefs and hats. The two escorts politely push back the nearest people of the crowd, clearing a path for Samuel to walk through. He is elated by the experience. As he greets and shakes hands while walking through the crowd, his thoughts rush through him like a waterfall. *What a beautiful moment. The people are here verifying their belief in me and confirming my trust in them. I can feel my heart pound and my body filling with a feeling of warmth and goodness all around me. Are they so sure I am elected President?* Samuel notices Mary, Sarah and the other ladies through the sea of people as he makes his way to the front steps of the mansion. He acknowledges them with a wave of his hand and they wave back. While he moves through the swells of well wishers to the front steps, he continues to express his pleasure with their overwhelming approval of his future Presidency. The entire day has been surreal to him and he knows that it doesn't get any better than this.

Mary, leaning toward Sarah, quietly says, "He has aspired to this goal for such a long time. I can hardly believe it is happening."

Sarah places her hand on Mary's arm. "I would be honored to be his wife and your sister-in-law, Mary. However, Samuel must be proper and ask for my hand. So far, I've heard no indication of interest from him."

Mary is pleased by Sarah's declaration. "My brother is a New England gentleman. If it is you he chooses, then he will ask proper."

Finally, as Samuel makes his way up the steps to the women, he reaches out to Mary, takes her hand and kisses her on the cheek. He greets the other ladies by taking each of their hands. Taking a moment, he turns and waves to the crowd again, before turning back to the door and entering the house with the women. Once inside the house, they can all still hear the crowds chanting Tilden's name in the background.

⟋⫟⟍

In an area of the street not far from the house, a large group of reporters from newspapers all across the country are scribbling notes. Amongst this group is John Reid, Managing Editor. He is not full of merriment like the rest of the assembly. After a few minutes of observing the throng of people around him, he frowns and then begins to walk the few blocks down the road to where his horse is tied at a hitching post. He can still hear the roar and chanting of Tilden's name in the background. With a slight show of disgust on his face, he stuffs his notebook into his saddlebag, mounts the steed and trots away from the Gramercy park event. He's dismayed and somewhat surprised by the large crowds and their great enthusiasm for the Democratic candidate he despises. He is also all the extra convinced and more determined than ever to do whatever he can to derail Tilden's entrance into the White House.

Inside the mansion, Samuel and the ladies have moved into the Reading Room, discussing the day's events. Their chatter is boisterous and is disturbing Mr. Smith and his assistant from doing their work. The telegram machine keeps ticking non-stop and Mr. Smith continues deciphering telegrams at his desk. With the help of his assistant, they continue to translate the pulses of current, deflecting the electromagnet marker, which produces written codes onto strips of paper – dependant upon the telegraph.

In the year to follow, 1877, a rival technology will be developed that will again change the face of communication. Alexander Graham Bell's notebook entry of 10 March 1876 describes his successful experiment with the telephone. Speaking through the instrument to his assistant, Thomas A. Watson, who is in the next room, Bell utters these famous first words, "Mr. Watson – come here – I want to see you." At the time of this current Presidential election, telephone technology is not yet available, but will be wired into the White House during 1877, thus making it the new-fangled way to communicate across the nation.

Smith, while reviewing one of the wires briefly looks up for a moment at Samuel. Catching his glance, Samuel asks," More good news?" Smith nods in agreement, motions a brief wave and returns without further pause back to translating the messages. Samuel, being a man of good work ethic and concentration himself, is not offended by the short response from Smith. He realizes the chattering ladies are distracting Mr. Smith's from completing his work and he politely suggests to the women," Perhaps we should go into the next room to chat and have a bite to eat." He leads the ladies toward the buffet, favoring Sarah whom he has on his right arm. As they walk into the next room they see a beautifully arrange buffet of fresh fruits, teas, sandwiches and flowers, Samuel comments to Sarah, "This is turning out to be an eventful day."

Sarah, without hesitation responds, "Poor Mr. Hayes – He never stood a chance against you." While filling a small plate with food, Samuel replies, "The Ohio Governor is a worthy opponent."

"He may be worthy, dear brother", Mary chimes in, "but he's no match for your popularity in this election." With a smile on his face and a gleam in his eye, Samuel turns to Sarah, "I don't know what I would do without her."

A few minutes later everyone is seated comfortably and eating. Sarah turns to Samuel and declares, "I have a lively new pink silk I will wear to your Inaugural Ball. I claim the first dance with you."

Due to his shy nature and the boldness of her declaration, Samuel, with cheeks flushing, replies, "I'd be honored Sarah, to have the first dance with you." The other women display some disappointment by Samuel's promise to Sarah, but they do not express their feelings out loud. Mary, now standing next to Sarah glances at her and reaches over and takes her hand gently and firmly squeezes it into hers as she nods her approval. Samuel notices the gesture and makes no further remarks

regarding the friendship between the two as he continues trading pleas-
antries with the other ladies.

Mary leans over and whispers into Sarah's ear, "He needs a strong,
take charge woman by his side." Sarah softly smiles and the two join in
the ongoing conversation in the room.

CHAPTER FOUR

Hayes Admits Defeat

The Republican candidate for President is Rutherford B. Hayes. He is fifty-five years young as he challenges Tilden for the Presidency. Born October 4, 1822 in Delaware, Ohio, he is a retired solider who sustained injuries during the recent Civil War. He was still in the Army when the Republican Party ran him for a Congressional seat. Declining to leave his duty as a brevet major general during the campaign he stated, "An officer fit for duty who, at this crisis, would abandon his post to electioneer for a seat in Congress ought to be scalped."

At the conclusion of the war and thus the end of his military obligations, Hayes served as a member of the U.S. House of Representatives from 1865-1867. After leaving Washington he was elected governor of Ohio, where he served two separate terms not consecutively. One of the Governors in between Hayes was a man who later helped him and the Republican Party to overturn the disputed Florida electoral votes from the Democrats amid charges of fraud and incidents of violence. Two years later, a congressional investigating committee absolved Noyes of charges that he had improperly influenced the Florida canvassers by promises of political favor. Hayes' first term as Ohio's Governor was 1868-1872 and his second term has just started this year, 1876, when he decided to answer the call for the Republicans candidate for the highest office in the country. Along with his military record, Hayes is educated in law, a graduate from Kenyon College and Harvard Law School.

Rutherford Hayes married Lucy Webb Hayes in 1852. She is a devout Christian and has obtained the nickname Lemonade Lucy because she does not approve of alcohol in her home. Lucy, a graduate of Wesleyan

Female College, is a very well educated woman for her time. She and Rutherford have eight children: Birchard, the oldest at age 26, is followed by James 20, Rutherford 18, Joseph 15, George 12, Fanny 9, Scott 5 and young Manning, who sadly died before his first birthday.

It's early in the evening and supporters for Hayes have surrounded his thirty-one room estate. They have assembled just outside the gates and can be heard chanting his name while holding their campaign signs in the air. The beauty of the colorful red, burnt orange and gold autumn maple, oak and birch leafs swirl and dance in the wind, making their descent to the ground over the people. The magnificence of color is ignored though because the Republican supporters have only one thing on their minds—Hayes being elected their 19th President.

Inside the Hayes home, Lucy tries with all the courage she can muster to hold back her tears of disappointment. Several men, Republican Senator W.T. Sherman of Ohio, Rutherford Hayes and other republican campaign managers have gathered in the living room of the Hayes home. They are all equally revealing glum expressions because it is being confirmed by popular vote that Tilden has defeated Hayes in the election. Rutherford, while comforting Lucy in his arms sympathetically says to her, "There, there Lucy. It was not meant to be."

Lucy is displeased with her husband's calm submission. "It's shameful. You are more suited for the Presidency than he." Rutherford continues to comfort her, but she pulls away from him asking, "What about all those poor colored folks in the South? Who will tend to their needs?" Wouldn't you agree Senator Sherman?"

The Senator looks up and replies, "I do, my dear lady. It is quite shameful."

Rutherford stares at Sherman for a brief moment before responding, "The colored folks in the South will continue to argue for Federal Reconstruction and I'm confident President elect Tilden will do right by them."

Lucy moves away from Rutherford and walks toward the stairs. Before climbing them, she turns to the gentlemen gathered in the room and says, "Please excuse me. I feel I am becoming ill." She continues up the stairs without further comment. Hayes watches her for a brief moment and turns his gaze to the floor, feeling a wave of his own disappointment come over him. But for him, it is not only his disappointment in the results of his campaign, but a feeling that he has failed the party and the woman he loves so dearly. *Unfortunately, there's nothing I can do about it now,* he thinks to himself. Gathering his inner strength, he turns and walks back to the men gathered in the room, who have continued their conversation about the election. Hayes admits, "The voters must have gone for Tilden due to the fame he gained with Tammany Hall and his Canal Ring reforms. It seems we Republicans had little hope for success… because of *his* success."

CHAPTER FIVE

Democrats Celebrate

Back in New York at the Everett House the mood is elated. The crowd is cheering with the good news about their candidate's apparent victory. Tilden has won the popular vote by over 254,000. His die-hard fans and supporters wait to hear more about the ballot returns. Out on the streets, fires are built in garbage cans and people huddle near them to stay warm as they pass the time to hear more election news.

At the Tilden mansion the crowds of people have swelled, filling the streets for blocks. The community waits and chats amongst themselves regarding the good news. They cheer every time Samuel comes to the window to wave to them. Their boisterous roars fill the air and delight the many guests Mary has invited to celebrate her brother's victory. These people, who Samuel trusts and loves, honor him on this election night of November 7, 1876. His victory is being celebrated across the nation.

Inside the mansion, are several of his distinguished friends and family, a mixed but cultured crowd. Politicians, notable stage actors, musicians and writers gather together for a private victory party. A variety of socialites, along with Sarah, Mary, John Bigelow, Mr. Magone, Mr. Smith, Congressman Hewitt and William Pelton are included in the mix.

Standing by the staircase Mary says to Samuel, "I truly am exhausted."

For Samuel it has been a long day and he too needs rest, but he's too busy enjoying the moment to think of sleep. William enters the room and stands close to his mother and uncle. Samuel smiles and asks Mary, "Are you bored?"

Mary smiles, "Not bored, just simply tired. So if you don't mind, Mr. President elect," Mary says as she leans over to Samuel first then her son giving each a kiss on the cheek, "Tomorrow is another day." As Mary is taking her first step on the stairs, she is stopped by William, who says, "But mother, the night is still young."

"It may be, but I am not," she replies with a grin.

Samuel teases, "She's had a long day William – entertaining the ladies so she can marry me off."

Mary, never one to let her brother get the last word defends herself. "I have made no such effort."

Samuel interrupts, "Don't think I didn't notice you and Sarah."

Mary grins, realizing Samuel is on to her matchmaking efforts, "She is one of the finest ladies in New York – and would make a wonderful First Lady." Samuel smiles and says, "Be that as it may, she does not make my heart thump."

Mary responds with sarcasm, "Make your heart thump? If you are in dire need to have your heart thump before you marry, dear brother – may I suggest you try running quickly up and down these stairs a few times."

Samuel, William and others near-by chuckle at Mary's humorous remarks. Mary wishes all a good night and retreats to her room for a good night's rest.

Samuel and William continue to discuss Mary's job as hostess. William remarks, "She will bring class to the role of hostess. Does she know you mean to give her the position?" Before Samuel can answer, he is interrupted by John Bigelow and a boisterous toast. John raises his champagne glass and bellows, "A toast to Governor Tilden – our newly elected President!" The crowd raises their champagne glasses and repeats in unison, "Our newly elected President."

The spectators in the street see the toast through the large pane glass windows and begin to chant, "Tilden, Tilden, Tilden." The party continues, not ending until sometime in the early morning hours at which point Samuel has finally had enough and decides to go to bed, firmly believing he has been elected the real 19th President of the United States

CHAPTER SIX

Conspiracy to Steal
a Presidency

Between eleven and midnight Reid and his editors at the *New York Times* are gathered together inside the five-story building that is nestled between several other major print outlets nicknamed *Newspaper Row*. A messenger enters the room and hands Reid, who is seated behind his desk, a note. Reid unfolds the paper and reads it silently. He holds the note in the air for the others to see, "Gentlemen. This is from the Democratic Chairman United States Senator Barnum of Connecticut. He's asking what news we have from Louisiana, South Carolina, Oregon and Florida." The others in the room seemed stunned by the question because they all have agreed that Hayes has lost to Tilden. Reid stands from his chair and blurts out, "Don't you see? The Democrats are in doubt about the returns from Louisiana, Oregon, South Carolina and Florida. It's a close vote and we must stop the press and claim the victory for Hayes."

John Reid ponders the consequences, *If my headline and editorial casts doubt, then maybe others will follow my lead. The worse that can happen is other news organizations will question the results. It's a long shot I'm willing to risk.* Reid scribbles the headline on a notepad for the morning news, "A Doubtful Election."

Edward Cary, a member of the NY Times Board, walks up to Reid, who has now turned his attention to studying the returns on the tote, and asks, "Hewitt wants to know by what majority Tilden has defeated Hayes?"

"One moment," Reid answers. He takes an eraser in his hand and erases numbers below the Hayes and Tilden's columns under the states of Florida, South Carolina and Louisiana and then places question marks in the blank spaces. Reid turns to Cary, "Tell him Tilden has won by none." Without pause, Cary responds, "But the numbers say otherwise." Reid points to the board and snipes, "Tilden has not yet won this election."

Cary takes a moment to review the numbers on the board. "He's won by over two hundred fifty thousand votes."

Reid points with his finger to the Electoral College vote column and explains, "True, but he has *not* won the 185 electoral votes needed."

Reid walks away from Cary toward his desk where his coat is hanging over a chair. He picks up the coat and hurriedly puts it on. Turning back to Cary he announces his intentions. "I must go find Chairman Chandler to report this news." He then hands Cary the piece of paper he had earlier scribbled his headline on. "Rewrite your article and cast doubt on the election returns. Use this headline."

Cary reads the headline, raises his eyebrows and questions, "A Doubtful Election? The Democrats have won by over two hundred fifty thousands votes. Every newspaper in the country is reporting a Tilden victory."

In an arrogant tone Reid tells Cary, "*They* may be, but *we* are not! The rest of us in *this* room are in agreement."

Annoyed and confused by Reid's demand, Cary checks his watch for the time. Reid walks toward the door and before he goes he fires back, "I am going to find Chairman Chandler so that I can change his mind about conceding." Cary, now thinking Reid a fool, sarcastically reminds him of the hour. "It's the middle of the night. He'll be asleep."

Walking through the door, Reid snaps back, "Then I shall wake him!"

⟞⟝

The *New York Times* set to ink this editorial for the morning paper dated November 8, 1876: "A Doubtful Election" At the time of going to press the result of the presidential election is still in doubt. Enough has been learned to show that the voting has been unprecedentedly heavy. Both parties have exhausted their full legitimate strength, while the peculiar Democratic policy, for which such extensive preparations were made in the large registry of this city, and in the enormous registry in Brooklyn, have had its effect.

Conceding New York to Mr. Tilden, he will receive the electoral votes of the following states:

Alabama	10	Arkansas	6	Connecticut	6
Delaware	3	Georgia	11	Indiana	15
Kentucky	12	Maryland	8	Mississippi	8
Missouri	15	New Jersey	9	New York	35
North Carolina	10	Tennessee	12	Texas	8
Virginia	11	West Virginia	5		
				Total	**184**

"Governor Hayes will receive the votes of the following States:

California	.6	Colorado	.3	Illinois	21
Iowa	11	Kansas	5	Louisiana	8
Maine	7	Massachusetts	13	Michigan	11
Minnesota	.5	Nebraska	3	Nevada	3
New Hampshire	5	Ohio	3	Oregon	22
Pennsylvania	29	Rhode Island	.4	Vermont	5
Wisconsin	10	South Carolina	7		
				Total	**181**

"This leaves Florida *alone* still in doubt. *If the Republicans have carried that State, as they claim, they will have 185 votes* – a majority of one.

With the above editorial rolling on the presses for the morning news, Reid's conspiracy is now in forward motion. Hayes and the Republican party Chairman, who had already conceded the Presidency to Tilden, went to bed not knowing the election returns were being rigged and manipulated by Reid and his editors at the New York Times.

November 8, 1876

At about 2 a.m. John Reid drives his horse and carriage to the front of the Fifth Avenue Hotel that houses the Republican campaign Headquarters and stops. He jumps down from the drivers' seat onto the muddy street and ties his horse to a post. Pausing, he looks up at a lighted window for a moment then enters the building.

Once inside the empty lobby he walks quickly past the front desk. There are two uniformed clerks working behind the registration desk. At first, neither takes notice, but the older of the two clerks' looks up and glances at Reid as he passes by. Raising his eyebrow, he glances at the clock mounted on the lobby wall. Noting the hour he murmurs under his breath "A little late for visiting."

"What's that you say?" asks the other clerk.

Shaking his head, the older clerk replies "Nothing. Just noting the late hour and looking at all this paperwork we have to finish."

Down the hall from the lobby, Reid enters the campaign headquarters' and sees that the room is strewn with papers from the Election Day events. W.E. Chandler, the national committee man from New Hampshire is seated alone, slumped in a chair at the far end of the room, staring blankly at the election tote board. He's obviously depressed and has a *Tribune* newspaper in his hand. The headline reads, "Tilden Defeats Hayes."

Reid hurries over to him and asks, "Where would I find Chairman Zach Chandler?"

W.E. looks up at him wearily, his eyes bloodshot from lack of sleep. "Have you seen the *Tribune*? It's a disaster."

"Yes, quite the disaster. Now again, where would I find Chairman Chandler?"

W.E. glances at the clock on the near wall. "At this hour?"

Getting annoyed at the man's lackadaisical attitude Reid raises his voice and barks "I *must* speak with him now!"

W.E. brushes off Reid's urgency and looks back down at the newspaper in his hand. "He's probably drunk and sleeping it off in his room."

Reid quickly looks around the room to see if there is anyone else he can get to help him in his quest. There is no one available and he says to W.E. Chandler, "I must speak to him immediately.

Looking back up wearily, W.E. asks, "For what reason?"

Reid blurts back, "I need his permission to send wires to the Southern Republican Party leaders." The *New York Times* is not conceding to Tilden" Reid explains. "Hayes may still win this election if we hurry."

W.E. pauses to stare at John for a moment, then stands up and does not say another word and walks out of the room. With a last quick glance at the tote board, Reid turns and follows him.

Zachariah Chandler, originally from Bedford, New Hampshire is the chairman of the Republican National Executive Committee for the 1876 election. He is a former Senator from Michigan and ran as an unsuccessful campaign as a Whig candidate for Governor in 1852. He was elected to the United States Senate in 1857 and was reelected in 1863 and again in 1869. He was unsuccessful as a Senate candidate for reelection in 1874, and was appointed Secretary of the Interior by President Ulysses Grant from 1875 thru 1877.

W.E., with the anxious New York Times editor behind him, approaches Zach Chandler's hotel room door and knocks on it. He puts his face to the door and says, "Zach, it's me, W.E.—Zach, I need you to wake up."

Inside the room, Zach Chandler lies on his bed dressed in a rumpled bed nightshirt and cap, half-asleep. There's an empty whiskey bottle next to his bed on the floor. He hears more knocking, stirs and puts a pillow over his head. He yells out, "Go away—I'm sleeping."

Reid now joins W.E. with the door knocking. W.E. pleads, "Please Zach—wake up and answer the door. We have important news concerning the outcome of this election."

Zach struggles to get up. He climbs out of the bed, annoyed, goes to the door and peeks through the peephole. In a grumpy voice he asks, "What is it? And who is that with you?"

"I have Mr. Reid, the Managing Editor from the *New York Times*. He says he has news about the election."

Zach, now a little more alert, recognizes the name Reid. "Yes, I know who he is. What does he want?"

Reid, getting impatient with the conversation through the closed door, interrupts. "Sorry to wake you Chairman—but the news I have may change the outcome of the election. Can I please come in and discuss this with you?"

With an audible sigh, Zach opens the door and motions for the men to enter. Reid and W.E. Chandler enter and stand just inside the door as Zach lies back down on the bed, placing an arm to cover his eyes. The chairman now annoyed with this interruption of his much needed sleep, demands, "What news is so important that you wake me at this hour?"

Reid begins to blurt out his explanation. "Sir, we have a chance to turn this election around to favor Hayes. After a careful examination of the results by me and the staff at the *Times*, we—well I—realized that the Southern States of South Carolina, Florida and Louisiana are in doubt."

Removing the arm covering his eyes, Zach, now more alert, sits up. "There was no doubt by any election reports I received."

"Those three states are under Reconstruction and Federal control, Chairman," Reid replies.

"Yes—Republican control," Zach answers, narrowing his eyes. "And what of it?"

Reid sees that Zach may finally be catching on. "Yes that's right—Hayes can take this election from Tilden by the Electoral College if we can convince the Republican state leaders to count Hayes the winner." Zach turns to stare out the window for a moment, allowing these thoughts to sink in and asks, "What is it you want from me?"

Reid steps closer to Zach, "Your permission to send wires to the Republican Chairmen of these states."

Zach ponders the request for a moment and asks, "Any others?"

Reid figures, *why not ask for more* and adds, "Oregon, Nevada and California too."

Zach contemplates the request for a moment and questions Reid's motives. "Mr. Reid, you must really despise Tilden to be doing this."

"He's a Democrat. Isn't that reason enough?"

Zach stands up and approaches him. Looking the editor directly in the eye he replies, "Very well. Go ahead—do whatever you think is necessary—although I think you're insane and are probably wasting everyone's time."

Finally, Reid thinks to himself, *we'll see if he feels the same in a couple of days!* Zach and Reid shake hands. Then Reid turns, giving W.E a quick nod, and walks briskly out of the hotel room.

While listening to Reid's receding footsteps, Zach leans over into W.E.'s ear and says, "Follow him W.E.—and report his actions back to me."

Moments later, W.E. rushes through the lobby, in an effort to catch up with Reid. They both walk to the telegraph office in the hotel lobby and find a *Closed* sign on the window. Reid moves to an empty desk, pulls out a chair and sits down. W.E. follows, and stands behind him.

Reid rustles around until he finds a pen and some paper in the desk. He motions with his hand to W.E. to sit in the chair next to the desk. As W.E. sits, Reid hands him the pen and paper.

Across the room at the registration desk, the older desk clerk that had observed them earlier, strains to listen to Reid and W.E.'s conversation. The younger clerk also takes notice this time and asks in a lowered voice, "What do you supposed those two are up to?" Perturbed at the other man's interruption of his eavesdropping, the older clerk replies quietly, "I'm sure I don't know. Just mind your business." The younger man shrugs off the remark and goes back to his work, noting that his older co-worker continues to observe the two men across the lobby. Not realizing the clerk's interest, nor caring if he did, Reid says to W.E., "I'll dictate, you write."

W.E., with the paper in front of him, and pen in his hand, asks "Ok, but how will we send these?" He then motions to the "Closed" sigh on the telegraph office door.

"The main wire office will be open," Reid replies. "We must hurry though, as there is little time." W.E. Chandler writes the information as Reid dictates, "To D.H. Chamberlain—South Carolina. Hayes is elected if we can carry South Carolina. Can you hold your State? Answer immediately. Sign it Chairman, Zach Chandler."

Reid waits for W.E. to finish writing and says, "We'll use the same message to the other states. We can fill in the names of the other States and their Chairmen when we get to the wire office."

Approvingly, W.E. responds, "Of course," as he finishes with the message. They both stand from their chairs and walk toward the hotel's front entrance door.

Back at the front desk, the older hotel clerk watches Reid and W.E. leave the hotel. He goes to a nearby coat rack and pulls his coat off the stand. He turns to the younger clerk and says, "Keep an eye on things. I have something I need to attend to." He puts on his coat and walks out the front entrance.

It is about three a.m. when Reid and W.E. arrive at the 23rd Street telegraph office. The telegraph clerk behind the counter is reading back the message to be sent. Both Reid and W.E. become impatient while waiting for him to finish.

"Is there a problem?" Reid questions the clerk.

The clerk asks, "Who is going to pay for these?" W.E. steps forward and says, "The Republican Party committee. I'll authorize it."

The clerk shakes his head disapproving, "My apologies, sir, but I'll need approval directly from the Chairman." Reid grabs the invoice from the clerk and signs his name to it and writes down an account number. He then pushes it back to the clerk, and barks, "Here! This is *my* account number. Charge it to the *New York Times*." The clerk pauses for a moment, examining the signature on the invoice. He looks back at the two men, then turns and walks over to the telegraph machine and proceeds to send the wire.

CHAPTER SEVEN

Day After Election

The morning after Election Day, at around nine a.m. inside the Tilden mansion, Mary is seated at the dining room table having breakfast. She beams with delight when Samuel enters the room and walks to the table. He seats himself in a chair and a butler walks over to him and pours him a cup of coffee. Mary cheerfully says to her brother, "Good morning Mr. President. That was some party last night. What time did you get to bed?"

Samuel smiles and responds "It was late – sometime after two. And not to correct you dear sister, I'm the President elect – I've not been sworn in yet."

"A mere technicality," she quips. "When will you resign your Governorship?"

Samuel takes a sip of his steaming cup of coffee then responds, "Many preparations need to be made and I'll be in need of your assistance." Mary takes a slice of toast, butters it and scolds, "Don't overdo it or you'll get yourself sick. You know how easily you catch colds."

Mr. Smith, Tilden's personal assistant, enters the room with a glum expression on his face. Without saying a word, he walks over to Samuel and hands him a few telegraph wires. Before reading them, Samuel invites Mr. Smith to have breakfast with him and Mary. "Well...good morning to you Mr. Smith. Please, have a seat and join us for breakfast." With a nod to Mary, Smith sits in a chair and the butler walks to the table and pours Mr. Smith a cup of coffee.

Mr. Smith, still glum, tells Samuel, "I need you to read those wires." Noting the look on Smith's face, Samuel begins to read the wires Smith has handed to him. Mr. Smith sits back in his chair and observes Samuel expression as he read the wires.

Mary, sipping her coffee innocently asks, "Is there a problem?" Smith glances at her for a moment then looks back to Samuel. Without looking up from the telegrams, Samuel queries calmly, "What other editors are reporting problems?"

"So far, just these," Smith replies. "It's rumored that the managing editor from the *Times*, John Reid, is behind this. I received an early morning message from an old friend of mine that works at the 5th Avenue hotel. He says that Reid was in the lobby devising a conspiracy with W.E. Chandler, the republican from New Hampshire."

Samuel places the telegrams on the table and resumes eating his breakfast as if nothing is wrong. Smith continues, "I haven't seen the *New York Times* yet, but I have heard that the paper is trying to cast doubt about your win." Samuel coolly replies, "Certainly this newspaper man has not the authority to influence or change an election outcome with a wishful headline."

Mary reaches over, picks up the telegrams and reads them. Samuel says to Smith, "You and I will visit headquarters after breakfast. I think we need to find out if there's any real need for concern."

Smith pushes back his chair and stands, "I'll go alert your body-guards and ready your carriage." As Smith walks out of the room, Mary says to Samuel, "The voters elected you, not Governor Hayes." Samuel after taking another sip of his coffee replies, "There's no need for concern, my dear. This is probably a last ditch ploy by the Times editors to create doubt about my win." Mary stands and walks toward her brother, "They can fabricate headlines without obligation to their readers?" Samuel smiles and places his hand over Mary's, "Reporters do it often. They use words such as; doubt, could have, may have, might have. It's how they sell newspapers."

❦

On the day before Election Day of November 7, 1876, Rutherford B. Hayes had penned his thoughts in his diary. *"A cold but dry day. Good enough here for election work. I still think Democratic chances the best. But it is not possible to form a confident opinion. If we lose, the South will be the greatest sufferer. Their misfortune will be far greater than ours. I do not think a revival of business will be greatly postponed by Tilden's election. Business prosperity does not, in my judgment, depend on government so much as men commonly think. But we shall have no improvement in civil service—deterioration rather, and the South will drift towards chaos again."*

Now on the morning after the election, outside the Hayes mansion, crowds of displeased Hayes supporters stand by the main gates and watch as Hayes talks to reporters. All of them listen while reporters take notes. One of the reporters shouts to Hayes, "The *New York Times,* along with several other papers that followed the headline, claims this race is not yet decided. Any comments Governor?"

Hayes answers, "Yes, I've heard the rumors – though I think we are defeated in spite of recent good news. I am in the opinion that the Democrats have carried the country and that Tilden has been elected."

Another Reporter pipes in asking, "Does that mean you are conceding the race, Sir?" Some of the supporters standing close by jeer at the question while a small group of Tilden supporters wave their signs and cheer. More reporters begin asking questions simultaneously, "Sir, answer the question? Are you conceding? What now Governor? Governor, just one more question?"

Hayes, not yet wanting to confirm his concession, waves to the crowd. "Thank you. Thank you all for your support." He then turns and walks away from them, back toward his house.

Days later, Hayes will write in his diary, Saturday, November 11, 1876

"The election has resulted in the defeat of the Republicans after a very close contest. Tuesday evening a small party assembled in our parlor to hear the news. General Mitchell and Laura, our boys, Birch and Webb, Governor Dennison, a reporter of the Chicago Tribune, Mr. Huntley, W. K. Rogers, Rutherford Platt, and a few others at times.-Emily Platt, Dr. Fullerton, and Fanny. We all felt that the State of New York would decide the contest. Our last dispatches from our committee in New York were very encouraging -full of confidence. Mr. A. B. Cornell, Chairman New York State Committee, Said in an experience of ten years he had never seen prospects brighter on the eve of an election. But we all knew – warned by the enormous registration in the cities of New York and Brooklyn and other facts- that we must not count confidently on carrying the State. The good omen from Ithaca was accepted with a quiet cheerfulness. Almost at the same instant came a gain of thirty-six in Ballville, the township nearest my own home. This was good. Then came, one at

a time, towns and precincts in Ohio. The comparison was made with the vote in 1875, instead of with the vote of October last. This was confusing. But soon we began to feel that Ohio was not doing as well as we had hoped. The effect was depressing. I commanded without much effort my usual composure and cheerfulness. Lucy felt it more keenly. Without showing it [her depression, she busied herself about refreshments for our guests, and soon disappeared. I found her soon after abed with a headache. I comforted her by consoling talk; she was cheerful and resigned, but did not return to the parlor. Without difficulty or much effort I became the most composed and cheerful of the party. At- P. M., or thereabouts, we heard that in some two hundred districts of New York City, Tilden had about twenty thousand majority, which indicated fifty thousand in the city. The returns received from the rural districts did not warrant the belief that they would overcome such a large city majority. From that time, I never supposed there was a chance for Republican success. I went to bed at 12 to 1 o'clock. Talked with Lucy, consoling her with such topics as readily occurred of a nature to make us feel satisfied on merely personal grounds with the result. We soon fell into a refreshing sleep and the affair seemed over. Both of us felt more anxiety about the South—about the colored people especially- than about anything else sinister in the result. My hope of a sound currency will somehow be realized; civil service reform will be delayed; but the great injury is in the South. There the Amendments will be nullified, disorder will continue, prosperity to both whites and colored people will be pushed off for years. But I took my way to my office as usual Wednesday morning, and was master of myself and contented and cheerful. During the day the news indicated that we (had) carried California; soon after, other Pacific States; all New England except Connecticut; all of the free States West except Indiana; and it dawned on us that with a few Republican States in the South to which we were fairly entitled, we would yet be the victors. From Wednesday afternoon the city and the whole country has been full of excitement and anxiety. People have been up and down several times a day with the varying rumors. Wednesday evening on a false rumor about New York, a shouting multitude rushed to my house and called me out with rousing cheers. I made a short talk, saying (as reported by the papers): "Friends.—If you will keep order for one half minute, I will say all that is proper to say at this time. In the very close political contest, which is just drawing to a close, it is impossible, at so early a

time, to obtain the result, owing to the incomplete telegraph communica-
tions through some of the Southern and Western States. "I accept your
call as a desire on your part for the success of the Republican Party. If it
should not be successful, I shall surely have the pleasure of living for the
next year and a half among some of my most ardent and enthusiastic
friends, as you have demonstrated tonight." From that time, the news
has fluctuated just enough to prolong the suspense and to enhance the
interest. At this time the Republicans are claiming the election by one
electoral vote. With Louisiana, South Carolina, and Florida, we have
carried one hundred and eighty-five [electoral votes]. This creates great
uneasiness. Both sides are sending to Louisiana prominent men to watch
the canvassing of the votes. All thoughtful people are brought to consider
the imperfect machinery provided for electing the President. No doubt
we shall, warned by this danger, provide, by amendments of the Consti-
tution, or by proper legislation, against a recurrence of the danger.

It's now mid-morning, the day after the election, and Zach Chandler
is standing with John Reid and W.E. Chandler inside Republican headquarters. The three men are reviewing telegrams and responses from
Republican leaders across the country. Several campaign workers busy
themselves in the room, shuffling paperwork and chatting amongst
themselves.

Reid looks to Zach and remarks, "Several newspapers across the
country have followed the *New York Times* lead and are reporting Hayes
may have won the election by Electoral College votes."

Pleased by this news and telegraph responses, Zach replies, "Florida
has wired a favorable response to the wire you sent last night."

Delighted, Reid smiles, "What say South Carolina and Louisiana?"

Zach hands over the wires from the two states. "The same—favorable."

Reid takes a moment to review them. "And the western states? Are
they offering Republican majorities as well?"

"There is no reason to doubt the correctness of the reports. Once
confirmed, Hayes is assured a majority in the Electoral College. One
vote in the electoral is all we need to take the election from Tilden. With
nineteen now in question, your little plan to overturn the election might
just work... Well done Mr. Reid."

Over at the Democratic Headquarters, Tilden and Mr. Smith, along with his two body guards, make their way through the crowd of well wishers. Samuel greets them with enthusiasm and shakes hands with several people before entering the building.

Inside the campaign headquarters, John Bigelow, Congressman Hewitt and William Pelton are reviewing the returns as Samuel and Mr. Smith enter the room. Noting his arrival, William walks up to his uncle visibly upset and says, "A friend of mine from the *Times* reported back to me that Reid, the managing editor of the *New York Times*, is behind all of this."

Samuel frowns, "So I've heard from another source."

William continues, "Well *my* source claims he was in the editorial room when Reid received a dispatch from Magone, asking to him to confirm the results."

John Bigelow steps up beside the agitated William and says, "This is obviously a combination of Reid's bitter partisanship combined with a gambler's wish. The Republicans desperately want to steal this election from you."

"They cannot steal a voter's majority," Samuel calmly states. "The law of the Constitution will conclude the result…not any wishful thinking on the Republican's part. What are our Democratic leaders of the disputed states reporting?"

Standing a few feet away, Hewitt declares, "Louisiana reported and confirmed we have defeated Hayes by some twenty-thousand votes."

Samuel takes a moment before responding, "We must not mislay our focus, Gentlemen. We need confirmation. Let's begin by wiring all our party leaders at once." He pauses again and commands, "And cipher the wires. There is no need to let anyone know outside of this room what we are doing." He pauses again for just a moment. "Now if you'll excuse me, Mr. Smith and I have a few other matters to attend to." A slight smile crosses his face as he continues, "I must prepare for the festivities planned for this evening, or…" and he looks directly at William, "you and I will have to answer to your mother." He then looks back at the men gathered around. "Please keep me apprised, gentlemen."

⁓—⫘—⁓

Later that afternoon, back at the Tilden mansion, Mary and her staff are busying themselves prepping for her brother's victory celebration.

Samuel, dressed in his formal attire, walks out onto the porch with his sister Mary. As Mary welcomes the guests filtering through the crowd, Samuel declares, "I think I'm going to take a few minutes and talk to some people out here before the merriment begins inside."

"Not too long." Mary counters. "We have numerous guests arriving and I can't fit anymore guests than the ones I've invited into the house." Samuel kisses her on the cheek and walks down the steps. Mary enters the brownstone and stands just inside the entry hall, so that she can continue to greet the arriving guests and at the same time, through the open door, keep a protective eye on her brother as he works the crowd. Learning their lesson from the previous days concerning crowd control, there is a roped off area so that the carriages can come and go to drop off passengers safely. There are hundreds of people waiting to congratulate Samuel and he is taking great pleasure in the attention. The curious spectators are respectful and peaceful as he greets and shakes hands with them. The mood of the crowd is upbeat. It's a surreal experience for Samuel. He realizes, *I have won the hearts of these people... regardless of other news they have read stating otherwise.* Meanwhile many of Tilden supporters continue to hold up their campaign signs while others wave their hats and handkerchiefs.

There are also several reporters present, including John Reid, standing closer to the mansion. Most of them have easy access to Samuel as he works the crowd. As the invited guests for the victory party arrive dressed in formal attire Samuel figures they could use the free publicity too and waves several over to him. Several reporters call out to Samuel, "Mr. Tilden, a moment please! Mr. Tilden, any comment?"

Samuel acknowledges their questions with a wave of his hand but continues to walk through the crowd and greet his loyal supporters. For a brief second, he catches the glare in John Reid's eyes. Quickly turning, he doesn't let on that he saw Mr. Reid, as he continues his meet and greet session.

Meanwhile, the carriages continue to arrive, stopping to unload passengers, and the invited guests are seen showing their invitations in order to enter the mansion. Men of position and wealth are wearing their best suits and the ladies of high society, married and unmarried are dressed in elegant designer bustle gowns, tightly fitted at the waist with long sleeves. Their make-up is subtle and natural and their long hair is twisted up and decorated in the latest styles off their necks with expensive jeweled hair pins that hold their locks in place.

After a time of visiting with his supporters, Samuel makes his way back toward the mansion. Just as he is nearing the top stair, John Reid shouts out loudly, "Mr. Tilden, what about Chairman Chandler's claims concerning the Electoral votes?"

Upon hearing this, the crowd tones down to a low whispering hush, and many start to boo Reid's question. Samuel stops, turns back and stares directly into Reid's eyes for a moment, and then turns his attention back to his supporters, as their whispering chatter grows louder. Samuel holds his arms in the air to quiet them and after a few moments the noise level lessens. Samuel looks again toward Reid and then back to the crowd. "My election victory was due to the issues. I received a great number of Republican votes. The election was decided in part, on my record as Governor of New York as the closeness of the contest shows. The opposition I had to overcome, well—I did not expect a large majority in the Electoral College. That is all for now. As you can see, I have many guests arriving."

Not missing a beat, another reporter standing near Reid shouts a negative question. "Governor…isn't it too soon for a victory party?"

The jeers begin again and Samuel looks over at Reid again. He decides to ignore the last question and shrugs his shoulders. He turns back toward the crowd and holds his arms in the air. This action gets the people cheering loudly again and they begin to chant Tilden's name while waving their campaign signs, hats and handkerchiefs. Samuel bows to his encouraging audience and puts his hand to his heart and thumps his chest in a sign to thank them for their support. The crowd roars even louder.

Mary who has been watching and listening to the verbal exchange, steps through the open door back out onto the porch and casually says to her brother, "You have guests inside vying for your attention too." Now that she realizes who John Reid is she casts a glare of contempt to him that he takes notice of. Samuel busy with his well wishers doesn't notice the exchange and when he turns to look at his sister, she flashes a big smile back at the crowd while taking Samuel by the arm to escort him inside.

CHAPTER EIGHT

Which Candidate wins?

A few minutes after 9 a.m., two days after the election at Democratic Headquarters, everyone in the room is busy counting election returns. Three men enter the room. Two are body-guards and the third is their charge, the new Tammany Hall Boss, Honest John Kelly. Honest John Kelly was born in New York City and raised by Irish Catholic immigrant parents. He never finished high school because his fathers' death forced him into the responsibility of supporting his family. He started a grate-setting business and became popular when he became Captain of his ward at the local target-shooting club. Kelly was also a volunteer fireman, an amateur boxer and actor, known well for his for Shakespearean roles. Kelly's political career started in the 1840s when he was elected to the city's board of aldermen. A decade later he ran successfully for congress and won by 18 votes. He was the only Roman Catholic in Congress at the time. He served on the powerful House Was and Means Committee, and was reelected in 1856. Two years later, Kelly resigned his seat in Congress and then went on to win another election making him the city and county sheriff, a job that offered no wages, but garnered him a percentage of all the legal fees collected. He was a savvy businessman and real estate investor and he shared his wealth by donating large sums of his earn-ings to the Catholic Church. His generosity and honesty in business dealings is how he attained the nickname "Honest John". Before rising to his current position, Kelly had become increasingly dissatisfied with the way William "Boss" Tweed ran Tammany Hall. In 1868, he agreed to run for mayor on a Reform Democratic ticket against Tweed's candidate, Oakey Hall. After losing, Kelly went on an extended tour of Europe. He returned in the fall of 1871 when press revelations of the "Tweed Ring" corruption and subsequent legal prosecutions were crippling Tammany as a political force. Democratic reformers who helped topple Tweed and his cohorts did not want to see Tammany Hall dismantled, so they offered Kelly the leadership of the organization.

In the first three years after the Boss Tweed scandals were exposed, Kelly rebuilt the powerful democratic machine almost single handedly. He reorganized the governing coalition of Tammany leaders who were not corrupted by the fraudulent transactions. And most importantly, in his view, he repaired the reputation to Tammany and the Democratic Party in New York City. His organization project was so successful it was used in other cities and small towns across the country to create Democratic "machines" known for their loyalties to the party. As a Catholic he understood how the Catholic Church hierarchy worked and he used the same formula to organize the party machine. Each election district of a few hundred to one thousand people would have a precinct captain or county committeeman; the same as a Parish Priest does in every church. These Captains would report back to district leaders, like a priest reports to a Bishop and the Bishops to the Cardinals and Cardinals to the Pope. Kelly's plan made sure every district issues were attended to fairly and openly. He was confident in his abilities as a leader, as a straight shooter and more organized than most, and did not like it when people questioned his sincerity.

Leaving his body guards at the door, Kelly strolls over to John Bigelow, William Pelton and Congressman Hewitt. All three have noticed him come in, but they keep their focus on reviewing election results at the tote board. As Kelly walks up to them he taps a rolled up newspaper against the palm of his hand. In his usual confident gruff voice he announces his presence. "Good morning Gentlemen."

John Bigelow, somewhat annoyed, continues to review the tote board and snipes back without looking at John, "Good morning yourself, Mr. Kelly. Where have you been hiding lately?"

Kelly, ignoring Bigelows' arrogance, stops tapping the paper and replies flatly, "Busy with Tammany business." Narrowing his eyes at Bigelow he asks, "Where is Samuel?" Bigelow doesn't respond. William realizing the tenseness between them chimes in, "He'll be here shortly."

Noting the negative mood, Kelly decides to change the tone of the conversation with some comical sarcasm. "Well I'm not at all happy with

the doubtful news reports. I have a very large wager on this election."
Congressman Hewitt, one of the newer members of Tammany, puts in
his two cents, "I'm sure Governor Tilden has no concern with your wager,
Mr. Kelly. And neither do we. At the moment, we are busy confirming
results to confirm his presidency."

Kelly realizing his joke has backfired places his newspaper in his side
jacket pocket, then raises both of his hands, palms up in a noncom-
mittal manner. "Relax Congressman—my ten-thousand is on Tilden's
win—not his loss."

Bigelow, realizing that Kelly was only jesting to lighten the mood,
relaxes his stance and replies, "Then your wager is safe."

Kelly is inwardly grateful for Bigelow's gesture to be nice to him, *these
men are not angry with me, but at the situation now confronting them.* He,
along with the rest of the Democrats across the country, believes that
regardless of what some newspaper men are reporting, there is no argument. Tilden has won the election by a large majority of the popular
vote. Kelly inquires, "How many votes are in dispute?"

Hewitt explains, "It is not the votes, John. He has over a two-hundred-
fifty-four thousand plurality. It is the Electoral College count—we appear
to be shy the one vote needed to claim victory."

Kelly, like millions of others across the country, believes the two go
hand in hand. He naively asks, "If he won the popular vote by that many,
then shouldn't the Electoral votes confirm it?"

"Not exactly," Bigelow replies.

Curious by the Bigelow's response, Kelly asks, "What do you mean
by *not exactly?*"

Bigelow turns back to the tote board and points at the count. "The
popular vote determines which of the candidates Electors go to Congress
with certificates. Each state has differing laws pertaining to how their
Electors vote. You know this because you were a Congressman yourself."

Kelly doesn't argue. "Yes, I understand how the popular works with
the electoral. So what is all the hoopla about? We have the popular vote
by two hundreds fifty-four thousands."

Bigelow explains, "The 'hoopla', as you put it, concerns these *differing*
state laws. Not all of them are bound by party loyalty to vote by way of
the popular vote."

After a moment of thought. Kelly replies, "Are you suggesting nation-wide election fraud?"

Hewitt jumps back into the conversation. "Maybe and hopefully not. We have made arrangements to send our best party leaders from the North to the South to review the Returning Boards of these southern states. We must secure our Electors there and will need your help to organize this effort."

"You know as well as I that the Republicans, under Grant's Authority, will try anything to swindle their way to victory," Bigelow complains. Kelly nods in agreement while staring at the tote board himself.

At that moment, Samuel enters the room and pauses for a moment to look at the two Tammany Hall guards. He gives them a slight nod with a smile, then moves forward to where Kelly, Hewitt, William and Bigelow are gathered. Samuel is in good spirits, regardless of the situation. He reaches out to shake Kelly's hand. "Honest John, it's good to see you. You missed a fantastic party last night."

Kelly's response is more serious than Samuel expects. "Samuel." He then turns and points to the tote board. "What do you know of these state leaders in the South? Can we trust them?"

Samuel looks at the board. "Hmm, yes the southern states." He looks back to Kelly. "Our friends in Louisiana need our moral support and my personal endorsement. Bayard, Thurman, Barnum, Randall, McDonald Dorsheimer, Kerand and a group of others are on their way to New Orleans as we speak A strong demonstration there will defeat the designs of the Returning Board."

John calculates in his head Samuel's detailed response and does not waiver because he knows everyone Samuel is talking about. "And Florida?" Kelly asks.

Samuel replies, already knowing every detail of the plan after being informed by Mr. Smith. "Henry Watterson will go to Florida with Beck and McHenry. They are requesting funds for reinforcements to resist the radical pranks expected. Coyle and a few others are heading down to South Carolina. Those fiery zealots of the Republican Party may attempt to count me out, but I don't think the better class of the Republicans will permit it. Don't worry John, we will prevail."

"It's good to hear you are confident but – "

"I won this election fairly by over two-hundred fifty-thousand popular votes." Samuel declares, then adds, "I am lacking only the one vote in the Electoral which will secure my Presidency."

Both Kelly's face and tone becomes serious. "Trust no one Samuel— the stakes for this Presidency are high and your reform tactics, honorable as they are—have gained you many political enemies."

Samuel replies, "I'm in agreement. Even with the states that are under Republican control and reconstruction, I need only but one," He raises a finger to emphasize his point, "of the nineteen electoral votes from those disputed states to win. Now, not being a gambler like yourself, I believe, and even you must admit, that those are very good odds."

⁓⁓

President General Ulysses Simpson Grant, the current two term president of the United States resides at the White House. Born April 22, 1822, he has a previous history of failure at every business he ever tried, including farming. Only his career as an army solider, followed by his rise to the presidency, marked the only true positive accomplishments in his life. But even these successes were riddled with poor policies and a poorer personal reputation. His administration is seen by many as corrupt and quid pro quo cronyism.

During his time in the military, Grant was quickly elevated to the rank of General in the Union Army, and he succeeded in getting General Lee to surrender the South during the bloody Civil War.

After the Civil War, a thankful President Lincoln appointed Grant commander of all the U.S. armies, complete with the rank of lieutenant general; a rank only George Washington had held before.

In 1868, Grant accepted the Republican presidential nomination and campaigned using the slogan "Let Us Have Peace." Once in office, Grant did everything in his power to unite the South and the North, including dealing with the Ku Klux Klan, the white supremacist group. Grant also met with notable Native American Indian tribal leaders in order to develop peace policies between their respective nations. He also took steps to repair the damaged economy during his two terms, but his good intentions were derailed by his own corrupt administration. One of the financial scandals that scarred his Presidency was Black Friday, September 24, 1869 when the U.S. gold market collapsed.

After his rise to the presidency, and during his two terms in the White House, Julia Dent, his wife and First Lady, enjoyed extravagantly entertaining dignitaries worldwide and living in style. She dreaded the thought of leaving the lifestyle she'd grown accustom to while positioned in society as the First Lady. During the disputed election she has busied herself by making plans for her and Grant to travel the world once his term was over. She is convinced that her husband's memoirs will be a valuable asset for their financial future. And although he doesn't yet know it, she has arranged for her husband to meet with Mark Twain so he could write them.

At present, just outside the White House, large crowds of Hayes and Tilden supporters are marching, holding up political signs in support of their candidates. Horse carriages with their drivers fill the streets. From inside the Oval Office, President Grant sees the crowds through the window.

Just having returned from a visit at the Centennial event in Pennsylvania, Grant lights a cigar and takes a few moments to watch the political supporters as they march. After a short time, he walks back to his desk and sits down. While he was away, he was not aware of or let in on the scheme that his fellow republicans had in mind to steal the election. He was secure in his belief that Tilden had won the Presidency and was now trying to comprehend the motive as to why his Secretary of War was diverting troops to South Carolina without his authority.

With these thoughts running through his mind, he calls his personal assistant Orville Babcock into the office. Grant is suspicious and not exactly sure what his party is plotting or concealing from him – but he knows he does not want to be responsible for their actions. His goal before leaving office is to do what is necessary to keep the peace in the three Southern states of Louisiana, Florida and South Carolina under his command during reconstruction. This election fiasco is the last thing he expected before leaving office to enjoy the world tours his wife Julia planned for them. For a brief period of time he had considered running for a third term, but dismissed the idea after finding out that he would not get the support he needed from the Republicans that had helped him in the past.

Before dictating a telegram to his assistant, Grant leans back in his chair, puffs on his cigar, and says," Please read aloud that telegram just received from General Sherman." His assistant picks up the telegram from W.T. Sherman and reads it out loud, "The Secretary of War, Cameron, has ordered me to send soldiers to Florida. Please confirm."

His assistant waits a moment then says, "From what I've gathered from the party leadership is that Governor Hayes' Electoral count is One-Hundred-Sixty-Six with nineteen votes still undetermined. Tilden's count remains at One-Hundred-Eighty-Four. The Democrats apparently need only one of those votes to win."

Through the cloud of cigar smoke, Babcock asks Grant, "How do you want – "

"One moment", Grant interrupts. "I do not want to lose my train of thought." He takes a few more puffs on his cigar, slightly rocks his chair and stares blankly for a few moments.

After a few minutes pass Grant dictates to Orville, "Address to General W.T. Sherman. Instruct General Auger, in Louisiana, and General Ruger in Florida." Grant waits for him to finish writing. "Tell them to be vigilant with the force under their command and to preserve peace and good order." He pauses for another moment then adds, "See to it that the legal Boards of Canvassers are unmolested in the performance of their duties. Should there be any grounds of suspicion for fraudulent counting on either side-", Grant looks directly at his assistant and says sternly, "it should be denounced at once." He waits for his Orville to finish writing and he says very loud, "No man worthy of the office for President would be willing to hold the office if counted in or placed there by fraud. Either Party can afford to be disappointed in the result, but the country cannot afford to have the results tainted by the suspicion of illegal or false returns."

Orville nods in agreement and knows better than to argue with the President. He has heard from gossip within the party that a newsman, John Reid from the *New York Times*, had started this scheme to hijack the election. He decides it would be better if the party Chairman, not Reid, questions the results of the election. Orville pauses for a moment and watches as Grant rises from his chair and walks around to the front of his desk, still puffing on his cigar. Grant looks at Orville square in the eyes and says, "Tell them to keep it honest and to make sure the colored men of the South are treated with respect."

In Ohio a large and unruly crowd of Hayes and Tilden supporters have gathered in front of the Hayes estate. Several reporters wait with them for Hayes to come outside to speak with them. A smaller group of Tilden supporters argue with Hayes supporters, suggesting rather forcefully that Hayes should get it over with and concede the election. A Tilden man bickers with a Hayes campaigner and angrily shouts, "Tilden's won this election! Hayes should back off!"

A Hayes's man fires back, "Tilden ain't won nothing yet! The votes ain't all counted!"

Another Tilden supporter fires an insult. "You're a horse's ass," and then reaches out and takes a swing at the man he is arguing with. The two wrestle each other to the ground and the crowd gathers around them. The reporters move in closer and one reporter says to another, "This kind of action will sell hundreds of papers."

While the melee commences outside, inside the mansion Hayes and his wife Lucy are seated at the dining room table. Two of their children, Fanny their nine year old daughter and Scott their six year old son, are with them at the table. They hear the commotion erupting outside and Hayes tries his best to ignore it, but Lucy won't let him.

"These people say you are the President," she blurts out to him.

Fanny not wanting to be left out of the conversation asks her father," Is it true? Are you the President?"

Scott protesting asks, "Do we have to move? I don't want to move from here."

Hayes, trying to calm his annoyed wife and children commands, "Please finish your lunch."

Lucy, realizing he is annoyed by the outbursts, reprimands her children. "Mind your father." Both children know better than to argue with either of their parents and start to eat again. But after a moment they are disrupted when they hear someone outside shout, "We'll fight 'til the end for you, Governor!" Then another demand, "Come outside and talk to us!"

Fearful that the people outside are getting out of hand, Lucy pleads with her husband, "Rutherford—Please—Go out there and talk to those people. Tell them to stop fighting. They are frightening our children."

Little Scott jumps up in his own defense and runs to his father's side, "I'm not afraid!"

Hayes affectionately pats his son on the head and sensing his wife's fears, he pulls his chair away from the table, stands and walks toward the front door with Scott trailing right behind him. He stops and firmly orders Scott, "Back to the table young man and finish your lunch."

Lucy, who has now gotten up from the table as well, walks over to Scott and takes him by the hand. "Come with me young man. I have something special for you." Scott looks up at his mother as she grips his hand and walks him toward the kitchen. "I have fresh cookies in the kitchen, want one?" Scott nods his head yes. He likes the idea of fresh baked cookies and stops complaining after her offer of one. Fannie, who is still eating her lunch, pushes back her chair and chases Scott when he sticks his tongue out at her. "You've been tricked," she blurts out to her younger brother. Lucy turns and scolds her, "Fanny...don't tease your brother."

Outside the mansion, Hayes walks down the path to the front gates. His supporters cheer him while the Tilden supporters are rude and jeer. Arriving at the gate, he holds up his hands for silence from the crowd. It takes about a minute and they finally settle down. Loudly, so they can all hear, Hayes states, "Friends, if you will keep order for me half a minute—I will say all that is proper to say at this time." The crowd quiets to a whispering hush and he waits until there is silence for him to continue speaking. The reporters ready their cameras while others scribble notes on their notepads.

After a moment, Hayes begins his announcement. "Thank you. Thank you all for coming. In a very close political contest, it is impossible at so early a time, to obtain a result. The telegram communications from some of the southern and western states are still incomplete."

He is interrupted when one of his over exuberant supporters shouts out, "Hayes is elected!" More cheers and jeers fill the air. Hayes again holds up his hands up for silence. The crowd quiets down. "I accept your call as a desire on your part for the success of the Republican party. If it should not be successful, however, I shall surely have the pleasure of living for the next year and a half among some of my most ardent and enthusiastic friends, as you have demonstrated here today."

The Hayes supporters cheer again and this time the Tilden supporters remain respectfully quiet. Hayes waves to the cheering crowd and then turns and walks back up the path toward the house.

In New York City, Samuel is seated at his office desk reading the Thanksgiving Day Proclamation he has just finished writing. It is his duty as Governor of New York to have it signed and ready for the media by the ninth of November. He reads silently to himself, *Proclamation by Governor Tilden, The unfailing mercies of God of which another year has given witness, call us to renew our acknowledgment of Him in thanksgiving and prayer. We are specially reminded of His protection, in the absence of any great disaster or calamity throughout the Commonwealth; and of His bounty, in the large and generous returns of nature. Let us rejoice in the spirit of order and of charity and of the hopefulness which has pervaded all classes under the depression in the industries and trade, and in the growth of the public sentiment toward wise and humane methods of dealing with want and suffering. Let us give thanks for the maintenance of our social and religious institutions in their integrity, and improve the Divine blessing upon all efforts in behalf of good government and a true morality. In common with the people of the other States of the Union, we recall, at this time, the blessings which we hold by inheritance. It becomes us, with them, to gratefully and humbly acknowledge the God of our fathers, whose mercies have been from generation to generation, beseeching Him for the continuous of His favor to the nation of His planting, that He may not "deliver our glory unto another." I do, therefore, set apart and appoint Thursday the 30th day of November, recommending to the people that on that day they put aside their usual employments, and in their homes and in their respective places of worship, render thanks to Almighty God for His mercies to us as individuals and as a State. Done at the Capitol, in the City of Albany, this sixth day of November, in the year of our Lord one thousand eight hundred and seventy six.* Satisfied with the proclamation, he takes a pen and signs it.

Just as Samuel is signing his name, his good friend, campaign manager and Gramercy neighbor John Bigelow enters the room. Samuel stands up from behind his desk, a broad smile spreading across his face. "John, come on in.

"Maybe we can go out for some fresh air today. I thought we could take a carriage ride through Central park?"

Samuel likes the idea and nods his approval. "Now that sounds like a very good idea. I've been cooped up in the house long enough." He walks toward Bigelow and grabs his friend by the arm and asks "Where did you park the carriage?"

"Out back," Bigelow replies. "This way no one will follow us when we leave."

"Good thinking. A spirited ride would do me some good." Releasing Bigelow's arm, Samuel walks over to Mr. Smith, who is seated at his desk and adds, "We can also discuss the days' news." He hands his assistant the freshly signed proclamation. "Here you are, Smith. It's signed and ready." Smith takes the document and nods in agreement. "I'll deliver it at once." Samuel pats Mr. Smith gently on his back to thank him then walks over and picks up his coat off the rack and says a new favorite phase he coined, "See you later." After slipping his arms into the coat he reaches over and picks up his newspaper and says to Bigelow, "I'll take this too. I haven't had time to read it yet."

Dressed in lightweight overcoats, both men walk out of the room toward the back of the house. As they both walk toward Mary she protests at Samuel, "You'll catch cold dressed like that."

Samuel reaches over and gives Mary a kiss on her cheek. Frowning, Mary glances over to a butler who is standing off to the side. Without a word, he walks to the rack and retrieves a hat and scarf and brings them to Mary. She turns, handing them to Samuel and says, "Humor me… please." Samuel knows better than to argue with his sister. He smiles and takes the items from her and turns back to Bigelow who is waiting at the door. With his back to Mary, he rolls his eyes and gives his friend a quick shrug and they both laugh.

About an hour later Samuel is holding both horses' reins with a loose but steady grip as he drives the two horse team at a steady pace in the chilly air. The sun is shining and the sky is a glorious blue with hardly a cloud in it. The two men make their way through the marked paths that are cut out through the park. The sweeping meadows and large lake complete the countrified landscape called Central Park. Odd shaped rocks stand firm and decorate the man made walkways. The horse paths are lined with hundreds of trees, shrubs and plants that have already gone into hibernation for the winter months. Once spring comes the flowers, shrubs and trees will bloom in splendor, the lake will thaw and New Yorkers will enjoy their country hide away that is nestled in the middle of a fast growing concrete metropolis.

As Samuel trots the team of horses through the park, Bigelow holds a firm grip with his right hand, trying not to get bounced off the carriage. The scarf Mary gave Samuel to wear is tied loosely around his neck and the hat he is supposed to be wearing to prevent head colds is resting on the seat between him and John. While holding on with his right hand, Bigelow holds the newspaper Samuel wanted to read in his left. Bigelow reads out loud, "Nip and Tuck. Tilden still has one-hundred-eighty-four votes to Hayes' one-hundred-sixty-six. Nineteen votes are still undecided."

Samuel slaps the reins and the horses start to trot a little faster. "What else does it say?"

Bigelow grabs the side of the bouncy carriage tighter and complains, "Samuel—You may be my closest friend, but by God, man, you are making it most difficult to stay in my seat"

Samuel lets out a huge laugh and pulls the reins back to slow the horses to a walk. "Better?" he asks John.

Bigelow relaxes his grip and replies, "Much, thank you" as he straightens the newspaper and continues to read. He then chuckles at something he has just read in the article. Samuel turns to him and says, "Humor me." With a smirk, Bigelow reads the article out loud. "It says here – Tilden's a most accomplished and astute politician—less confiding and more distrustful than Grant. A man of modest, unobtrusive personality—stooped and hence looks smaller than he is – a small boyish face—round head bent with that sleepy droop in the left eyelid – caused by Ptosis. He dresses with plainness."

Un-offended, Samuel thinks the remarks are interesting. "I like the boyish face remark but I do not think my suits are plain."

Intrigued, Bigelow continues to read aloud. "There is a paragraph here—Governor Marcy predicted you would be President, except for your physical stamina."

Samuel now gets somewhat defensive by this last statement. Frowning, he asks, "Marcy commented on my physical stamina?"

"He claims it is like putting a two hundred-horse power engine in a craft built for only a one hundred horse-power. He states that you have too much mind for your body."

Samuel continues to walk the horses at a slow pace then says, "He actually could have said worse. After all, I certainly have of him." Both men laugh.

Suddenly, and without warning, a black stallion with a beautiful woman in the saddle dressed in a very fashionable outfit races past them, spooking Samuel's horses. As the horse gallops pass them at lightening speed, the woman turns in her saddle and tips her hat in apology for the upset. Samuel, who only sees the woman for a brief moment during the encounter, estimates the woman possesses not only class and beauty but also has remarkable riding skills.

Vivacious, he thinks to himself, while he steadies his agitated horses to a halt. Both men are awestruck by the woman's spirit and the skill of her riding. Her long deep brunette hair bouncing off her back is all they can see as she distances herself from them.

The talented rider's name is Celeste Stauffer and she is from New Orleans, Louisiana. Though not an area of the country Samuel or John have frequented in the past, it is an area they are now connected to because of the election dispute in that state.

"Now that's a feisty female," Samuel remarks. "I've never seen one ride with the skills she possesses."

While watching Samuel's reaction to the surprise interruption Bigelow realizes his best friend is smitten with the young woman. He nudges Samuel's arm and notes, "She looks young."

Samuel elbows his friend's arm back and says, "I'm may be cerebral, John, but I'm not blind."

Recovering his thoughts and realizing that they are sitting still, Samuel snaps the reins against the horses' backs and maneuvers the team to turn back toward his home. "You know, I could love a woman that knows how to handle spirited horses. Age means nothing."

As the horses get back on track and pick up the pace, Bigelow again grips his hand to the side rail to steady himself. "And it shouldn't—but romance will have to wait for another day Mr. President elect. Your schedule at the White House should prove to be very hectic in the coming years." Samuel nods in agreement as he guides the horses out onto Fifth Avenue and they trot away from Central Park.

CHAPTER NINE

Fearing the Worse

It is the first Monday in December and President Grant is inside the Oval office standing at his usual spot by the window. He watches with concern, knowing that the tension is still high, as the protestors continue to march. After almost a month, they are relentless in their support for their candidates. Orville Babcock, Grant's assistant, is in the Oval Office, reviewing a telegram response from General Sherman.

Without turning away from the scene outside the window, Grant, while chomping on a cigar, asks Babcock, "What reports have come in?"

Babcock reads the telegram response out loud. "From General Sherman. Disruption is being reported throughout the union. The Republican and Democratic parties are both taking action in the streets to resolve the issues concerning which candidate will succeed you. It has also been reported that many military veterans, even though out of uniform, remain a threat."

Frustrated and angered by the events, the President turns from the window and slams his hand down on the desk, startling Babcock. "This country cannot afford another bloody battle! *We* must maintain order and *Congress* must respond to their Constitutional duty by the sixth when the electoral votes are submitted. As I see it, Tilden has won the popular vote and is elected." Babcock places the telegram on the President's desk and walks out of the office.

Over at the Capitol building, several Senators and Congressmen are discussing the situation as they stroll outside, their Aides following closely behind. As they near the entrance of the building, they try to avoid the protestors vying for their attention. Once inside they continue to the House Chambers where they will begin hearings and debates regarding the latest news and events concerning the election dispute. Congressman John Goode, a colonel in the Confederate Army during the Civil War, is currently the Democratic representative from Virginia. He enters the Chamber with one of his aides. He begins tapping a folded up newspaper against his left palm as he walks toward the front of the room to where the Speaker of the House desk is located.

A few other Congressmen, including Speaker of the House, Democrat Samuel J. Randall, are standing near the desk and are in mid discussion when he arrives. They acknowledge him then continue to talk amongst themselves. Goode hands the paper off to his aide and in a hushed voice tells him, "When I signal, please read the Grant statement out loud." His Aide agrees then Goode turns back to the gathered congressmen.

Clearing his throat to gain the other men's attention Goode says, "Excuse me Gentlemen, I need your undivided attention for a moment so you can hear the statement made by the President." He signals with his hand for the Aide to begin and the Aide straightens the paper out and begins to read aloud, "It says that President Grant and the Republicans will have the regular army but the Governors of the Democratic States will have to call upon the militia if needed." The man stops and looks at the gathered Congressmen. There is a moment of awkward silence. He then looks back to Goode. "Would you like me to read more?"

"No, and thank you. That will be all."

As Goode turns back to face his fellow Congressmen, Speaker Randall and the others mumble some words between themselves. After a few hushed comments, Speaker Randall walks up to the Speakers' podium. Still standing, he picks up his gavel and bangs it a few times on the desk. The other congressmen know that this is the signal for their Aides and the Tellers in the room to take their prospective seats. They all scatter to different areas of the Chamber, sitting and standing in areas designated to them. Goode turns to his Aide, "It's time, go and take your seat." The man walks up the aisle and stands with some others not politically elected in the room.

One of the other Congressmen, standing near Goode, says to him, "The fear amongst us is heightening with the threats of violence surrounding this election."

Goode fires back with sternness in his voice, "We are the lawmakers and we should abide by the Constitution."

The other man slips his hand into his jacket and pulls back the front of his suit to show Goode he has a pistol in his inside coat pocket. He says to Congressman Goode, "The Constitution is not going to protect us from those violent protestors out there in the streets."

With a look of disgust, Goode puts his hands on his hips and puts his face inches away from the other man. Keeping his voice low and controlled, he asks, "Do you really believe that is necessary?"

Without hesitation, the Congressman in his own defense declares, "I'm not the only one walking the streets in fear. Several Representatives are armed. And yes, I would suggest you do the same to protect yourself."

Before Goode can respond, he is interrupted by Speaker Randall, who begins banging his gavel once again to quiet the noisy room. He shouts out, "The House will come to order." Within moments, the Congressmen respond with silence and take their seats. The feeling of tension in the room is running high.

John Goode stands to his feet and says out loud so all can hear him, "Mister Speaker, one Party or another must surrender or we must fight!" He then turns to face the assembly. "Are the Gentleman prepared for a fight?" Without pause, all the Congressmen rise to their feet and shout out with a fiery cry, "YES!" The room fills with voices of noisy chatter. John Goode is stunned by the quick and maddened response and slowly falls back into his seat. Once more, Speaker Randall bangs his gavel several times and shouts, "Order! The House must come to order!"

Another Congressman, standing close to Goode, leans over to the seated Virginia Congressman and says, "If it does come to war, at least the Republicans will have the regular army." Without looking up at his colleague, Goode lets out a sigh.

CHAPTER TEN

Soldiers Ordered to Keep the Peace

A group of angry protestors, a mixture of white and black men, have surrounded the Republican headquarters in Tallahassee Florida. The men carry and wave political signs for both Hayes and Tilden. Soldiers, who are dressed in confederate uniforms, surround the social unrest. Although these soldiers are under federal control, they have yet to be issued their blue uniforms standard for the National Government. Since the end of the recent Civil War and with the country at peace, the funds and supplies have been slowed to a trickle to the South. These soldiers have just been called up again and are struggling with the crowd to prevent riots from breaking out. They are there to keep the protestors from crossing the roped off barriers located a few hundred feet from the entrance of the Republican headquarters. The soldiers have been ordered to do the best they can without harming anyone. So far, there have only been a few minor incidences with protestors fighting amongst themselves and not much work for them. Although their tempers do flare from time to time, the crowd remains relatively calm. Their mood changes every time a horse drawn carriage filled with politicians carrying political VIP passengers' moves into the area. Some of these notable politicians are; former Governor Noyes from Ohio, William Chandler, General Ruger, Florida's General Lew Wallace, Florida's Governor Marcellus L. Sterns and W.E. Chandler, from New Hampshire.

As the carriage works its way through the crowd, the protestors' wave their campaign signs and start shouting obscenities at the political men passing. The carriage driver halts his horses at the barrier line manned by the soldiers when he realizes he can go no further. The driver abruptly decides he is not willing to risk life and limb or his horses to protect the politicians by getting them a few feet closer to the door. Turning in his seat, the driver leans back and says, "Sorry gentlemen, but this is as far as I go."

The men inside the carriage are not pleased by his announcement and a few look apprehensively at one another. After a moment of hesitation, they decide there is nothing else they can do and begin, one by one, to climb out of the carriage on to the street. A few of the soldiers rush over to the carriage and assist the politicians by creating a human barrier for them to walk through. As the men of importance make their way toward the front entrance of Republican headquarters, a few of the protestors manage to slip through the barriers and race toward them. Much to their dismay they are quickly halted by the soldiers and escorted back behind the roped line.

The rowdy crowd continues to rant and rave and shout their obscenities at the politicians. Tempers flare and the protestors, in support of Tilden, shout out in anger, "Tilden or Blood!" The Republicans supporting Hayes wave their signs and rant, "Recount—recount."

Now free of his charges, the carriage driver maneuvers his horses and turns his carriage away from the shouting throng of protestors, departing as quickly as he can to get away from the noise and confusion.

As the political men make their way toward the entrance of the headquarters William Chandler notes the insignia on the uniform of one the soldiers close to him. Over the noise of the angry crowd, he shouts, "Are you the commanding officer? You should push these people back further down the road." The officer grunts as he pushes a protestor back, and then turns back to William Chandler and snipes, "We're doing the best we can, sir, without shooting them."

Upon hearing this exchange, Noyes chimes in, "If you must shoot them, danmit, then shoot them."

General Ruger barks back, "I gave them strict orders not to do that Mr. Noyes, unless someone fires upon them first."

Noyes now turns to William Chandler. "This is going to cost the party more than the two thousand you've already paid, Mr. Chandler. I will authorize your Elector Certificates, legal or not—but the party *will* pay for this disruption."

W.E. nuzzles himself into the conversation and states, "Whatever it takes, Mr. Noyes, whatever it takes."

Now Wallace leans over to William and says, "We will need at least another five-thousand to be rendered soon." William snaps back as they all enter the building, "You'll have your money Mr. Wallace."

Once safely inside the Republican Headquarters the political VIPs observe campaign workers scattered throughout the room shuffling paper work in preparation for the recount. William turns to Sterns and promises, "Funds will be on hand to meet every requirement as long as you can guarantee those certificates for Hayes."

Turning to face William, Sterns replies, "It has been reported to me that the Governor of Georgia is here representing the Democrats in the State Board of Canvassers."

William Chandler, seeking more answers, asks, "How many other Democratic Statesmen from the north do you know of that have arrived ahead of me to secure the ballot boxes?"

"I've heard of several." Then, to assure William that he's got it under control, Sterns adds, "Secretary of State McLinn and Comptroller Cogwell, once persuaded, will balance the ballot boxes quite easily for Hayes."

William smiles, "That's good news. It's been told to me that George Drew is suing for a recount to take the governor's office in Florida. If the Republican count goes to Hayes you can rest assured Florida *will* get a Republican Governor."

Sterns and William Chandler walk toward the campaign office to the right of the room, leaving behind W.E. Chandler and the others who are busy talking with the campaign workers. Once inside, William watches Sterns as he moves to the chair behind his desk and pulls opens his desk drawer. From this drawer he retrieves a bottle of whiskey and two glasses and places them on his desk. Starting to pour the whiskey Sterns says, "So…I've heard you're a whiskey man." With a wink he continues, "This is the best in the south and will make you cry. Give her a try?"

Raising an eyebrow, William Chandler nods and takes one of the glasses off the desk. He swirls the amber liquid around the bottom of the glass. Then in one swift motion, shoots the hard liquor down his throat in one gulp. His eyes water and he coughs from the sting and says, "Not bad." He reaches out for another and Sterns fills his glass again.

"Most Yankees can't handle southern whiskey," says Sterns with a slight mischievous smile. Before gulping down the second shot, William Chandler raises his glass in the air, "To President elect Hayes." Stern's nods in agreement and raises his own glass, "And the Republican Party." Both men then empty their glasses, the second one going down a little easier for William, who adds, "and the best money can bribe – I mean buy."

⁓⟊⟊⁓

In New York City at Democratic Headquarters', Samuel, his nephew William Pelton, Congressman Hewitt and John Bigelow are busy reviewing the returns. All of the campaign workers who fill the room assisting them are convinced that Tilden has won by the popular vote and none of them want to hear otherwise.

Hewitt turns to Samuel and says, "Floyd in Florida claims he needs ten thousand dollars more." Samuel is not pleased by the request. "For what purpose?"

"To guarantee strong and honest men in every precinct. He's offering to put up one-thousand dollars of his own money."

Samuel appreciates Floyd's offer but decides to refuse the request. "No more money goes out." Then, with a firm tone of dignity in his voice, he adds," This election must be kept honest."

At that point, William chimes in and complains to his uncle, "It is the Republicans that are not being honest. They are spending hundreds of thousands of dollars to influence men to steal this election."

John Bigelow adds with a sarcastic tone," All that and a free Federal army, courtesy of President Grant, to help them do it." He pauses for a moment and adds, "They're promising to remove the Federal troops along with the Carpetbaggers in the reconstructed states if Hayes wins. My concern is the southern Democrats may turn on us."

Samuel starts to get agitated at the direction this conversation is taking. Bristling, he fires back, "I do not *care* what the Republicans are spending. It is fraud to buy votes—I will not buy my way into the back-door of the White House!" After a quick moment, he softens his demeanor and calmly adds, "I also believe that Governor Hayes is an honorable man and that he will not allow his party to act improperly either."

All the other people working in the room witness the outburst. All of them admire Samuel for his integrity. Many of them think it is naïve' of him to believe the Republicans, regardless of what he may think of Hayes' integrity. As Democrats, they know from past elections that the Republicans are capable of buying, bribing and stealing whatever they want to win.

CHAPTER ELEVEN

Legal Electors

For the 1876 presidential election, each state is required by law to submit their Electoral Certificates to Washington by December 6th for Congress to count. Democratic Governor L.F. Grover of Oregon is seated behind his huge colonial style desk signing papers. His assistant, seated a few feet away, is holding a copy of the U.S. Constitution in his hands. Looking up from his paperwork and eyeing his assistant, the Governor asks, "Please read aloud the Twelfth Amendment."

"Eighteen o- four (1804)," the man begins, "The Electors shall meet in their respective states and vote by Ballot for President and Vice-President, one of whom, at least, shall not be an in-habitant of the same state with themselves; they shall name in their ballots the person voted for as President, and in distinct ballots the person voted for as Vice-President, and they shall make distinct lists of all persons voted for as President, and of all persons voted for as Vice-President, and of the number of votes for each, which lists they shall sign and certify, and transmit sealed to the seat of the government of the United States, directed to the President of the Senate;—The President of the Senate shall, in presence of the Senate and House of Representatives, open all the certificates and the votes shall then be counted;—The person having the greatest number of votes for President, shall be the President, if such number be a majority of the whole number of the Electors appointed; and if no person have such a majority, then from the persons having the highest numbers not exceeding three on the list of those voted for as President, the House of Representatives shall choose immediately, by ballot, the President."

At this point the assistant pauses for a moment when he hears Secretary of State Steven Chadwick, who is also a Democrat, enter the room. Again, Grover looks up from the paperwork before him and waves a hello to the Secretary. "Mr. Secretary, good day to you." He then motions for him to sit in a chair close to his desk. "Come on in and take a seat." Trying to keep the interruption to a minimum, the Secretary quickly walks to a chair across from the large desk and sits. Little does either the Governor or Secretary of State realize at the time, that in a few short months, Grover will resign his office and that Chadwick will be sworn in as the new Governor of Oregon.

Grover then looks back to his assistant. "Please continue."

Clearing his throat, the man starts again. "But in choosing the President, the votes shall be taken by states, the representation from each state having one vote; a quorum for this purpose shall consist of a member or members from two-thirds of the states, and a majority of all the states shall be necessary to a choice. And if the House of Representatives shall not choose a President whenever the right of choice shall devolve upon them, before the fourth day of March next following, then the Vice President shall act as President, as in the case of the death or other constitutional disability of the President. The person having the greatest number of votes as Vice-President, shall be the Vice-President, if such number be a majority of the whole number of Electors appointed, and if no person have a majority, then from the two highest numbers on the list, the Senate shall choose the Vice-President; a quorum for the purpose shall consist of two-thirds of the whole number of Senators and a majority of the whole number shall be necessary to a choice. But no person constitutionally ineligible to the office of President shall be eligible to that of Vice-President of the United States." The assistant stops reading and asks, "Would you like me to continue?"

Taking a moment to think, the Governor answers, "No – there is nothing in there that will help me change the popular result."

"But Hayes has won our state by one-hundred-thousand votes," Chadwick complains.

The Governor settles back in his chair, removes his reading glasses and tosses them on top of the paperwork on his desk. Looking up at the ceiling, he begins to rub the weariness from his eyes and states, "My only recourse to save this election for the party is to use the law in Article

2 and disqualify Watts. It will give Tilden the one electoral he needs to claim victory."

Chadwick promptly adds, "It clearly states; no senator or representative, or person holding an office of trust or profit under the United States, shall be appointed an elector." He pauses for a moment, thinking. Then he slowly smiles and says, "This may just work."

A day later, the Republicans get word that Governor Grover is going to disqualify the Republican Elector J.W. Watts because of his postmaster position. They decide to counter his decision with more confusion and deceit. They are not about to let the Governor and his lot hand over the one electoral vote needed for a Tilden victory without a fight.

Waiting in the hallway outside the Governor's office are the Oregon Republican Electors J.W. Watts, John Cartwright, William Odell, John Miller and John Parker. Across the hall are Democrat E.A. Cronin and Secretary of State Chadwick. The Secretary of State makes the first move and walks up to the Governor's door that is slightly ajar. He knocks first, then peeks his head inside the door and asks, "May I come in?"

The Governor is seated behind his desk. The argument and dispute that he has been expecting, is about to begin. "Of course, I've been waiting all morning "

Chadwick enters the office and walks to Grover's desk. Keeping his voice low, he says, "Odell and Cartwright have brought two witnesses, Sir, along with Mr. Watts."

Though he's been expecting a negative reaction by the Republicans over his decision to disqualify Watts, Grover feels his blood pressure rising. Slightly surprising even himself, he states loud enough for everyone to hear, "This dispute has been settled! Are they are here to argue?"

"They claim they are not," Chadwick responds, keeping his own voice in an even tone. Not expecting this response, Grover becomes a bit calmer and somewhat confused. "Okay," he reluctantly agrees, a puzzled look now crossing his face. "Fine… show them in."

Chadwick walks back to the door and motions to the men in the hallway. As they all enter the room, the Governor stands from his chair to greet them. "Good afternoon gentlemen." He then picks up the three

Electoral Certificates from his desk and hands two of them off to Odell and Cartwright. "These are signed and ready."

The Republican Electors take the two certificates from him and begin to review them. As they are doing so, the Governor walks over to E.A. Cronin and hands him the third certificate. "This one is yours, again, signed and ready." Taking the certificate, Cronin replies, "Thank you Sir."

The Governor now walks back behind his desk and seats himself in his chair, waiting to hear the complaints and arguments that he knows the Republicans Watts, Cartwright and Odell are going to make. He figures, *why wait for them to start the fight,* and says, "The Elector's certificates have been authorized with my signature. Complete and express them to Congress for the count by the sixth of December as required by law."

Odell, who is angered by the switch, knows that the Governor has the law of the Constitution on his side, but asks just for the sake of argument, "And where is Mr. Watt's certificate?"

"We have been through this all before, gentlemen," the Governor answers.

Cartwright then jumps into the dispute. Pointing at Mr. Watts, he declares "We stand firm that Mr. Watt's is here as an official Republican Elector."

"He is not official," Grover interrupts. "Mr. Watt's forfeited his right as an Elector when he delayed his resignation as Postmaster at Lafayette. As a result of that delay, Mr. Cronin here will fill the vacancy. He has received the highest amount of votes required by law to appoint him, by Secretary of State Chadwick here, as the new elector."

Odell refuses to accept the decision. "But Mr. Watt's *has* resigned his Postmaster's position..."

Not giving Odell a chance to continue, Grover interjects, "He did so a day after the law required it. The Constitution clearly states that no elector can hold an official federal office."

"But Governor, Mr. Cronin is a Democrat," Cartwright complains. "He will vote the certificate as a Democrat for Tilden."

Grover, noting how Cartwright almost spat the words 'Democrat' and 'Tilden', sits forward in his chair and steely looks back to Cartwright. "Mr. Cronin may vote as he deems fit. If it *is* for Tilden..." he pauses slightly for effect, then raises an eyebrow and continues, "then it *shall be* for Tilden." Sitting back in his chair again, he waves his hand. "Now gentlemen, if you please, I have other matters to attend to. This matter is now closed and not open for any further debate."

Angered by the Governor's nonchalant attitude Odell shouts out, "Governor Grover, we hereby officially object to this decision, on the grounds that you yourself are a Democrat! We also want it noted that you want to use this opportunity to hand Tilden the election!"

Grover, annoyed by the outburst and accusation, narrows his eyes at Odell. Keeping his voice steady, he sternly counters, "Are you challenging my authority Mr. Odell?" Trying to make his point, he starts tapping with his index finger on his desk. "I have followed the law in this case and I am doing my sworn duty as the Governor of this state. I suggest *you* do the same as an Elector. Now…Good Day, Gentlemen!"

All six electors, hearing the Governor's dismissal and realizing that there is nothing more to gain, leave the room without further argument. Once in the corridor, they walk toward another room in the Capitol building and enter. The room has a few empty desks and several chairs. Mr. Cronin walks over to one of these desks with his electoral certificate, seats himself in a chair and begins to fill out the document. The five Republicans, Parker, Miller, Watt's, Odell and Cartwright stand close by and watch him. After a moment, Odell interrupts, "Mr. Cronin." Without looking up and continuing his task, Cronin answers, "What is it?"

"Cartwright and I are declaring our positions vacant and are appointing Mr. Parker and Mr. Miller to replace us."

Surprised by the announcement, Cronin stops writing, looks up at Odell and says, "That is not a legal option Mr. Odell."

"It is and we shall do so," Cartwright adds defiantly. He then takes the two certificates from Odell and hands them to Parker and Miller. "Mr. Parker, Mr. Miller… Mr. Odell and I declare that you are to fill our vacancies as the Republican Oregon Electors. Please complete these certificates and give them to Mr. Cronin to express to Washington immediately."

Miller and Parker take the certificates, walk to another empty desk in the room, seat themselves and begin to fill out the Electoral certificates. Cartwright, Odell and Watts walk out of the room back into the corridor. Cronin stands up from the desk from which he was seated behind and walks over to Parker and Miller. As Cronin waits for the men to complete their forms Miller says without looking up, "Mr. Parker and I will be finished momentarily." Cronin, obviously angered by the switch barks, "This is illegal and you two know it."

Parker nonchalantly responds, "It's as legal as the Governor appointing you to replace Mr. Watts."

Meanwhile, Cartwright, Odell and Watts have already left the building. They enter a small restaurant where a few people are dining. The three men walk to a table and quietly seat themselves. Cartwright reaches into his jacket pocket and pulls out three new sets of Electoral certificates. He hands one each to Watts and Odell and quietly says, "Mr. Watts—Here is your certificate. Mr. Odell and I are declaring your vacancy filled. Complete this certificate as a true and official Oregon Elector for the Republican Party."

Odell turns to Cartwright and says, "I'll wire Chairman Chandler of our actions."

"Yes. Immediately," Cartwright replies. Odell nods in agreement and Watts asks, "What about Cronin?"

Cartwright smirks and says, "No need to worry about Cronin. By the time he explains what we've conspired to the Governor, our second set of certificates will be on their way to Washington." Then he turns to Odell and says, "Be sure to send the Five-thousand back to Tilden's nephew Pelton untouched. His bribe should justify our actions in appointing Watts."

"I'm betting Mr. Tilden will not be pleased when he discovers his nephew's attempt to pay us off," Odell answers with a chuckle.

Back in Governor Grover's office, Cronin enters with his certificate in hand and walks over to the Governor's desk. Secretary Chadwick is still present and is surprised by Cronin's sudden entry.

"Is there a problem, Mr. Cronin?" Grover asks. Without hesitation, Cronin begins to explain. "Odell and Cartwright have both declared their positions vacant. That is why they brought Parker and Miller – so they could appoint them positions and give them their certificates from you. I believe these men are planning to send a second set of Electoral certificates from Oregon to Washington."

Grover stands and pounds his hand on his desk, "They are not authorized to do that!" He turns to Secretary Chadwick. "Send a wire immediately to Mr. Pelton in New York. Tell him the certificates have been granted accordingly, and that the third Elector is a Democrat, filling the vacancy of Republican Postmaster Watts." The Secretary takes a piece of paper from Grover's desk and writes down the message. Grover waits for him to finish and instructs, "Also, wire back the money that Mr. Pelton sent for the Republican Electors and me. Let him know that the Governor of Oregon need not be paid to uphold the law." Grover waits again for Secretary Chadwick to finish scribbling the instructions and then adds, "As for the actions of the others—inform Mr. Pelton there may be an illegal second set of Electoral certificates headed to Congress. Tell him that I am not party to that action. —nor can I stop the Republicans from violating federal election laws."

Chadwick completes his notes and confesses to Grover, "I can send back only half of the money."

Grover angrily questions, "Only half?"

"Odell took five thousand of it for expenses," Chadwick explains. Grover tightens his fists and thinks to himself, *Those Scoundrels!*

CHAPTER TWELVE

Scandals and Assumptions

The cold months of winter in New York City can be harsh but are rarely a distraction to the Northerners who are used to the frigid climate. Nothing short of a blizzard would keep them from being outside to take care of their daily business. The fresh snow and slippery ice decorating the front side-walks of the Everett House is being enjoyed by several children who are bundled in their warm coats, hats and mittens.

Through an office window, William Pelton watches as people busily rush along the sidewalks with their packages. He smiles when he sees a few children frolicking in the snow. At this moment he is wishing his life was a little more like the strangers he sees outside. If he could he would put aside his work and join in the festivities of the upcoming holiday season, but his loyalty to his uncle is more a labor of love. He will not give up until he knows he has done all he can to see Samuel in the Presidency. After a few moments, he turns from the frosty scenery outside his window. With a small sigh, he walks back to his desk and takes a seat across from Mr. Smith to assist in deciphering the incoming telegrams from around the country.

Once seated, William looks wistfully back at the window from which he was watching his fellow New-Yorkers. Then a determined look crosses his face as he thinks to himself, *the light-hearted joy of the holiday season will have to wait. There is too much work to be done and I will do whatever it takes to stop those thieving Republicans from stealing this election from my uncle.* He then picks up a telegram from Oregon and while decoding the message with his pencil to the paper he becomes confused. Placing the document aside, he searches for a moment through some of the other telegrams on his desk and finds a second cipher from Oregon. He reviews it immediately and once done he leans back in his chair and is more puzzled than before. Raising his eyes up from his work, Smith looks over at William and realizes there may be a problem and asks, "What's wrong?"

"The money from Oregon has been returned in two separate wires... untouched." Crooking an eyebrow, Smith stands and takes the two telegrams from the desk. He takes a moment to review them both, and then replies, "It's no matter. Hayes has won Oregon by over one thousand popular votes. We must keep our focus on the Southern states."

William, who is not completely convinced, ponders on the remark for a moment then says with concern, "If my uncle hears of this—I think I should inform him."

Smith returns to his seat. To reassure William, he says, "The money has been returned and there is no proof of any wrongdoing." By the look on William's face, Smith realizes he needs to be more convincing. "There is no need to anger your uncle over something that did not work out. If the money subject comes up, we can easily justify the situation."

"Easily justify? How?"

"We will say that you simply sent the funds to cover legal expenses for the dispute."

Thinking for a moment, William nods that this is a good explanation and then asks, "What about the two different sets of certificates Oregon is submitting?"

"If Oregon sends two sets—it will force an investigation in Congress" Smith answers. "Then Hewitt will use it to prove Republican fraud."

Back at Republican Headquarters in Tallahassee, Florida, Lew Wallace hands a telegram to Zach Chandler. He quietly watches as Zach reads the wire and waits for his response. Finishing the document, Zach smiles and says, "This is good news from Odell in Oregon. He has positive proof of a Democratic fraud by money received from Tilden's nephew, Pelton, to purchase an Elector's vote."

Wallace is not won over by Zach's enthusiasm. "It also states that they are sending in duplicate sets of certificates—Good trickery, but is it legal?"

Zach smirks and replies smugly, "Just as legal as what we are doing in Florida by using an ex-governor to authorize them."

Seeing the confidence in Zach's face, Wallace begins warming to the deceitful game plan. "Do you think it wise for South Carolina and Louisiana to send duplicates as well?"

Zach realizes that Wallace is enjoying the moment and adds, "It's not only wise, but a genius move."

Just then a thought occurs to Wallace. "Not if Congress decides to throw out the second set."

"Your conclusion is quite correct, Mr. Wallace," concedes Zach. "But consider this. The President of the Senate is a Republican. If he throws out *any* votes it will more likely be the Democrats."

"You sure this is legal?"

"He's a loyal party man. He'll do whatever needs to be done to seat Hayes."

Pondering this, Wallace sits down in his chair and thinks to himself, *These people have deep pockets. I should have asked for more money.*

⌐⫘⌐

Back in New York, Samuel and Mary are seated with John Bigelow in the front parlor in Tilden's Gramercy home. They are all near the glow and warmth of the fire that is burning in the handsomely carved mahogany framed fireplace. Enjoying after-dinner cocktails, they are talking about current and upcoming events for his Presidency. Bigelow turns to Samuel and asks, "You realize this matter will be settled soon. It's only a couple of days before Congress conducts the count and announces the results. Do you have any concerns?"

"I have a few, but am secure the Electors will push me over the one-eighty-five needed."

Mary chimes in, "I despise dirty politics. Deceit and trickery is shameful. Women would never stoop so low if they were in charge." Samuel reaches out to pat his sister's hand. "They might if the stakes were high enough." Mary frowns at his remark then Samuel adds, "But I would still support a woman's right to vote."

Mary smiles, "I will hold you to that promise, dear brother."

"I didn't say promise – I said support." Mary pulls her hand away and glares at her brother. For a moment there is an awkward moment of silence and Bigelow, who is very good at changing the subject quickly, asks Samuel, "Have you considered your choices for Cabinet?"

Samuel is thankful for the break in the tension, "I have and I'll wait before making any announcements."

Mary not skipping a beat scolds, "Procrastination may signal to the opposition you are in doubt of your election."

Samuel doesn't agree with her negative opinion but Bigelow sees her point. Sitting back in his chair, he motions toward Mary. "You know Samuel, Mary may be right concerning this matter."

Samuel still does not agree and attempts to clarify his position. "There is already anarchy in the streets. I am trying to avoid fanning the fires for fear of sparking riots. The voters have given me the majority by over two-hundred and fifty four thousand. I have faith that they will not allow the scoundrels on the Republican side to over-rule their decision to have me elected."

John and Mary glance at each other for a moment and then both nod in agreement that Samuel's assumptions are correct. Raising his glass, Bigelow proclaims, 'To the voters."

Both Samuel and Mary raise their own glasses, "To the voters."

CHAPTER THIRTEEN

Certificates Are Opened December 6th

Samuel J. Randall, the Democratic House Speaker, is inside the House Chambers on Capitol Hill and members of Congress on both sides of the aisle are readying themselves for the battle that is about to begin. They have all gathered for the official legal count of the Electoral Certificates and are aware of the problems that will ensue. Randall, now at his podium in the front of the Chambers begins banging his gavel numerous times to quiet the boisterous voices filling the room. It takes a few moments, but the congressmen finally settle down and sit in their designated seats. In the back of the room, off the official floor, there are several reporters from newspapers across the country surrounding the *New York Times* editor, John Reid. Through one of his many connections in the Capitol, he has secured himself a front row view. He is anxious to see if his half baked scheme to confuse the electoral count will play out to his satisfaction. He impatiently watches and listens with great anticipation.

The President of the Senate, Thomas Ferry, stands next to Randall, ready to witness the count. When the room finally settles Randall announces loudly, "The States of Oregon, Louisiana, Florida and South Carolina have submitted two sets of electoral certificates. We must decide today which votes are legal." All the Congressmen stand and jeer. John Reid, surprised by the announcement, smirks while writing notes in his pad. He thinks to himself, *this will surely give Hayes the opportunity to win.*

Congressman Hewitt stands and shouts out, "I have prepared a draft for President Tilden—The people must assemble to protest against this fraud—they should not be robbed of their choice for President." A Republican Congressman stands and hollers, "Fraud? There is no deception here! Republican Chairman Zach Chandler has announced to us that Hayes is elected." Immediately all the Democratic Party members of Congress stand again, booing and jeering in protest. The demonstration is deafening and Speaker Randall continues to bang his gavel to quiet them. "Order! Order! Gentlemen we must have Order in the House!"

Unaware at the moment of the dispute happening at the Capitol building, President Grant stands in front of a window in the Oval Office. He thinks to himself while watching the marching protestors; *don't these people have businesses or families that require their attention?* Lost in thought, he doesn't notice as one of his Aide's walks in. Clearing his throat, the Aide stops, holding out a message on paper. With an audible sigh Grant turns away from the spectacle and takes the message from the mans' waiting hand. The Aide nods and quickly leaves the room. Grant unfolds the paper, reads the message and then crumples it in his hand. He then turns back to the widow and resumes his vigil on the marching protesters.

A moment later, his wife Julia enters the room, walks over to her husband and puts her arms around his waist from behind him. Reaching her lips close to his ear, she says to him in a soft voice, "Deep in thought?" Welcoming the touch of her thin arms around him, he reaches down and gently takes her hands into his and lifts them to his lips and kisses them. "I always have time for you—my sweet Julia." He turns to face her and she can see he is disturbed about something.

"Is something wrong?" she asks, "What's going on?"

Grant slips out of her embrace and walks over to his desk and heavily sits in his chair. "I have just received word that the election has been compromised." Julia moves and positions herself behind him and rubs his shoulders. "How so?" she asks.

The President attempts to explain. "By duplicate Electoral submissions from the South and the state of Oregon."

Julia continues to massage his shoulders, "Oregon? What do they have to do with it?"

"In my opinion this entire election is a fraud. Every day that passes, the country falls deeper into division and violence."

Julia moves away from him and walks to the front of the desk and she seats herself in a chair. "As President, can't you declare a winner?"

"No—It is not the job of the President to declare the outcome of an election. The Electoral College process has caused some minor problems in the past… but none like we are witnessing today."

Julia indicates agreement with a nod and remains silent, waiting for the rest of his explanation. Grant continues and articulates, "In 1804 the system was modified by the Twelfth Amendment which delegates the election of President to the House and leaves the determination to the Vice President." He takes a deep breath, "Who, by the way, is in charge in the Senate."

Julia, bored by how the process works, asks, "So the Vice President and *not* the President decides? That hardly seems proper."

"He is the President of the Senate. In the event no candidate wins a majority of the electoral votes—but wins the larger majority of the popular vote the electors should reflect it." Noticing that Julia has a blank look in her eyes, he then asks her, "Am I confusing you, dear?"

Julia jolts back to reality. "Is this going to take a long time to resolve?" After all, she wants him to guarantee that their departure from the White House is going to happen on the time schedule that she has planned. If they do not she will have to reschedule all their travel arrangements that she has so meticulously prearranged.

"If the Liberal Republicans have their way it can," Grant answers. "They are narrow-headed men with their eyes so close together that they can look out of the same gimlet hole without winking."

Both of them are startled when they hear gunshots coming from outside. The President, followed by Julia, rushes over to the window to see what is happening. They can see the protestors, who have dropped their signs but not their torches, are now fighting with the soldiers who have been stationed near the crowd to keep order. Horse and carriage drivers begin trying to maneuver their charges away from the commotion, but are having a difficult time because the animals are getting spooked by the violent outbreak. The ones not tied down start to scatter in different directions.

"Damn it!" Grant growls. "This situation is getting out of hand!" A few of the protestors take their torches and move toward some nearby trees and set them on fire. A large number of people in the crowd shriek and begin to run to escape the intensifying confrontation.

The President and the First Lady, still watching from the window, witness the peoples' violent activities. Julia raises a hand to her mouth and cries out in horror, "Those people are setting fire to the trees!" The President tries to calm her. He knows she does not like hostility of any kind. A moment later an officer of the guard enters the room, walks to the President, salutes and says, "The perimeter guards are having a difficult time with the demonstrators, sir."

Grant points back to the window and fires back," I can see that, Captain. Get more men out there immediately! Those people may protest but they can not and will not be allowed to destroy public property. Get this situation under control at once!"

The captain quickly salutes. "Yes Sir." He then briskly walks out of the room.

Grant, with arm still around his wife's shoulder, grips her closer to him and consoles her saying, "No need for worry, this will all be over in a few minutes."

━━✦━━

That same evening at the Governor's office in Tallahassee, Florida, Governor Sterns is having similar problems with his own set of protestors. Like President Grant, Sterns is watching a mob from a window inside his office. As in the nation's capital, this crowd is also becoming violent and the protestors begin fighting amongst themselves. The political signs they carry to support their respective candidates start to become makeshift clubs and are being used to hit each other. The soldiers, who are acting as guard, gather up in formation. On order from their officer, they fire a volley into the air above the heads of the crowd. Although this action succeeds in scaring off some of the rowdy protestors, many others stay to continue the brawl.

One of the soldiers, a Major who has just recently received and is now wearing his federal blue uniform, enters the Governor's office to report the rioting. The man realizes that the Governor is watching from the window and he states, "We are trying our best to control the situation, sir."

"Your 'best' does not seem to be good enough!" Sterns growls. "This situation is impossible. I can barely enter the building anymore without fear of being bumped on the head."

The Major walks to a window next to the Governor and looks out at the fighting mob. "My men are controlling the situation as best they can, sir. Unfortunately, these riots are becoming rampant throughout the city."

The Governor walks over to a coat rack in the room and takes a coat from it. As he slings the garment over his shoulders he says, "Major, get my carriage at once—and four of your best men. I'm going to tour the city."

The soldier walks away from the window and faces Sterns. "With all due respect, sir, I'm not sure that would be a good idea. It's mighty dangerous out there right now, sir. Small parts of the city are becoming uncontrollable."

The Governor, annoyed by this warning, fires back, "Don't argue with me Major. It is my duty as Governor of this state to protect it. And I can't perform that duty unless I know what is exactly going on out there."

With a note of resignation in his voice, the soldier replies, "Yes sir. I'll assemble the required troops, sir."

As the Major walks out of the room, Sterns turns back to the window. He watches as his escort guard is assembled next to his carriage and horses. With a satisfactory grunt, he turns and walks out the door to join them.

CHAPTER FOURTEEN

Negotiations Begin

Tilden, along with his sister Mary and his nephew William Pelton are seated in the living room at the Tilden mansion. Accompanying them are John Bigelow, Mr. Smith and Senator William Thurman from Ohio. The Senator reaches into his jacket pocket and pulls out a telegram. He hands it to Samuel. The Senator and others wait in silence while he reads the message, anticipating his reaction.

Finishing the cipher, Samuel crumples it in his hand, a look of anger clouding his face. After a long moment of tense silence he looks to the Senator and asks, "Why did Congress call off the count?"

"Two and three sets of different certificates being submitted apparently is the cause," Thurman replies.

Surprised by the declaration, Samuel's anger turns to confusion. "*Two* and *three* sets of certificates?"

Standing, William suggests, "Uncle—Maybe we can persuade the Oregon Electors."

Samuel stands to look his nephew in the eye. With his anger returning, he fires back, "I will not be part of any fraud to buy votes."

Defending her son's suggestion Mary chimes in, "Samuel, there is no need to scold William. He is just making a suggestion."

Still agitated by the news Samuel fires back, "Not one I will consider." He then looks over to Bigelow, who has been standing silently off to the side, his hands in his pockets. "What are your thoughts?"

"A peculiar situation, Samuel. The representatives must be up in arms," Bigelow says.

"Indeed they are," the Senator replies.

Samuel argues, "Maybe so—but not the ones party to this fraud. The violence and harm being done to a free government is spreading across the country like wildfire. I will surrender this election before I see another day of bloodshed."

Mary disagrees. "Samuel, you must fight this and consider any deals the southern Democrats may be making behind your back." Mary pauses for a moment and William chimes in, "The Republicans want to gain control of their property stolen by the Carpetbaggers."

Samuel walks over to a window, pulls back the curtain and stares out at his faithful supporters. He stands there for a moment, watching the campaign marchers outside. These people, many of them Civil War Veterans have been enduring the cold weather ever since Election Day to let Samuel know that they are loyal and want him to be their President. They have been doing this since the controversy began and they stay late every night, no matter what the weather. They anxiously wait to hear any words or commands from their duly elected Commander and Chief on whether he needs them to fight or not. They are willing, able and ready to do whatever he asks.

Samuel turns back to his sister and the others gathered in the room. "You all know that it is not in my nature to support violence. I pride myself on high principals, discipline and reason—strategies of the mind. I have never used ruff and tumble politics in place of justice."

Bigelow, who Samuel can always count on to change the tone of a conversation, asks, "Did Mr. Hewitt send any advisement on how Congress will decide which certificates are legal?"

Samuel, calmer now, his recent anger abated, looks up to the ceiling. "He doesn't know, John—The Framers of the Constitution never anticipated or provided a law for election fraud of this magnitude."

Still stinging slightly from his uncles' rebuff, William cautiously says, "Mr. Hewitt suggested to me before he left for Washington, that we should organize the Democrats across the country to protest."

The others nod in agreement to this and then the Senator adds, "The way I see it, Samuel, you have three choices. We can fight, we can back down or we can arbitrate."

Looking at no one in particular, Samuel ponders this suggestion. He then turns to Thurman. "Violence is never a good solution, Senator. We have just emerged from one Civil War and it will never do to engage in another- it could very well end in the destruction of our free government.

At the same time, however, 'backing down' is not a solution that I find very appealing. I've never 'backed downed' from anyone or anything in my life and I do not wish to start now." He pauses for a moment, before continuing. He quickly looks at everyone in the room and then turns his gaze back to Thurman. "That leaves your third solution, Senator." Again, he pauses just for a moment, a grim look crossing his face. "We must arbitrate."

"Arbitrate?" Bigelow fires back. "Samuel! Your supporters are angry at this outrage. You've won the popular vote and they want their candidate elected."

Samuel stares at his friend and shakes his head in agreement. After a moment of thought, he walks over to a table and picks up a book. He believes he may have discovered a solution to end the controversy peacefully. He waves the book in the air and says, "Open hearings, full Congressional debates- no secret agreements should be allowed."

The others let out a moan and William looks at the floor, mumbling unintelligibly under his breath. Bigelow shakes his head and says sarcastically, "Why not just throw names in a hat and break the deadlock?"

Annoyed, Samuel fires back at them, "I may lose the Presidency, but I will not raffle for it. Arbitration is a much wiser solution."

Again, Bigelow shakes his head in disagreement. "Samuel, the Constitution says nothing about a lawyer's arbitration. Or even about which certificates are legal."

"That's true, John," Samuel responds, looking at the book he is still holding in his hand. "Only the President of the Senate has the power to decide which certificates are valid."

Senator Thurman is somewhat surprised by Samuel's decision to choose arbitration, even though it was his own suggestion. But with the mention of the President of the Senate, he interjects "I don't think I need to remind you, Samuel, that the Senate is currently controlled by the Republicans. They would vote along party lines and give credit to the certificates for Hayes. What would your legal argument be to stop that action?"

Samuel smirks, puts the book back on the table and places his hands in his pockets. "To throw the election into the House of Representatives, where it belongs."

Bigelow's frown fades as he nods in agreement. "And the *Democrats* have control of the House." Samuel is happy to see that his friend finally understands what he is thinking, but he also realizes his plan is not flaw-less. "Unfortunately, since the Twenty-second Joint Rule was repealed earlier this year, the Republicans will refuse to adopt it."

As the others are thinking about how the plan could work, William adds to the confusion when he negatively says, "The death of Grant's Vice President could complicate the issue further—with Republican Senator Ferry acting as Vice President – he would obviously be bias and back Hayes."

Samuel smiles at this. "His bias be damned…I must start immediately to write and publish a case." He walks back to his desk and sits down. The others move closer to the desk and await his instructions. Samuel looks to the Senator and says, "Please send Congressman Hewitt and the others a wire and tell them to start working with the Republicans to get the best deals they will offer."

CHAPTER FIFTEEN

Chance Meeting

People fill the Forty-Second Street area of New York City near Fifth Avenue with many of them carrying loaded shopping bags filled with merchandise from local merchants. Consumers scurry past the election protestors that continue to march in support for their candidates Hayes or Tilden. The sound of clip-clopping horses pulling taxi style carriages and their drivers fills the air as they move gracefully east and west on the holiday decorated Avenue.

John Bigelow, Mary and Samuel are also out this morning buying gifts and enjoying the festive season. They are standing on the sidewalk as their driver busies himself loading their packages into the coach. Mary watches anxiously and directs the man in hopes that none of the items will be broken or damaged. Seeing that his sister has the matter well in hand, Samuel turns and waves to the protesting marchers. They call out to him, "Demand what is yours and the people will sustain you." A second protestor shouts, "Issue the call that our liberties are best preserved by the sword." Then a third bellows, "Fair count or fight." Without replying to these enthusiastic supporters, Samuel tips his hat to the men and climbs into the now loaded carriage.

Once inside the coach he looks to the window to his left in time to see another carriage pass by at a fast clip, with the horses in full trot. As this rapidly moving carriage passes to the front, its' rear wheel catches a rut, throwing mud and water directly at two nicely dressed women who have been chatting with each other nearby. Their packages fall to the sidewalk and both women scramble to retrieve them. In the midst of this scuttle, the older of the two women falls to the ground and the other lady starts to laugh while struggling to help her up.

From inside the carriage, Mary says, "Oh John, those women are in need of assistance. Would you be so kind?" Nodding, Bigelow curses under his breath, "Damn taxi drivers!" and retrieves his hat that he had just taken off. While holding his hat in his hand he carefully maneuvers his exit from the coach. Once he is outside, Samuel leans out his window, winks at John and says, "Do not get too distracted – I'm going to need you today."

John smiles while positioning his hat on his head, "No need to worry—I'll meet up with you at headquarters." Samuel nods his approval and motions for his driver to go forward.

Samuel's driver snaps the reins in his hands and the horses move forward into traffic. Samuel and Mary watch from the carriage window as John and a few of the protestors who have put down their signs, rush over to assist the ladies. Samuel waves at them as his carriage passes. At that moment, he realizes that the younger woman is someone he has seen before, but does not know personally. As this thought races through his mind, the young woman, Celeste, raises her head in Samuels' direction and their eyes meet for a brief but defining moment. While concentrating on the fallen packages, Bigelow doesn't remember or recognize her as the woman that sprinted past them in Central Park a few weeks earlier.

Mary notices Samuel's obvious attraction to the younger woman and scolds, "Really Samuel—put your eyes back in your head. She is half your age."

Samuel smirks and says coyly, "I was just making sure John is alright. But since you mentioned it—the beauty of that young woman is quite… exquisite."

"Need I remind you, there are other matters that are more important right now than flirting?" Samuel brings his hand to his chest and thumps it gently against his heart, "I always have time to admire a beautiful woman."

Back outside on the sidewalk, Bigelow hands the packages back to Celeste and her mother, then asks the older woman, "Are you in need of any medical attention?"

The older woman smiles, "No, no," then asks, "Was that Samuel Tilden in the coach with you?"

"Why yes, it was." Bigelow answers.

Celeste is surprised that her mother has recognized anyone in New York City and asks, "Mother, how do you know who that man was?"

The woman winks at Bigelow and says with a slight snicker to her daughter, "All the society ladies in New Orleans read the papers – that is Samuel Jones Tilden, our newly elected President. You would know this, my dear, if you paid more attention to the news."

Celeste is not amused by her mother's remarks or the mud-spattered situation which has now begun to soak through her clothing. "What do I care what man is elected President?" she sarcastically responds. "Women are not allowed a say in such matters of politics." She then turns to Bigelow, "Thank you, sir, for your kind assistance. We can handle it from here."

The mother reprimands her daughter, "Celeste, your manners," and turns to Bigelow and says, "I'm sorry sir – I did not hear your name." Bigelow touches the brim of his hat and slightly nods, "John Bigelow, M'am," The woman tries unsuccessfully to swipe some of the mud from the front of her dress and she smiles and states, "Your reputation precedes you sir. My name is Mrs. Stauffer, of New Orleans. My husband is in pharmaceuticals. And this lovely lady is my daughter Celeste Stauffer, who, as you now know, speaks her mind without pause."

Bigelow is impressed with her family's credentials. "Mr. Tilden's father was in the same business." Mrs. Stauffer replies, "Yes I know, my husband often spoke of his successes with cures." The three commence walking toward the entrance of the Fifth Avenue Hotel. Bigelow turns to Celeste and asks, "And if you could vote?" This question from John takes Celeste by surprise and she pauses for a moment before answering him, then replies, "If women were more ambitious about equal rights and the laws that guide us—this country would be better for it. We are, after all, half the population and there would be *none* without us." John smiles and nods in agreement at her response.

Before entering the hotel, Mrs. Stauffer stops and reaches her hand out. "I thank you again, for your assistance, Mr. Bigelow. And please excuse my daughter—she has become very anxious with all the protesting and violence. We have been in the city for only a few weeks and are traveling abroad in the morning to visit family."

"I can speak for myself mother!" Celeste snipes. She turns to Bigelow and shakes his hand rather vigorously. "Mr. Bigelow—Thank you for your assistance. I wish you and Mr. Tilden a victorious outcome as well as a Merry Christmas."

Again, tipping his hat and smiling in amusement, Bigelow replies, "Maybe someday we will meet again under better circumstances and Merry Christmas to you as well, Miss Stauffer." *Not in this lifetime.* Celeste thinks to herself as she watches John walk away.

CHAPTER SIXTEEN

Publishing the Case

Inside the Republican Headquarters at the Fifth Avenue Hotel, on December, 20th, Reid is reviewing Tilden's recently published case, the *Presidential Counts*. The booklet was placed on every member of Congress' desk in the capital. A few feet away from Reid, Zach Chandler sits behind his desk, busily working on another project. Pausing from his review, Reid walks over to Zach, with the pamphlet in hand and asks, "Have you read this yet?" Zach, trying to concentrate on his own work, briefly looks at the cover and mumbles, "No."

Reid waves the booklet in the air to get Zach's attention and gripes, "John Bigelow wrote the introduction and it's quite effective. It could possibly sway some of the Republican Senators to vote for Tilden."

Zach, annoyed by Reid's interruption, stands up from his desk and moves away from Reid and counters, "You started this election fiasco—don't complain." Walking over to a volunteer, he hands off a slip of paper to him. "Please send this immediately." The clerk nods in agreement and takes the message from Zach and exits the room. Zach walks back to his desk and sits down. He continues with his work and without looking up, says to Reid, "Go ahead, read it aloud while I finish this report."

Reid frowns. He is not overjoyed about being brushed off but begins reading. "It starts; it is shown that in Seventeen-Ninety Three—two Houses, by concurrent Resolution, prescribed the mode of the counting, which was followed down to Eighteen-Sixty-Five."

Within the same time frame, others, in different locations are reading Samuel's Presidential Counts.

Seated behind his desk in the Oval office, President Grant is leaning back in his chair, smoking a cigar. Relaxed, he listens to the words of Tilden's *Presidential Count*, being read to him by his wife Julia. General Sherman is seated in a nearby chair, chewing on his own cigar, and with his legs crossed and arms folded, he too, listens as the first lady reads, "Subsequently, a standing rule of Congress for counting prevailed in Eighteen-Sixty-Five, Eighteen-Sixty-Nine and Eighteen-Seventy-Two. The two Houses invariably appointed tellers to make the count—two for the Lower House and one for the Senate."

Inside the living room at the Hayes home in Ohio, Senator Sherman is seated by a desk, reading aloud his copy of the *Presidential Counts* to Lucy and Rutherford Hayes, who are seated comfortably on a couch next to each other. "In this survey, with citations to sources, Tilden contends: that the two Houses have exclusive jurisdiction to count the electoral votes under their own rules and had exercised that power."

Back at the nation's capital, as protestors continue to march in the streets outside the White House, Julia continues reading out loud, "From the beginning of the Federal Government, the President of the Senate merely opened the votes and presented them to the two Houses for action, but it's never gone beyond that limit-"

Over at the Capitol the Senate President Ferry reads out loud the *Presidential Counts* to a couple of other Senators seated near him in the room, "Function in a single instance. To allow him to count the votes would permit him to disfranchise a State, and even to elect himself President. Three, that the two Houses had-"

Inside House Chambers Speaker of the House Randall stands by the door reading the *Presidential Counts* out loud to Hewitt who is seated in a chair near Randall's desk, "Authority to decide upon the legality of votes and might go behind the returns to do so."

Back in Republican Headquarters after Reid finishes reading the *Presidential Counts*, Zach stands and stretches. He then reaches over and takes the booklet from Reid. "Tilden makes a notable case."

"His writings are good." Reid admits.

Zach looks over at Reid. "Worried Mr. Reid? Go ahead and print it. Most people won't understand the content. In fact, most are amazingly ignorant when it comes to politics." Raising an eyebrow, Reid gives Zach a devious grin. "I'm counting on it," he replies.

Little does either man realize, but just outside the hotel lobby on the sidewalk several protestors are huddled near a fire and are reading Tilden's *Presidential Counts* that have just been published in the *New York Sun* newspaper.

CHAPTER SEVENTEEN

Messages Galore

The following day, a large group of Tilden's supporters are gathered in front of the mansion, carrying signs and calling out for Samuel to claim his Presidency. George, the local Postman, is having difficulty maneuvering his horses and mail carriage through the crowd. He finally pulls up to the curb and halts. He jumps down from the carriage and struggles with his heavy mailbag, trying to make his way through the crowd.

Mary, not far from him, walks past the crowd with her arms filled with shopping bags. As she too, struggles through the crowd, she calls out, "Coming through. Excuse me please." She finally makes it to the stairs and climbs the stairs while listening to the protestors yell out, "Demand what is yours and the people will sustain you. Fair Count or Fight! Tilden or Blood! Our liberties are best preserved by the sword!"

Giving a sigh, Mary turns and looks back out over the crowd and notices George struggling with the heavy mailbag. As he finally gains the stairs and starts to make his way up, she says to him, "I am so sorry, George. Carrying *all* this mail every day must be a nuisance."

George drops the heavy bag onto the front porch. It lands with a rather loud thud. "It seems your brother is getting letters from the entire country on this matter." With her free hand, Mary opens the door to the house and invites George in. "I'm afraid you're right, George, and, yes, he tries to read them all, but it is quite impossible. Come on inside and warm up."

With a grunt, George picks up the heavy sack, slings it over his shoulder and follows Mary into the house. Once inside she puts her own bag down. A butler saunters over to retrieve them and carries them away. Mary instructs George to put the mailbag down on the floor near the stairwell, "Right over there will be fine." George walks to the staircase and unloads the mail bag with another loud thud, onto the floor near the bottom of the staircase. "There you go Mrs. Pelton."

Mary smiles and says, "Please George, don't be so formal—call me Mary." She opens her purse to get money for a tip. "Would you like something to drink? You must be parched."

Just as George answers, "no thank you," with a wave of his hand, Samuel appears, descending down the staircase and greets George. "Well, Good Morning to you, George. I see you have the daily cart load of mail." He peeks into the mailbag and Mary says to him, "He has been carrying this load for weeks. You would think the Postmaster would get him an assistant."

"Not likely," George replies. "He has a budget to keep." George makes his way back toward the door and waves his hand. "You folks have a good day, now"

As the mail carrier opens the door, he pauses for a moment when Samuel says, "You too, George. And don't worry, all this chaos should be over soon and then my mail will be diverted to Washington."

Still standing at the open entry, George looks at Mary and asks, "Will Mrs. Pelton be going with you?"

Mary saunters to the door to see George out and asserts with a smile, "No I will not—When he moves, I will finally have some peace and quiet around here!" Mary holds the door open and watches George as he descends down the stairs. He stops mid-way and turns to look up at her. "So you're not moving with your brother?"

Mary grins, "Actually, that has not been decided."

George continues his decent down the stairs, "Oh—well—I'd like it if you stayed."

"Why thank you George" Mary says shyly. She waves to him, then turns and closes the door. She watches George as he makes his way back through the busy street to his waiting mail carriage.

At the bottom of the inside stairs, Samuel is poking through the mailbag when Mary walks back into the foyer. Samuel always looking to poke a little fun back at his sister teases her when he asks, "Does George make your heart thump Mary?" Mary walks past Samuel toward the living room. "Mind your own business, Samuel."

Forgetting the mail for the moment, Samuel follows her into the living room where Mr. Smith is working at his desk.

"Mr. Smith, there is more mail at the entrance," says Mary. Mr. Smith stands from his desk and looks at Samuel. "You're in a good spirits today, sir."

"He has been, ever since he finished the publication," replies Mary. Samuel smiles and walks toward the dining room table where there is a dish piled high with cookies. He selects one, holds it up and looks at Mr. Smith and his sister. "It's the holiday; of course I'm in good sprits."

Smiling, Smith walks over to the mail bag. His smile turns to a frown as he starts to drag the heavy sack across the floor to his desk. Once at his desk, he straightens himself and gingerly rubs his lower back. He says to Mary, "The response from the public has been... over-whelming—and I must say, I have a new, profound respect for George, our postman"

Samuel chuckles while eating his cookie and walks over to Mr. Smith's desk. He takes a few telegrams off the desk and finishes eating his cookie. His tone changes to serious as he flips through the messages, "It has been overwhelming—but it's the violence worries me. I had an offer today from one man pledging himself and his five sons. Hundreds are pledging their lives and their fortunes to fight for my Presidency."

Smith nods. "I have read many and I am amazed by the support."

With all signs of his earlier light-heartedness now gone, Samuel replies, "I feel blessed by the thousands that have offered to fight for my office – but I will not endorse any bloodshed on my behalf." Mary walks over to her brother and places her hand on his arm as Smith again nods in agreement.

CHAPTER EIGHTEEN

New Rules

Outside the Capitol building, it is just days before Christmas. Members of Congress are walking the outside grounds, discussing their options regarding election laws. While outside, they keep a safe distance from the protestors and reporters on the street and watch as soldiers keep the boisterous crowds at bay. Their biggest fear is that some of the more violent demonstrators will get past the guards and possibly surround and harm them. They also realize that the reporters that are present would enjoy the chaos because the headlines would sell more newspapers.

Inside the Capitol building on this December 22, 1876, the members of the Committee on Privileges, Powers and Duties of the House of Representatives are assembled. Representative J. Proctor Knott of Kentucky, who is the chairman of the committee, is seated at the center of the table. He is surrounded by the other eleven Congressmen who make up the committee and they are reviewing all the election documents. Their focus is to make any major decisions and possibly write any new laws pertaining to the current election rules.

Rising from his chair, Congressman Knott takes a moment and looks around at the men gathered before him. He picks up some of the papers laid out before him and begins to read out loud the final decision of the rules. Congressman Abram Hewitt is one of the twelve on this committee and he sits listening attentively while Knott reads the resolution out loud.

"The resolution is complete as follows; One, that the Constitution does not confer upon the President of the Senate the power to count the electoral votes for President. . . Two, that he may only receive, preserve and open them. Three, that the Senate and House only may examine and ascertain the votes to be counted. Four, that in the exercise of this power the House is at least the equal of the Senate. Five, that no vote can be counted against the judgment of the House." Knott places the document back on the table and looks at the other members. "If there are no further questions or remarks, then this meeting is adjourned."

⸺⸺

In the first months of 1876, never suspecting any issues with the upcoming election between Hayes and Tilden, the Republican controlled Senate had repealed Joint Rule 22. This rule provided for both houses of Congress during an electoral count that both houses would have to see eye to eye, meaning that they would agree on counting a certificate as legal or it would be thrown out.

Now on this December day, in the hallway just outside of the committee room, Democratic Congressman and Speaker of the House Samuel J. Randall waits for Congressman Abram Hewitt, one of Tilden's campaign managers, to leave the room. At the conclusion of the resolution vote Hewitt exits the room. Without saying a word to one another, the two turn and walk down the hall, away from the committee room.

After gaining a safe distance out of ear-shot, Randall says to Hewitt, "With the Twenty Second Joint rule repealed and this new Resolution passed by committee, the Republican Senate must abide by the law of the Constitution. We can object in the House and a certificate can be thrown out."

"Senator Thurman offered Tilden three courses to follow," Hewitt replies. "Fight, back down or arbitrate... Tilden has chosen the latter of the three."

Slowing his stride, but continuing to walk, Randall takes a moment before answering. "If it was my presidency, I would fight." Hewitt grunts at the remark and turns to look at Randall. Randall stops, raises an eyebrow and looks Hewitt in the eye, "Good thing it's not my choice, aye, Hewitt?"

Hewitt nods his head and grins but doesn't answer. The two continue their walk toward the exit, each lost in his own thoughts. At the door, they stop and shake hands.

"I am meeting with President Grant today. I'll meet up with you later at the train station to relay the outcome of the meeting. How long do you intend to be in New York?" Randal asks Hewitt while shaking his hand good-bye. As their hands separate Hewitt warns, "Be careful, Mr. Randall. The President may not be very receptive to the words of a Democratic Representative."

Randall smirks. "Grant is a fair man. Samuel will want to know his thoughts." Hewitt nods in agreement and the two men give each other a quick wave as they go their separate ways.

A few hours later, Randall is outside on the White House grounds. He has just concluded his meeting with the president and is walking briskly toward the street in order to hail a horse and carriage driver to take him to the train station where he will, as planned earlier relay, Grant's thoughts about the election to Congressman Hewitt. As he walks toward one of the taxi carriages Randall realizes he will not be able to avoid the large group of sign waving protestors, soldiers and reporters that have surrounded the White House grounds. The demonstrators are barricaded by the guards near the transport area and several reporters that are there know he has just come from a meeting with the President. All of them are anxious to interview him so they can get the latest news for the morning papers.

Trying to avoid the media, Randall walks past them and climbs into the closest coach available. One of the reporters calls out asking, "Mr. Speaker, what did the President say?"

From inside the coach, Randall leans out the window. "My apologies sir, but I have no comment at this time." He then motions with a wave of his hand for the driver to go. The driver moves his horse slowly forward through the gathering on the street. A few more reporters follow the slow moving carriage and one yells out, "The president told me he would not seat any man in the White House—but would be bound by the action of Congress whether the choice is Tilden or Hayes."

Randall is intrigued by the reporter's declaration. Again he leans out the slow moving carriage window and says to the driver, "Halt the carriage for a moment." The driver pulls back on the reins and stops the horse. Randall then looks out at the people surrounding the coach, and eyes the man who has just gained his interest. "Did you just say you talked to the President and asked who he preferred?"

"Well actually – no. I did not – the president came out here earlier to talk to us."

Astonished, Randall smiles and says," That is the cheekiest thing I've ever heard a President to do."

"I heard Congress is going to count Hayes in rightly or wrongly" interjects another reporter. "I heard he will be seated in the White House—Any comments from you?"

Randall had decided beforehand not to comment to any reporters about his meeting with President Grant. He decides now, however, to find out what else the reporters have heard. Again, he directs his comment to the reporter that claimed to have spoken to President Grant. "I do not know who told you that, but believe me when I tell you; Congress will be fair to both candidates."

A tongue-tied moment of silence follows his statement, during which he motions his driver to move on. Still leaning out the window, he addresses the men still gathered around. "I'm sorry Gentlemen; I have a train to catch." As he leans back inside the carriage, the driver cracks his whip and the horses once past the crowd, clip-pity clops down the street.

The correspondents scribble more notes and one of them complains to the other journalists, "I thought we'd get a better response from him."

"I did too," another newsman complains. Then he motions with his hand adding sarcastically, "Politicians all look and act the same. All La-ti-da—if you know what I mean." The crowd laughs at the reporter's gesture and he bows to thank them.

⁓───⁓

Early in the evening at the Tilden estate, a fire burns brightly in one of the mansion's several fireplaces. This particular hearth is located in the reading room. Nearby, Samuel is snuggled into one of his favorite chairs and is reading a book. To Samuel, reading books is more than just a way for him to pass the time. He enjoys absorbing every written word on the pages. Since he was a child, he has collected hundreds of leather bound manuscripts that he displays on built in shelves in his reading room. He values these books more than he does his own personal wealth. To him, books are the ultimate source of great literature, imagination and creativity. He has spent many nights entertaining and dining at home with some of his favorite authors and actors, discussing the fictional characters that they portray on stage. Normally he cherishes his time alone, but tonight he is anxious to hear the latest news from Washington regarding his Presidency.

No longer able to concentrate on the words he is reading, Samuel closes the book, and with a sigh, stares at the dancing flames flickering in the fireplace. Someone should have gotten to him with news from the capital by now. After a few moments he hears voices just outside the room. As if on cue, one of Samuel's household butlers opens the door and announces the arrival of Abram Hewitt. Hewitt follows the butler through the now open door and walks over to Samuel, who places his book on a nearby table and stands to greet the man. The two shake hands. "Abram, I was just thinking about you." Samuel says with a grin spreading across his face. He then offers his Gramercy neighbor and friend a drink and instructs the butler to pour a glass of wine for them. The butler carefully dispenses two drinks from a lead crystal decanter as both men talk. He hands Samuel and Abram their drinks then he leaves the room, quietly closing the door behind him.

Both men take a sip of the deep red wine and Samuel politely offers his friend a seat beside the chair he was just sitting in. After both men are comfortably seated Samuel is more anxious then he realizes. Samuel quickly prompts his friend "So Abram, what did the committee decide?"

Before answering, Hewitt takes another sip of the delicious vintage and takes pleasure in the growing warmth in his belly after his rather long and chilly ride from the capital. "First I will tell you of President Grant's exact words to Randall. He says that no man can take the office of President unless the people believe he has been fairly elected."

Samuel nods in agreement and sips another mouthful from his wine glass before placing the glass on a nearby table and says with a slight tone of sarcasm, "I've been elected by an overwhelming majority and he knows it. The president is loyal to his party—make no mistake of it. He orders the army on a daily basis to assist the Republicans with their frauds in the South."

Hewitt nods in agreement. "Randall also said that Grant claims he believes South Carolina has gone for Hayes and so has Florida by a majority of forty."

Aggravated by the Republican's claim, Samuel complains, "A majority of forty-five? I've heard from our visiting statesmen that *my* majority in Florida was ninety-three."

"Of that I'm not sure. Although he *does* think that Louisiana gave you the majority by six to eight thousand votes."

Samuel stands and moves closer to the fireplace to warm himself. Like a magnet, his eyes are again attracted to the dancing flames. More thinking out loud for himself than replying to his friend, he asks aloud "Is that so?"

Hewitt takes another sip from his wine glass and adds "Randall concludes that Grant stated he thinks that due to the irregularities of the vote from the last named state, it should be thrown out, leaving the House to elect the President."

At this, Samuel grins and sardonically asks, "Did he guarantee Randall that he would not interfere if that happens?"

"He said he would not, unless either side called up armed forces. If *that* should happen, then he would be obligated to call up the army to save public property."

Samuel not pleased by Grant's remarks turns back toward Hewitt and fires back, "He has *already* called up the army to assist the Republicans in the Southern states."

"I understand your concern, Samuel, but Randall and I are convinced that Grant believes you have been properly and legally elected."

Still defiant, Samuel barks, "I *am* elected! The Republicans just won't give in to it. Florida is under their control by the Republican frauders." He then folds his arms across his chest trying to contain his anger. "Did you hear about Drew and the Florida Governor's race?"

Hewitt raises his eyebrows slightly, "I've heard Governor Sterns is taking full advantage and declaring the win for himself."

Samuel shakes his head in disgust. "Drew had to appeal and sue for a recount. The Florida State Supreme Court has authorized it." Samuel, who very rarely displays his temper to anyone, now walks over to the window to disguise it. "Maybe I should sue for a new election."

Continuing to look out the window, his mood suddenly lightens when he sees four of Mary's friends walking up the steps. Relaxing slightly, he waves at them from the window and calls out, "Mary, your friends are here for a visit."

Hewitt sees the change in his friend's demeanor and realizes that the discussion is over. Standing, he pulls a sealed paper from his jacket pocket and walks over to Samuel who is still standing by the window. He hands him the new committee resolutions to review. "These are the five resolutions. Review them and we will discuss this again in the morning." Samuel turns to Hewitt, takes the paper, nods in agreement and tucks the paper in his suit pocket.

As the butler proceeds to the front door to greet the new arrivals, Mary opens the door to the reading room. Upon seeing Hewitt she walks in to greet him, smiling. Hewitt leans over to give her a brief kiss on the cheek.

"Mr. Hewitt, it's good to see you again."

"You too Mary," he answers. The three of them move toward the adjoining living room, where they find Mary's friends already inside, having just been escorted in by the butler. Before moving to join her friends, Mary leans over and whispers in Samuel's ear, just loud enough for Hewitt to hear. "It's your affections they seek, dear brother, not mine." Without waiting for a reply, she quickly walks over to join her friends. Samuel turns to Hewitt and shrugs his shoulders, an amused grin on his face.

Hewitt chuckles at the remark then turns to Samuel. "We can talk again tomorrow." He shakes Samuel's hand and walks to the front door.

Just as he reaches the entry hall, Samuel calls out asking, "When do you meet with Speaker Randall again?"

"I return to Washington in the afternoon," Hewitt answers.

"Good" replies Samuel, as he walks Hewitt to the front door. "Please thank him for me for all his efforts. And yours as well. I know everyone in the party is working long hours and I want you all to know, I do appreciate all that is being done on my behalf."

Hewitt smiles, "It is our pleasure to serve you, sir."

Samuel stands at the open door and watches as Hewitt goes down the stairs and walks toward his townhouse, which is only a few doors away. After a moment, Samuel closes the door shutting out the cold night air and strolls back into the living room where the women are already engaged in a lively conversation. Samuel is aware he has more pressing issues to deal with concerning the Presidency, but decides that for the moment he is going to take a few minutes to chat with the ladies who he

knows will lighten his mood. The women pause for a moment acknowl-
edging his entrance with warm smiles, before they start chattering again
to update Mary and him on current events regarding the New York social
scene. Mary catches her brother's glance and winks at him. Samuel winks
back and continues to politely listen to the ladies babble.

～∦～

The next day, Congressmen Randall and Hewitt are inside the Capitol
privately conversing with each other while walking down the corridor.
Several other Congressmen nod their usual good-mornings and pleas-
antries as they pass by.

Continuing their conversation, Randall says to Hewitt, "I've been
informed that the Republicans have been intercepting our wires and
duplicating them." Hewitt's facial expressions reveal he is angered by
the information. "How did that happen?" he asks.

Randall lowers his voice, speaking softly so that the people passing
by cannot hear. "William Orton, a close friend of the Republican Party,
is President of the telegraph company."

Hewitt stops and leans against the wall. "Do you have any proof of
these wire duplications?"

"None that anyone would testify to for fear it would ruin their
careers."

Hewitt moves from the wall and the two begin to walk again, "I will
pass the word for our side to cipher all future wires."

Randall offers more worrisome news. "It is also rumored that the
Republican Chairman, Chandler, has evidence pertaining to Tilden's
nephew William paying to bribe an elector in Oregon."

Hewitt, fearful of how Samuel would react to this if he knew, declares,
"Samuel would disown William if there was any evidence of bribery...
nephew or not." Then, thinking of Mary, Hewitt frowns. "Both Mary
and Samuel would be angered to hear William did anything to disgrace
the family name. Honor and integrity is everything to them." The two
continue their walk in silence. After a few moments Hewitt asks, "Any
news from the Senate?"

"Word has come to me that they are planning to propose a special
electoral commission."

Stunned by the announcement Hewitt complains, "When did *this*
occur?"

"I do not have all the details yet", Randall replies, "but I will let you know as soon as I know."

As they near the exit, Hewitt discloses, "I'm leaving for New York in a few days and will tell Samuel what we've learned about the Senate committee meetings." He pauses for a moment then adds, "I'll arrange for another meeting to discuss any new developments for tomorrow night. Can you be there?"

Randall gives an affirmative nod and recommends to Hewitt, "Invite Thurman and Bayard from Delaware to sit in on the meeting as well. If we back another solution, we should all be there together in order to discuss the consequences it could bring to the party. Now is the time is now to keep the Democrats together as a party, no matter what the outcome."

CHAPTER NINETEEN

Christmas Eve 1876

Large crowds of people have been parading around outside the Hayes's estate with campaign signs in support of both Hayes and Tilden. A group of Christmas carolers moves ahead of the protestors and begin to sing holiday songs. Both Lucy and Rutherford are outside strolling through the crowd to shake hands with their supporters and even some of the Tilden people as well. Rutherford watches his wife with a protective eye as she works the crowd. In these situations, there's always that nagging fear that someone might do something to insult or harm her. After a few minutes Lucy waves good-bye and turns and walks back toward the gates. Upon seeing Lucy's retreat toward the gate, Rutherford lets out a silent sigh of relief. He turns back toward the crowd, smiles and waves his goodbyes and joins Lucy inside the gates.

Inside the Hayes's home Senator Sherman patiently waits with his wife for Rutherford and Lucy to come back inside. The mood is festive and the room is filled with friends and family members. Once Rutherford and Lucy enter through the front main door, Senator Sherman turns to his wife.

"Please excuse me, dear," as he points toward Rutherford, "business awaits."

"Why yes, of course," she replies and gives her husband a quick peck on his cheek. She watches Sherman walk over to Rutherford, and then starts a conversation with some other people standing nearby. Rutherford who is just handing off his overcoat to one of the servants says to the approaching Sherman, "This is an exhilarating experience. How are you doing?" The two men shake hands, "Fine, just fine." Sherman answers, and then adds, "There is talk of a special electoral commission being proposed by the Senate."

"I cannot influence the action of the Senate," Rutherford replies. "In my opinion, I believe only the Vice President has the Constitutional power to count the electoral votes and declare the results."

"I quite agree sir, but with Vice President Henry Wilson dying before Grant's term ending, well, we have this dilemma. I sometimes wonder what *he* would have done about the duplicates."

Rutherford smirks. "Henry had his own scandals to deal with. If he had lived to run for President there would be no dispute. He would have lost by a landslide. As for my thoughts about the electoral votes, Congress does not have the right to interfere in the process. If I am inaugurated President, I swear to you on this night that I will not seek a second term."

Across the room, Lucy looks over and waves her hand at Rutherford to join her. Catching her gesture, Rutherford turns to the Senator, "I believe our wives want us to put aside politics for the evening." Both men smile and walk toward their wives who are chatting with others in the room.

⌒╫⌒

On the street, just outside the White House, several carolers are singing holiday songs. Not far from them are several die-hard protestors who have refused to go home, even though it is Christmas Eve. A few soldiers stand guard at the front entrance, with a few more along the driveway that loops its way in front of the main entrance to the grand building. These soldiers, unlike the protestors and carolers, have to work the holiday to protect the President and his family in case any commotions occur.

Inside the Oval Office, President Grant and his wife Julia stand by the window in each other's arms, enjoying the entertainment. Grant says to Julia, "Do you hear it?"

"The music?" Julia asks softly enjoying the peacefulness of the holiday.

"Yes that too – but I meant the quiet, the serenity. No one is arguing tonight."

She snuggles closer to him, "Hmmm—yes."

Grant leans over to her ear and says softly, "Are you going to miss being First Lady when we leave? All the attention and gifts will not be at your disposal."

"No, not at all," she replies.

"No?" he asks, surprised by her quick response.

"I'll happily turn over the duties to the new First Lady, whoever she may be. Next year at this time we will be abroad, enjoying our civilian life and publishing your memoirs."

At the mention of his memoirs, Grant lets out a moan and walks over to his desk. He reaches out and picks up his partially smoked cigar from an ashtray. Smiling to herself, Julia follows him and takes the cigar from his hand and places it back in the ashtray. "I understand you're uncomfortable about writing your memoirs, my dear." Julia pauses for a moment then adds, "I know of a very talented writer that is willing to work with you." Raising an eyebrow, Grant picks up his cigar again and lights it.

Julia boasts, "His name is Mark Twain. I've heard he's one of the best."

Grant turns and looks back out the window at the people outside. As a wisp of cigar smoke curls around above his head, he adds, "Twain, huh? Never heard of him."

⌒⫘⌒

Back in New York City, hundreds of Tilden supporters surround his Gramercy Park estate. Several horse and carriages arrive and then leave after dispatching ladies and gentlemen dressed in their best attire in front of the mansion. Through the large plate glass windows of the mansion, people from the street can see the festivities inside which include a stringed Quartet.

Mary, dressed in a beautiful gown, is busy socializing with the guests, one of them being Honest John Kelly. Meanwhile, Samuel, along with his nephew William, Congressman Abram Hewitt, John Bigelow, Mr. Smith and Manton Marble, have all gathered together in the reading room. Marble, who is the editor of the *New York World*, has been a close friend of Samuel's for years and always attends Christmas functions not as a newsman, but as a close friend of the Tilden family.

In the main part of the house, outside of the reading room, the party is now in full swing. After finally catching his hostess's attention, John

Kelly invites Mary to dance. "Shall we?" he asks Mary, while taking her hand and leading her to an area set aside for dancing.

"You make it difficult to say no," Mary replies, putting on her best party smile.

At the same time, inside the reading room, Bigelow asks, "So Samuel, have you decided on any choices for your Cabinet?"

Samuel winks at his good friend, raises his glass of wine towards the big man and says, "You for one, my friend. And", he then looks at the other men gathered around, "I am considering Charles Francis Adams for Secretary of State."

Bigelow is delighted by the announcement and raises his own glass in acknowledgment. "Good choice—on *both* accounts." The other men agree and nod their approval. "Who else?" Bigelow asks.

Samuel takes a sip of wine from his glass, "Charles O'Connor for Attorney General and I'm thinking of David Wells for Secretary of the Treasury."

Again, Bigelow and the others nod their approval.

Samuel turns his attention toward Marble and Hewitt and says, "Lyman Trumbull, William Sumner and both of you, of course, for other posts." Then he turns to Mr. Smith and William, "I have not forgotten either of you. I need the best people working for me. Men I can trust." Both men turn and grin at each other.

"What have you heard from Hendricks?" Hewitt asks.

"Not much. I think he and the Tammany boys wish he'd won the nomination instead of me. Their support of him for President was very strong."

Replenishing his now empty glass, Bigelow pipes in, "It would do them and your Vice President good to realize that the Republicans would have shown Hendricks no mercy either." The men laugh at this and clank their glasses together.

Samuel then turns to Hewitt and, in a more serious tone, says, "We do need to resolve the reconstruction issue in the South. The democratic leaders in the confederate states want the federal troops out. On this, I agree."

"The loyal republican Negroes in south have received several promises by the Hayes people," Marble pipes in. "And assuredly none that they will give them."

"I'll make sure that their civil rights are protected and that the federal troops are moved out in a reasonable time frame," Samuel replies. He then turns his focus back to Hewitt, "We need to schedule a meeting soon to discuss this idea of an Electoral Commission. The thought of a few men deciding my Presidency is not what the people expect or what *I* want."

Hewitt frowns, but before he can respond, Mary appears at the door to the reading room. Upon her arrival, the men give a slight nod as Samuel asks her, "Is there a problem?"

Without saying a word, Mary walks over to the group and takes her brother by the hand. "Come this way Gentlemen—it is Christmas Eve and we have guests."

Allowing her to lead him out of the room, Samuel smiles and gestures his helplessness with his free hand. The other men chuckle quietly and begin to follow their host and hostess toward the party area. As they near the door to the main hall, Hewitt reaches out and takes hold of William's arm. He leans over into William's ear and in a hushed voice says, "I've heard a nasty rumor about you. It has been brought to my attention that you've tried to bribe an Elector in Oregon. Is there any truth to this rumor?"

Frowning, William responds, "It's not what you think, Abram."

Both men then notice that Samuel is staring at them, a questioningly look on his face. Hewitt smiles back at Samuel then back toward William and says in a low voice so only he can hear, "We'll discuss the issue at a more appropriate time." William nods in agreement.

As Hewitt walks on toward the party in the other room, William turns toward Mr. Smith, who had stopped and noticed the exchange. William glares at Mr. Smith as if to say, *I told you so*. Mr. Smith, not privy to hearing the accusation Hewitt has just implied, looks back at William and innocently shrugs his shoulders.

⟶⟨⟩⟵

Inside the New York Times editorial room there are several reporters rushing to finish their reports so they can go home to be with their families on this merriest of holidays. Standing off to one side are John Reid and Zach Chandler who are watching the bustle of activity with mild interest.

"What have you heard about the Electoral Commission being proposed?" Reid asks Chandler.

Chandler grunts and gripes, "That the Democrats are supporting it and we are not."

Concerned by his answer, Reid replies, "I didn't anticipate this. I thought once we confused the vote in the south that the republicans controlling those states would have easily counted the Democrats out."

"Don't jump to any conclusions just yet," Chandler barks back, finally taking his eyes off the hustling reporters in the room. With a stern expression on his face, he looks Reid in the eye. "The House and Senate have to agree on terms before any Special Commission is in place."

Still curious Reid asks, "How will it work?"

"I don't know," Chandler sighs, then adds, "Senator Conkling, who was not thrilled that Hayes took his nomination from him, wanted a different outcome." Looking back to the reporters working diligently, a look of frustration returns to his face. His eyes narrow and he practically spits out his words, "I swear to you that even though he is a loyal republican, I think he wants Tilden to win just to throw it in our faces for not nominating him."

Sensing Candler's frustration, Reid stuffs his hands in his pockets and doesn't reply while silently thinking about what he has just been told. After a brief moment, Chandler's demeanor calms a bit, as he reaches for his coat and hat hanging on a nearby chair. Placing his hat on his head and putting on his coat he says, "Time for me to go, John – it being Christmas Eve and all."

Reid fumbles with some of the papers on his desk, "Yes, quite right, Mr. Chandler, go on home. Enjoy the holiday with your family."

As Chandler heads toward the door, he stops and turns to face Reid again. In a calmer, softer tone, he adds, "Don't worry, John, we've been successful this far. I'm sure Hayes will be elected and *you* will be generously rewarded."

"I didn't do this for the money, and you know that!" Reid fires back.

Chandler smirks, "Maybe not, Mr. Reid, maybe not. But many men—even the ones who claim the highest of integrity—do." He then touches the brim of his hat, turns and walks out the door, leaving the editor with an angry look on his face.

Two days later, Samuel, Congressman Hewitt, William Pelton, Manton Marble, Mr. Smith and John Bigelow are all seated in the reading room discussing the day's business and the proposed Electoral Commission. Samuel stands, looking at a piece of paper in his hand, and announces to the men, "On the first, I will be at the Inauguration for Robinson when he takes my place as Governor. I should not be absent but a day." He then looks to the congressman. "Tell us more about the happenings in Washington, Mr. Hewitt."

"One moment, if I may" Bigelow chimes in. "What exactly is the Special Commission?"

Not turning away from the congressman, Samuel adds, "Before we complicate the issue about the Commission, wouldn't you agree, Mr. Hewitt, that there should be a resolution in the House first and then one later in the Senate?"

Hewitt looks at Bigelow and replies, "A Special Commission is being proposed to decide what Electoral Certificates are valid and to be counted."

Samuel pauses for a moment and then retakes his seat, placing the paper he has had in his hand on a nearby table. "With a resolution in the House asserting exclusive Rights of the House and Senate, they will be acting concurrently to count the Electors votes."

"They will until the duplicate certificates are presented," Hewitt counters.

"And then what?" Bigelow asks defensively.

With an incredulous look, Samuel asks, "Are you suggesting neither the House nor Senate will have any say about which ones are valid?"

"They will make an attempt to, yes."

"An *attempt*?" Samuel asks, raising his hand in the air. "Will they at least debate these certificates before the country in the House of Representatives?"

Hewitt leans forward in his chair, and begins to explain how he thinks the process will work. "There will be no debate regarding the disputed votes, Samuel. *That* is what the Special Commission is for."

"Ah, excuse me Congressman Hewitt," Marble interrupts. "Will this commission prevent the Republican President of the Senate from deciding the election on his own?"

"The President of the Senate will not be deciding anything on his own, as much as he would like to." Hewitt answers, looking to Marble. He then looks back to Samuel and adds, "He'll be blocked and rejected by rule of the House of Representatives, which as we all know, is controlled by us Democrats."

Contemplating the outcome, Samuel states, "I see no value in this proposed Special Commission. How does it serve us? What are Senators Thurman and Bayard advising?"

Hewitt, trying to keep his frustration out of his voice, tries to clarify. "Before leaving Washington, Senators Thurman and Bayard met with me and Speaker Randall to discuss the Special Commission. We agreed the creation of one would be two plans of action. One," he raises a finger, "to follow the Committee of Privileges for a decision with that body and two," raising another finger, "to create a new agency outside of Congress to encourage a Committee on an Electoral Count Bill. The latter would decide on the duplicate certificates issue. Keep in mind, gentlemen," he continues, looking around at the other men gathered, "the Republicans in the Senate are not happy either. They think their chances are better with the three states election returning boards, which are controlled by them and will give them the better odds to steal the Presidency."

Bigelow nods his head in disagreement, "It sounds pretty risky."

"It does to me as well," Samuel agrees. "But with the support of over two hundred fifty thousand popular votes on my side and needing just the one electoral vote to win—I don't know what more it will take to convince them that the Presidency is mine alone."

Bigelow, disgusted by the commission's proposal, articulates, "There are nineteen votes between those three disputed states and the Republicans are fearful Samuel may get the one with the aide of an Electoral Commission?" Looking down at the floor in front of him and shaking his head again, he continues, "Grant should have taken control of his party's antics and stopped them from using the military to cheat Hayes into the presidency. As President he should insist that Samuel be sworn in as the rightfully elected winner." They all agree, except for Samuel, who with a slight smile, says, "Grant would have me shot by one of his soldiers before he turned his back on his cronies."

The men chuckle at this and Samuel, folding his arms over his chest, continues, "Unfortunately my Presidency must be resolved legally before I can take the oath of office."

With the exception of Hewitt, none of the men agree that the Special Commission is the solution. They are frustrated and believe the Electoral Special Commission is a conspiracy created by the Republicans to cheat them and the country out of a Tilden Presidency.

Meanwhile, in the Oval Office of the White House, President Grant is seated at his desk reviewing paperwork when his aide knocks on the door. "Come in." Grant calls out, without looking up from the paperwork spread out in front of him. The aide peeks his head into the room and announces, "Pardon me, Mr. President, but Representative Conger, of Michigan, is here to speak with you." Grant shuffles some of his paperwork and barks, "Yes, yes, all right. Send him in."

Without pause, Congressman Conger strolls through the door and heads toward Grant's desk. The President stands and walks around the large desk to greet him and the two shake hands.

"Good Morning, Mr. Conger" Grant smiles, "Haven't seen you for a while." Then Grant raises his hand. "Let me guess, the election matter."

"To get straight to the point, I'm not one for idol rumors Mr. President," Conger replies with a slight frown, "but it has been told to me that Tilden was intending to take the oath of office, even at the risk of being shot. Would you order it, sir, if he did such a thing?"

Grant smirks and answers, "No Mr. Conger, I would not shoot Mr. Tilden – but I *would* have to arrest him." Seeming relieved by the President's response Congressman Conger relaxes. Grant then continues, "And what have you heard from Mr. Hayes?"

Conger walks over to a chair and sits down before responding. Grant watches him and asks again, "Have you *heard* from Mr. Hayes?"

Taking a moment to answer, Conger says, "He has written to me."

Grant reaches for a cigar from his desk and walks over and sits in a chair across from the Congressman. A moment of silence passes between the two as he lights his stogie and takes a few puffs. He looks straight at the Congressman seated in front of him and waits. Another silent moment passes, and then he asks," Well, Mr. Conger? Are you going to make me wait all day? What has he to say?"

Cautiously, Conger replies, "He is concerned about the proposed electoral commission."

"Is he now?" Grant remarks with a sarcastic smirk. He takes another puff, blowing the blue smoke above his head.

"He is questioning the authority of the Constitution on the matter."

At this, Grant raises his eyebrows and says, "Well Congressman, you can tell Mr. Hayes the next time you write him, that it is the duplicate certificates that created this situation and not the people's votes. You can also tell him that he lost the election by that tally by over two hundred and fifty four thousand votes." Conger looks at Grant's expressionless face. He is not sure if the President is angry or not, so he says nothing. Grant takes a few more puffs from his cigar and then leans forward and places the stogie in an ashtray on a table between the two of them. Still leaning forward, he looks Conger directly in the eyes and with the smoke curling up from the still lit cigar in the ashtray, Conger is not sure, but he believes he sees a brief moment of fury flickering in the presidents' eyes. "And yes, please Mr. Conger," Grant continues, "Tell Mr. Hayes for me that it is quite possible, in fact, that the Framers of our Constitution are to blame. After all, they made no provision for duplicate electors' certificates. In fact, I think they would consider it to be fraud, as do I, and would have disqualified any states that submitted them. And that's exactly what I would do…that is if I had the authority to do so."

Mustering what courage he has, Conger stands from his chair. "I'll, um-I'll tell him."

Grant picks up the still smoldering cigar and clamps it between his teeth as he stands. His stone face softens slightly as he smirks, "Have a good evening."

The Congressman indicates agreement, and nervously turns and makes a hasty exit. Grant stands alone for a moment, looking at the now empty space the congressman had just occupied. He then turns and walks back behind his desk and heavily sits down in his chair. Leaning back in the chair, he blows a large plume of smoke into the air, shakes his head and thinks to himself, *I should have pushed for that third term.*

CHAPTER TWENTY

The Special Commission Bill

A messenger holding a large envelope walks through the crowd gathered outside the Tilden estate. He is stopped when he reaches a couple of guards at the front steps.

Due to the election chaos and the resulting rising of violence across the country, Mary requested that Mr. Smith hire some security for the Tilden estate. Through his contacts at the local police precinct, Smith was able to procure a half a dozen off-duty officers. Though Samuel didn't favor this action, he realized it was necessary for the added protection for his family and friends.

One of the guards takes the envelope from the messenger, reviews it, and hands it back to him. The man then climbs the steps to the front door and knocks to announce his arrival. The envelope has printed on it *"Strictly Confidential" from Congressman Abram Hewitt.*

Inside the house, Mr. Smith hears the knocking and continues working at his desk. Concentrating on the paperwork before him, he takes little notice as one of the butlers walks to the door and opens it. He looks up as he hears a voice say, "Confidential, for Mr. Tilden." Hearing the door shut, he waits as the butler appears around the corner.

"An envelope for Mr. Tilden." The butler announces.

"Yes, yes, bring it here." Smith waves from his desk. He reaches out and takes the envelope from the butler, looks at the label, and then without pause, stands up and hands it back to the butler. "Mr. Tilden will want to read this now." The butler walks into the reading room and, without speaking a word, hands the envelope to Samuel. "Thank you,

Thomas," Samuel says. Again, without a word, the butler gives a slight nod and turns and retreats from the room.

Reviewing the outside of the envelope Samuel realizes it's the third draft of the *Electoral Special Commission Bill* drafted by Congress. He walks over to his chair, sits down, and proceeds to tear open the envelope. He pulls out several papers that are neatly packaged inside and just as he begins to read the contents, Mr. Smith enters the room. Samuel lays the papers down on the table and looks up and quietly asks, "What is it Mr. Smith?"

Smith is holding a telegram in his hand. "Sorry to disturb you, sir. You have just received another wire from Attorney Whitney."

Samuel nods, knowing Mr. Smith would never disturb him unless it's important. "Go ahead, Smith, read it to me."

Mr. Smith adjusts his glasses then starts to read the cipher out loud to Samuel, "He says; you should consider forcing a modification of the resolution in order to preserve the Constitutional right of the two Houses to participate equally in the count—That is all we want and the country is with us."

Samuel smirks. "Wire him back and tell him I will consider his proposal." Mr. Smith nods in agreement and walks out of the room. Samuel picks up the proposed bill from the table and begins to study it.

About fifteen minutes later Samuel hears another knock at the door. He listens as the butler again answers it. Then he hears a familiar, booming voice say "Hello Thomas, tell him I'm here, if he's not too busy." Smiling to himself, Samuel waits as John Bigelow enters the house. As Bigelow hands his coat and hat to the Butler, he says, "On second thought, never mind, I'll tell him myself."

For a rare moment, the butler breaks into a very brief smile. "Very well, sir." He knows that any interruption by Tilden's best friend will not be a problem. The smile instantly disappears as he turns and walks toward the coat room with Bigelow's coat and hat.

Bigelow watches as the man walks away, then proceeds to the reading room where Samuel is patiently waiting. Samuel smiles when he sees Bigelow and waves the papers in his hand at him. Bigelow walks up to him, "What have you got there?" He reaches out and takes the papers from Samuel's hand.

After reading the first few lines, Bigelow looks at Samuel and asks, "The McCrary House Bill? How did you get it so soon?"

Samuel winks and warns, "This is strictly confidential."

Bigelow smiles as Samuel hands him the papers and before starting to read them he asks, "You do not trust me?"

Samuel looks back at his closest friend and says, "You dare ask me that question?"

Bigelow answers with a huge smile, "I do."

Samuel decides to play along with Bigelow's teasing mood. "You are my best friend, neighbor and confidant. Who could I trust more?"

Bigelow gives an audible grunt, hands the papers back to Samuel and walks over to a table where coffee and some fresh fruit are beautifully displayed on the table. He picks up the coffee carafe and fills a cup. Then, with dissatisfaction on his face, he says, "I've heard secrecy has been imposed on all committee members."

Samuel stays in his chair and flips through the papers. "Revisions provide for a commission of fifteen members—five from the House, five from the Senate and five from the Supreme Court. The judges will be determined by putting the names of the Senior Justices into a hat and drawing out one. There's to be seven Republicans and seven Democrats. The draw for the fifteenth member would break the deadlock." Bigelow, still standing takes a sip from his coffee. "That's risky—suppose the odd man out is a Republican?"

Samuel frowns, "I could lose the Presidency by a name in a hat." Samuel stands and walks over to the bay window. He pulls back the curtain and looks out at the crowd in the street. Continuing to look out through the window, he says, "Hewitt will be here later to discuss the particulars. He seems to think this is the best solution. He says the others think so too. On the other hand, I do not agree with *any* of them." He turns back to face Bigelow, and points back out the window. "I cannot let these people, who have believed and fought so hard for my Presidency, think that I'll give it up so easily. They'll lose faith in me and our party."

Bigelow walks over to Samuel and places a beefy hand on his shoulder. "Those people won't lose faith in you. They would lay down their lives to protect you."

Samuel shakes his head in disgust, "They elected me to reform Washington—not to start another bloody war."

In the *New York Times* building, John Reid is sitting behind his desk reviewing stories for the newspaper. A knock on his door disrupts his work when a messenger arrives carrying a large envelope. He waves the messenger in and signs for the package marked: *Confidential, from Zach Chandler*. Reading the label he says to the courier, "Thank you, and please close the door on your way out." He waits until his door is shut before opening the envelope. He pulls out the enclosed paper work and reads: *The McCrary House Bill*. Realizing the proposed bill is not something anyone else should be privy to, including himself, he walks over to his door and places a do not disturb sign on his office window, closes the door and locks it behind him.

A few hours later at Tilden's house, Congressman Hewitt has arrived and is seated in a chair. He waits patiently while Samuel reviews the proposed revisions of the electoral commission bill. John Bigelow is still present and turns in his chair when he hears a knock on the adjoining doors to the living room.

Looking up, Samuel calls out, "This is not a good time."

Mary leans her head in and says, "I'm sorry, Samuel, but Mr. Marble and Hewitt is here." Samuel motions with his hand and says, "Send them in." Marble and Hewitt enter the room quietly and sits down next to Bigelow, who has recently traded his coffee for a glass of bourbon.

Samuel continues to review the proposal silently and does not notice when Marble leans over and whispers in Bigelow's ear, "I wonder how many others have this report?" Bigelow smiles and shrugs his shoulders, indicating that he doesn't know.

Samuel finishes reading and with a deep sigh, places the documents on a nearby table. He looks to Hewitt, who is sitting across from Bigelow and Marble. "We need to discuss details."

Nodding, Hewitt replies, "Bayard and Thurman are absolutely committed to this bill. They concur with the Republican members."

"How many oppose it in the House?" Samuel asks.

"Several." He pauses for a moment. "The House Committee has suggested killing it in the House." Samuel frowns and fires back, "Is it not rather late then, to consult with me?"

Defensively, Hewitt barks, "*They* will not consult with you. They are public men, Samuel, and they have their own duties and responsibilities. I consult with you."

Samuel looks Hewitt in the eye, "I know I cannot advise you or the other Democratic members to agree to the bill one way or another, but I will advise you as to the details." Hewitt can feel Samuel's intensity. It is a behavior Samuel displays rarely because his normal personality is one of being a very patient and calm intellectual. Hewitt nods his head in agreement. Samuel stands and waves the papers in the air, "This is a raffle for the Presidency and I know the voters would not approve of it. Nor do I."

Bigelow and Marble sit in silence as they watch the two men exchange heated words.

Hewitt fires back, "None of us in the party expect you to."

Samuel takes another moment to compose himself and says in a more calm tone, "The way I see it, arbitration should be adopted into the bill. Then it would be the duty of the arbitrators to investigate and decide the case on its merits. This should be mandatory and would eliminate the element of gambling." He starts to pace the floor. The men in the room knew when he is did this he was master-minding a solution to a problem. Samuel wrings his hands and continues, "Consider this. If you go into a conference with your adversary and can't break it off because you feel you must agree to something, you cannot negotiate. You will be beaten on every detail."

Hewitt chimes in and asks, "What about the danger of collision and force with President Grant?" Samuel looks at Hewitt and fires back a round of questions for Hewitt to think about. "Why surrender now? You can always surrender, at any time. Why surrender before the battle for fear you may have to surrender after the battle is over?" Bigelow, Marble and Hewitt nod in agreement. Samuel adds, "President Grant is in need of the next man to replace him, and I understand his position. He has served his country most of his life, fighting a bloody Civil war and then following that as a two term President. He's tired and wants to retire peacefully. There is nothing wrong with that. We all want the same—some sooner than later."

Hewitt asks, "Do you agree to the five justices? They will be playing a major roll in the Special Commission."

"There is no need for hot haste. We still have time to consult and to debate publicly. I do not like the secrecy surrounding this bill and I do not trust it. You must allow the others in the House to debate."

Hewitt knows they are running short of time and says, "Congress moves at its own pace and will not wait on this issue. We need to discuss what we will do if the bill is adopted."

Samuel looks over at Bigelow and Marble and shrugs his shoulders. "If that happens," he replies and looks back to Hewitt, "then they all act on their own judgments. I cannot be responsible for their actions. I am only advising you to bring the information before them to debate. I still have grave doubts any of this will succeed. It still amazes me that one newspaperman's last ditch scheme to rob the voters of a duly elected President has turned so many in high office against me."

CHAPTER TWENTY-ONE

Special Commission Act Passes

An angry group of protestors are standing in the street waving copies of the *New York Times* newspaper. The headline reads, *Dice Box VS Ballot Box*. One of the protestors yells out, "They might as well draw straws!" Another follows with, "The presidency is being raffled like a Thanksgiving turkey!" Supporters and protestors from both parties are frustrated by the electoral commission bill that President Grant has signed into law, creating the Special Commission. They are being held back from entering the Capitol by federal troops. No one in this angry crowd agrees that fifteen men have the right to decide which electors' votes are legal or not. They all have cast their personal ballots and now believe that the votes have been manipulated to steal the Presidency.

Many think another election should take place and many others are ready to fight to the death for their candidate. As the crowds continue to swell and surround the Capitol building, horse and carriages fill every available parking space. Dignitaries from other countries, as well as Senators, Congressmen and national newspapermen, are being protected and escorted into the Capitol building by federal soldiers. They have all assembled so that they can watch, report and participate in America's most controversial and disputed election ever. Everyone is there this day, with the exception of the two candidates, Hayes and Tilden. Both men have to wait it out in their home states to see which of them will be the next President. Neither one of them agrees to the Special Commission, nor are they able to have a voice in the decision process. Tilden thinks the House of Representatives should have made the decision because it is written law in the Constitution. On the other hand, Hayes believes he has won by a fair count in the Southern disputed states.

Act Creating an Electoral Commission, January 29, 1877

AN ACT to provide for and regulate the counting of votes for President and Vice President, and the decision of questions arising thereon, for the term commencing March fourth, anno Domini eighteen hundred and seventy-seven.

Be it enacted by the Senate and House of Representatives of the United States of America in Congress assembled, That the Senate and House of Representatives shall meet in the hall of the House of Representatives, at the hour of one o'clock post meridian, on the first Thursday in February, anno Domini eighteen hundred and seventy-seven; and the President of the Senate shall be their presiding officer. Two tellers shall be previously appointed on the part of the Senate, and two on the part of the House of Representatives, to whom shall be handed, as they are opened by the President of the Senate, all the certificates, and papers purporting to be certificates, of the electoral votes, which certificates and papers shall be opened, presented, and acted upon in the alphabetical order of the States, beginning with the letter A; and said tellers having then read the same in the presence and hearing of the two houses shall make a list of the votes as they shall appear from the said certificates; and the votes having been ascertained and counted as in this act provided, the result of the same shall be delivered to the President of the Senate, who shall thereupon announce the state of the vote, and the names of the persons, if any, elected, which announcement shall be deemed a sufficient declaration of the persons elected President and Vice President of the United States, and, together with a list of the votes, be entered on the journals of the two houses. Upon such reading of any such certificate or paper when there shall be only one return from a State, the President of the Senate shall call for objections, if any. Every objection shall be made in writing, and shall state clearly and concisely, and without argument, the ground thereof, and shall be signed by at least one Senator and one Member of the House of Representatives before the same shall be received. When all objections so made to any vote or paper from a State shall have been received and read, the Senate shall thereupon withdraw and such objections shall be submitted to the Senate for its decision, and the Speaker of the House of Representatives shall, in like manner, submit such objections to the House of Representatives for its decision, and no electoral vote or votes from any State from which but one return has been received shall be rejected except by the affirmative vote of the two houses. When the two houses have voted, they shall immediately again meet, and the presiding officer shall then announce the decision of the question submitted.

SECTION 2. That if more than one return, or paper purporting to be a return from a State, shall have been received by the President of the Senate, purporting to be the certificates of electoral votes given at the last preceding election for President and Vice President in such State (unless they shall be duplicates of the same return,) all such returns and papers shall be opened by him in the presence of the two houses when met as aforesaid, and read by the tellers, and all such returns and papers shall thereupon be submitted to the judgment and decision as to which is the true and lawful electoral vote of such State, of a commission constituted as follows, namely: During the session of each house on the Tuesday next preceding the first Thursday in February, eighteen hundred and seventy-seven each house shall, by viva voce vote, appoint five of its members who with the five associate justices of the Supreme Court of the United States, to be ascertained as hereinafter provided, shall constitute a commission for the decision of all questions upon or in respect of such double returns named in this section. On the Tuesday next preceding the first Thursday in February, anno Domini eighteen hundred and seventy-seven, or as soon thereafter as may, be, the associate justices of the Supreme Court of the United States now assigned to the first, third, eighth, and ninth circuits shall select, in such manner as a majority of them shall deem fit, another of the associate justices of said court, which five persons shall be members of said commission, and the person longest in commission of said five justices shall be the president of said commission. The members of said commission shall respectively take and subscribe the following oath: "I, _____ _____, do solemnly swear (or affirm, as the case may be) that I will impartially examine and consider all questions submitted to the commission of which I am a member, and a true judgment give thereon, agreeably to the Constitution and the laws: so help me God," which oath shall be filed with the Secretary of the Senate. When the commission shall have been thus organized, it shall not be in the power of either house to dissolve the same, or to withdraw any of its members; but if any such Senator or member shall die or become physically unable to perform the duties required by this act, the fact of such death or physical inability shall be by said commission, before it shall proceed further, communicated to the Senate or House of Representatives, as the case may be, which body shall immediately and without debate proceed by viva voce vote to fill the place so vacated, and the person so appointed shall take and subscribe the oath hereinbefore prescribed, and become a member of said commission, and, in like manner, if any of said justices of the Supreme Court shall die or become physically incapable of performing the duties required by this act, the other of said justices, members of the said commission, shall immediately appoint another justice of said court a member of said commission and, in such appointments, regard shall be had to the impartiality and freedom from bias sought by the original appointments to said commission, who shall thereupon immediately take and subscribe the oath hereinbefore prescribed, and become a member of said commission to fill the vacancy so occasioned. All the certificates and papers purporting to be certificates of the electoral votes of each State shall be opened, in the alphabetical order of the States as provided in section cne of this act; and when there shall be more than cue such certificate or paper, as the certificate and papers from such State shall so be opened, (excepting duplicates of the same return,) they shall be read by the tellers, and thereupon the President of the Senate shall call for objections, if any. Every objection shall be made in writing, and shall state clearly and concisely, and without argument, the ground thereof, and shall be signed by at least one Senator and one member of the House of Representatives before the same shall be received. When all such objections so made to any certificate, vote, or paper from a State shall have been received and read, all such certificates, votes, and papers so objected to, and all papers accompanying the same, together with such objections, shall be forthwith submitted to said commission, which shall proceed to consider the same, with the same powers, if any, now possessed for that purpose by the two houses acting separately or together, and, by a majority of votes, decide whether any and what votes from such State are the votes provided for by the Constitution of the United States, and how many' and what persons were duly appointed electors in such State, and, may therein take into view such petitions, depositions, and other. papers, if any, as shall, by the Constitution and now existing law, be competent and pertinent in such consideration; which decision shall he made in writing, stating briefly the ground thereof, and signed by the members of said commission agreeing therein; whereupon the two houses shall again meet, and such decision shall be read and entered in the journal of each house, and the counting of the votes shall proceed in conformity therewith, unless, upon objection made thereto in writing by at least five Senators and five members of the House of Representatives, the two houses shall separately concur in ordering otherwise, in which case such concurrent order shall govern. No votes or papers from any other

State shall be acted upon until the objections previously made to the votes or papers from any State shall have been finally disposed of.

SEC. 3. That while the two houses shall be in meeting, as provided in this act, no debate shall be allowed and no question shall be put by the presiding officer, except to either house on a motion to withdraw, and he shall have power to preserve order.

SEC. 4. That when the two houses separate to decide upon an objection that may have been made to the counting of any electoral vote or votes from any State, or upon objection to a report of said commission, or other question arising under this act, each Senator and Representative may speak to such objection or question ten minutes, and not oftener than once; but after such debate shall have lasted two hours, it shall be the duty of each house to put the main question without further debate.

SEC. 5. That at such joint meeting of the two houses, seats shall be provided as follows: For the President of the Senate, the Speaker's chair; for the Speaker, immediately upon his left; the Senators in the body of the hall upon the right of the presiding officer; for the Representatives, in the body of the hall not provided for the Senators, for the tellers, Secretary of the Senate, and Clerk of the House of Representatives, at the Clerk's desk; for the other officers of the two houses, in front of the Clerk's desk and upon each side of the Speaker's platform. Such joint meeting shall not be dissolved until the count of electoral votes shall be completed and the result declared; and no recess shall be taken unless a question shall have arisen in regard to counting any such votes, or otherwise under this act, in which case it shall be competent for either house, acting separately, in the manner hereinbefore provided, to direct a recess of such house not beyond the next day, Sunday excepted, at the hour of ten o'clock in the forenoon. And while any question is being considered by said commission, either house may proceed with its legislative or other business.

SEC. 6. That nothing in this act shall be held to impair or affect any right now existing under the Constitution and laws to question by proceeding in the judicial courts of the United States, the right or title of the person who shall be declared elected or who shall claim to be President or Vice President of the United States, if any such right exists.

SEC. 7. That said commission shall make its own rules, keen a record of its proceedings, and shall have power to employ such persons as may be necessary for the transaction of its business and the execution of its powers.

Approved, January 29, 1877 and President Grant signed it into law as soon as it was put on his desk.

CHAPTER TWENTY-TWO

A problem with the Independent Justice

After much deliberation and debate, the Commission members have finally been chosen. There are five Senators consisting of three Republicans and two Democrats. From the House of Representatives there are three Democrats and two Republicans and from the Supreme Court there are two definite Democrats and two Republicans with the last Justice being the odd man out.

This last Justice is not partial to either party, even though he was, at one time, a Republican. He is Justice David Davis from Illinois. Years before, he was a big supporter of President Lincoln and worked closely with Lincoln to be a founder of the Republican Party. However, after the Civil war, he switched his alliances after Lincoln was assassinated. He gave his devotion to the then Vice President, Andrew Johnson, after Johnson was sworn into the Presidency. The radical Republicans, annoyed by his disloyalty, thought of him as the odd man out. They believed he would some day run for President as a Democrat.

The Special Commission would probably not have been agreed to by the Democrats, if Davis wasn't chosen to serve on the commission. What no one, including Davis, realized at the time was that his name was being considered and voted on by the Illinois legislators to elect him as their Senator, which they did on January 25, just before the Special Commission passed. Tilden had known about the Illinois legislators' decision weeks before the vote took place and never said a word to Hewitt about it. In response, Davis accepted his new position as Senator and immediately resigned his position as a justice on the Supreme Court.

At that time, Congressman Hewitt, along with many other Democrats, were stunned by his actions. They believed the newly elected Davis would not be starting his Senate term until March 4th which would leave him with plenty of time to complete his obligations to the Special Commission and the disputed electoral certificates. But now, because of his immediate resignation from the Supreme Court, he will no longer be able to serve on the newly formed Special Commission. This instantaneous news thrills the Republicans, because they believed Davis would have gone for Tilden and not Hayes.

The other newly formed Electoral Commission members now have to first resolve the issue of who will take Davis's place. So far, the people serving on the commission are House Representatives Henry Payne (D-OH), Eppa Hunton (D-VA), Josiah Abbott (D-MA), James Garfield (R-OH) and George Frisbie Hoar (R-MA). On the Senate side it is Allen Thurman (D-OH), Thomas Bayard (D-DE), Oliver Hazard Perry Throck Morton (R-IN), George Edmunds (R-VT) and Frederick Theodore Frelinghuysen (R-NJ). The Supreme Court Justices are Democrats Stephen J. Field from CA and Nathan Clifford of MN and Republicans Samuel F. Miller form IA and William Strong of PA.

For the now empty fifth seat on the Commission, the remaining Justices decide on Republican Joseph P. Bradley, originally from New York, but now residing in New Jersey. He is chosen because he's known to both parties to be an independent minded man and always judges his cases with fairness.

Immediately following this last minute choice, the Democrats cry "foul" because President Grant had chosen Bradley for the Supreme Court in order to overturn the Legal Tender Ruling (Greenbacks) and there was now only 33 days left before Grant is to leave office. On the flip side, one of Hayes' older sons gets so excited by the news that Justice Bradley had been selected as a replacement for Davis that he wires his father, telling him that he's going to be the next President of the United States.

⚬─∦─⚬

On February 1, 1877 at one p.m. the Special Commission is signed into law by Grant, giving the fifteen men from the Supreme Court,

Senate and Congress the power to decide on who will be the next President. Eight of the fifteen are Republicans and seven are Democrats. Their primary duty is to decide which of the disputed Electoral Certificates, tossed to them by Congress during their electoral count, are valid and which are not.

After putting his signature on the document, President Grant felt like he had not a care in the world as he waits in the Oval Office. Relaxed, he is seated comfortably behind his desk, smoking one of his favorite cigars, and reading a book. He knows the matter is now out of his hands. Even though he has believed all along that Tilden rightfully won the Presidency by the peoples vote, as far as he's concerned, he has played his part and has been loyal to the Republican Party.

Inside the Capitol House Chambers, there is standing room only. Speaker of the House Randall is seated next to, but below, Ferry, the Senate President Pro Tempre. There are four tellers on the floor in the front of the room. They are ready to assist and chronicle the Electoral certificates as they are opened. These certificates will be opened alphabetically, verified, and then will be counted or rejected. The rejected certificates will then be immediately turned over to the fifteen members of the Special Commission. It will then be the Commission's responsibility to decide which of these rejected certificates will be deemed valid.

Standing close but not next to each other in the rear of the room are John Reid and Zach Chandler. Both men have come to observe the House activities, along with the hundreds of other spectators in the room. Some of these other spectators are visiting diplomats from other countries who want to witness this extraordinary event in American democracy. As people walk through the chamber, each finding their seat or, in some cases, just a place to stand, they can hardly hear themselves think as the room is filled with low tone of whispering chatter. The atmosphere grows tense and more exciting than a Shakespeare play ready for the opening curtain. Never in the history of American politics has there been such looming doubt or disagreement over a Presidential election. Every person present is anxious and wants to be a part of and bear witness to this unfolding event. And each quietly wonders *will it be Tilden or Hayes?*

The clock on the wall strikes one chime. Representatives Fields, Kassman and Senator Sargent watch Senator Ferry as he walks to the

House of Representatives desk which is normally occupied by the Speaker of the House. House Speaker Randall is sitting beside him. Senator Ferry clears his throat and shouts, "The Joint Session is now called to order. The Certificates will be opened in alphabetical order starting with the state of Alabama." He opens a wooden box and takes out the first sealed certificate from Alabama and hands it to one of the four tellers in the room. The teller opens the certificate and reads it out loud. "Alabama casts its ten electoral votes for Samuel J. Tilden."

The process continues smoothly until he comes to the state of Florida. There are three different sets of certificates submitted and as the tellers open them, they call out each of the three's results.

"Four votes for Hayes."

"Four votes for Tilden."

"Four votes for Tilden."

Senator Ferry calls out, "Are there any objections to the certificates from Florida?"

Representative Field stands and bellows, "I object to the first set of certificates."

Senators Sargent and Kasson stand and call out in turn, "I object to the second and third sets."

Senator Ferry scans the room with his eyes and asks out loud, "Are there any further objections?" He waits for a response and there is none. He then calls out loudly ruling, "There being none, the papers will be sent to the Electoral Commission." At that point, the Congressman and two Senators who voiced their objections stand and proceed to submit their objections in writing to the tellers. The voices in the room continue their low whispers and John Reid and Zach Chandler look at each other with sly smiles.

The counting process continues. More objections are voiced and submitted for the certificates submitted from the states of Louisiana, South Carolina, and Oregon. Finally, after all the certificates are opened and counted, the final tally leaves neither candidate with a clear victory. The certificates from the states of Florida, Louisiana, South Carolina and Oregon are then turned over to the Electoral Commission. It will be up to the commission to decide which are valid and to be counted.

Earlier in that year of 1876, before the election, the Senate had voted to eliminate the Twenty-Second Joint rule. If that rule had still been in place, then the states that submitted the duplicate and triplicate returns would have been tossed out and the states' votes would not have counted. In that case, Tilden would have won the Presidency without dispute. Tilden had received 184 Electoral votes and Hayes 165. In order to steal the Presidency away from Tilden, who had already beaten Hayes by 254,235 popular votes, the Republicans needed all of the twenty disputed votes to give Hayes a majority of one. The two Vice Presidential candidates, Republican Wheeler from New York and Democrat Hendricks from Indiana, were just as anxious for the outcome, and wanted to know if they had a job in Washington or not.

⸎

February 2, 1877

On the following day, inside a conference room at the Capitol Building, the five Senators, five Congressmen and five Supreme Court Justices chosen for the Special Commission are seated around a long table. They are in a small, cramped room where there is hardly any space for spectators. In the corner of the room, there is a large cuspidor (Spittoon) which stands out like a sore thumb.

Standing just inside the door, Speaker Randall motions to Congressman Hewitt to step outside into the hall with him. Catching this motion out of the corner of his eye, Justice Bradley looks up from the paper certificates in front of him on the table and gazes at both men when they walk out of the room. He is quite aware of the fact that he is the deciding vote on these disputed certificates and which ever way he decides, he is going to be disappointing a lot of good people. He also realizes that as a Republican, he will be critically judged and heavily scorned by his party if he votes on the side of the Democrats.

After quietly exiting the Special Commission room, Randall and Hewitt stand in the hallway, just a few feet away from the door. In a low voice, Randall says to Hewitt, "Justice Bradley has a reputation of fairness and honesty amongst his peers, but none the less, he is a Republican and loyal to his party. I have a bad feeling about this."

Hewitt nods in agreement. "I've heard some things I don't like."

"It's too late now to do anything about it now." Randall snipes. "We may have been better off if we'd listened to Mr. Tilden when he advised us to debate. At least that way, all of this would have been in the open and the public would have been aware." He then points back toward the room where the Special Commission has assembled and continues. "As it is, all of this secrecy is going to allow just one person to decide the Presidency!"

Hewitt looks around to see if anybody is listening. Then, almost in a whisper he replies, "I was told by Taylor and Gibson that they spoke with Justice Bradley at his home and he assured them he was going to give the Florida Electors to Tilden."

Randall, slightly raising his voice, fires back, "Governor Drew in Florida had his own problems. He had to sue the Republicans to get a recount. We don't have that option now."

Keeping his voice low, Hewitt places his hand on Randall's arm. "Bradley knows the truth. The only certificates that should be counted as legal from Florida should be Governor Drew's, since he is the legal Governor."

Randall smirks and snipes, "I heard two-hundred thousand is the going price these days for a change of heart."

Back inside the conference room, Justice Bradley looks back to the documents placed before him. He tries to concentrate on the papers, but, feeling the heavy burden placed on his shoulders, his mind begins to wander. Still looking at the papers, but not really seeing them, he thinks back to what happened a few nights before.

Early in that evening, Democrats Taylor and Gibson arrive at Bradley's house. He had had a brief talk with the two men, and all three men seemed in agreement. They shook hands and the two Democrats departed. When Taylor and Gibson left, they were convinced that Justice Bradley was going to write his opinion in favor of counting the Florida votes for the Democrats. But minutes later, after the two had departed, two unknown men waiting in a carriage out of sight of Taylor and Gibson, drove their carriage toward Bradley's home. Still standing outside, Bradley sees and waits for the men, watching as they climb down and walk toward him. He shakes hands with one of the men and the other hands him a large envelope and pats him on the shoulder. Bradley, not amused by the gift, tries to give the envelope back but the men refuse to take it. The two men then turn and walk away from him and climb back into their carriage waving as they drive off. Bradley is stunned when he rips open the envelope and pulls out a large stack of cash.

CHAPTER TWENTY-THREE

A *Republican Victory*

On March 2nd, the House of Representatives meets before the Special Commission to finalize their decision, which is expected to be announced on the following day, March 3rd. By a vote of 137 to 88, the House of Representatives adopt a series of preambles introductory to the following resolution:

Resolved by the House of Representatives of the United States

"That it is the duty of the House to declare, and this house does solemnly declare that Samuel J. Tilden, of the State of New York, received 196 electoral votes for the office of the President of the United States, all of which votes were cast and lists thereof signed, certified, and transmitted to the seat of the government, directed to the President of the Senate, in conformity with the Constitution and laws of the United States, by electors legally eligible and qualified as such electors, each of whom has been duly appointed and elected in the manner directed by the Legislature of the State in and for which he cast his vote aforesaid: and that said Samuel J. Tilden having thus received the votes of the majority of the electors appointed aforesaid, he is thereby duly elected President of the United States of America for the term of four years commencing on the 4th day of March, A.D. 1877; and this House further declares that Thomas A. Hendricks, having received the same number of electoral votes for the office of Vice President of the Unites States that were cast for Samuel J. Tilden for President as aforesaid, and at the same time and in the same manner, it is the opinion of this House that the said Thomas A. Hendricks, of the State of Indiana, is duly elected Vice President of the Untied States for the term of four years commencing on the 4th day of March, A.D. 1877."

At the Tilden estate in New York, Mary, Samuel and John Bigelow wait to hear the outcome of the voting. Samuel knows of the resolution being presented by the House of Representatives to elect him. He refuses to accept anything but the decision by the Special Commission, because it is now the rightful law to decide the election. He never agreed to its creation because he believed there never should have been any secrecy involved, and that the House should have debated it publicly. But since it was signed into law by President Grant, he feels bound by his ethics to abide by it.

Breaking his train of thought, he turns as Bigelow's booming voice snipes, "There are four disputed states, Samuel, and you only need one Electoral vote to end this charade."

Samuel smirks and replies with sarcasm. "With one honest judge— the cards are stacked against me with Bradley. He's a Republican and I have a strong sense he will vote strictly along party lines." The three continue to discuss the ramifications of the deciding vote by Bradley. But then all grow quiet when Mr. Smith walks into the room and places a telegram into Samuel hands. Samuel reads it and places it on a nearby table without saying a word. He watches in silence as Mary leans over and picks up the telegram, reading it silently at first. She then clears her throat and reads out loud, "By a party line vote they have decided 8 to 7." She looks up from the paper and into her brother's eyes. In a deadpan voice, she continues "Hayes is elected." Slowly returning her gaze back to the paper in her hand, she takes the telegram and crumples it in her hand. Angry, because she believes her brother did not put up enough of a fight, she snipes, "William was much more bent on going to Washington then you were and takes it more to heart."

Trying to keep his own anger in check, Samuel fires back at her, "Yes, and he's been counted out, too." He then turns and follows Mr. Smith out of the room. "Mr. Smith, I need you to send a wire."

Back at the House of Representatives, Hewitt and Randall argue in the House that the Commission is unconstitutional. It is March 3, 1877, 1a.m. The Congressmen and Senators are arguing fiercely with each other, with accusations flying back and from across the room. In the Spectators area, John Reid and Zach Chandler listen to their boisterous exchanges. Then Chandler smiles and puts his arm around Reid's shoulder and grips him tightly. "I think this is it my friend. Well done." Reid smiles back.

At the front of the room, Speaker Randall stands with Senator Ferry at his side. Ferry bangs the gavel to stop the men from fighting. Hewitt and the others ignore them and continue arguing with each other. Ferry continues to bang his gavel.

"Gentlemen we must have order… we must have order!" As the men continue to bicker, a messenger enters the chamber and walks directly to Randall. Without a word, in the midst of the chaos, he hands Randall a telegram and walks away. Randall reads the telegram, and then hands it to Senator Ferry. After reading the telegram, Ferry steps down off the center podium and Randall steps up. He takes the gavel and bangs it. He shouts out loud waving the telegram, "GENTLEMEN…I HAVE JUST RECEIVED A WIRE FROM MR. TILDEN!"

This gets everyone's attention and the men stop arguing and turn to listen. Randall shouts out, "Mr. Tilden is willing to let the count be concluded." There is a pause of brief silence and the men begin to fight again.

Senator Ferry steps back up to the podium and shouts, "HAYES AND WHEELER ARE HEREBY DULY ELECTED!"

Hewitt, after hearing the announcement, collapses to the floor. Several men run over to help him up and walk him out of the House Chambers. Back in the spectators' area, Reid and Chandler, along with some other Republicans, break out in smiles and quietly pat each other on the back for their win.

Chandler says to Reid, "If it wasn't for you and the *New York Times* editorial staff, this would have never happened." Reid grins and replies sarcastically, "As you can see, the Democrats are not fit to run this country."

Just a few days before Hayes is sworn in, *The World* newspaper reports that Mr. Tilden, under the alleged authority of General Woodford, the United States District Attorney for the Southern District of New York, is about to take the oath of office as President in New York and proclaim himself President of the Untied States. When asked by other reporters if this is true, John Bigelow responds, with Tilden's approval, by a written letter to the media.

After finishing his written response, Bigelow asks Mary to read it aloud for him and Samuel. Mary, standing a few feet away from them takes the letter from Bigelow and proceeds to read out loud:

"There were two contingencies in which it would have been lawful and obligatory for Mr. Tilden to have taken the official oath as President.

***First**, if Congress had performed it constitutional duty of counting the electoral votes and had declared that Mr. Tilden was chosen by the electoral colleges.*

The two Houses of Congress have all the powers for verifying the electoral votes which by the Constitution or the laws confer or allow. Nobody else in the federal government has any such powers. This exclusive jurisdiction of the two Houses has been exercised by without interruption from the beginning of the government. It is known to all those who came in contact with Mr. Tilden at this period that he concurred in this view of the powers and duties of the two Houses of Congress exclusively to count the electoral vote. He was perfectly free and unreserved in the expression of his opinions on this subject.

This contingency, however, never presented itself. Congress, before time fixed by law for counting the electoral votes, passed the electoral bill, wherein it substantially abdicated its powers and enacted that the Electoral Commission should, in the first instance, make a count and that its count should stand unless overruled by the concurrent action of the two Houses. The electoral tribunal counted Mr. Tilden out, and counted in a man who was not elected. Congress did not overrule their count: consequently the false count stood as law under the act of Congress.

***Secondly**, The other contingency, in which it would have been lawful and obligatory on Mr. Tilden to have taken the oath of office, was that the House of Representatives on the failure of a choice of President by the electoral colleges had itself proceeded to make the election, voting by States in the manner prescribed by the Constitution.*

"This contingency, like the first one, never occurred."

"The House of Representatives is required, by the express language of the Constitution, to elect the President when neither of the candidates can command a majority of the electoral votes.

The right of the two Houses to count the electoral votes and to declare that any person has a majority is a matter of implication, precedent, and practice. But the right of the House of Representatives to supply the failure of a choice is a positive constitutional command. It is not only a right, but a duty. The provision is mandatory. The House is a witness at the opening of the certificates; it is an actor in counting the votes by its own tellers and in its presence.

Having such and the best means of knowing whether a choice has been made by the electoral colleges , it is also expressly vested with a power and duty to act exclusively and conclusively in the event that no person probes to have been chosen by a majority of the votes of those colleges. The House acquires jurisdiction by that fact. The assent of the Senate to the existence of that fact is nowhere prescribed or required. No judgment, certification, or act of any official body is interposed as a condition to the assuming of jurisdiction by the House. When the House has once acted in such a case, no review of its actions nor any appeal from its decision is provided for in the Constitution. It is difficult to see why the House in such a case, like all tribunals of original jurisdiction and subject to no appeal, did not insist upon its rights as the exclusive judge of the fact and the law from which it acquired jurisdiction. It was, I am told, a fear that the Senate might lead a resistance to the rightful judgment of the House, and that General Grant would sustain a revolutionary policy with the army and navy and the militia of the great States in which the Republicans had possession of the governments, that deterred the House of Representatives from the assertion of its rights and induced it to abdicate in favor of the Electoral Commission.

But without speculating upon causes or motives, one thing is certain: the House of Representatives did not elect Mr. Tilden in the manner prescribed by the Constitution. On the other hand, it did concur with the Senate in anticipating and preventing the contingency in which it might have been compelled to act, thus providing an expedient which disarmed it. It adopted the electoral law and went through all the forms required for the execution of the electoral scheme. True, it afterwards passed a declaratory resolution condemning the action of that tribunal and asserting that Mr. Tilden had been duly elected; but the Constitution had not provided that a man should or could take office as President on a declaratory resolution of the House of Representatives merely. If that resolution could have had full effect to abrogate the electoral law which the House had assisted to enact, it would have created no warrant of authority to Mr. Tilden to take the oath of office. A vote by States that he should be the next President of the United States was still necessary to give Mr. Tilden any more title to the succession that General Grant, and that vote the House of Representatives never gave him.

I might have disposed of your question more briefly by simply saying that no contingency provided by the Constitution ever existed in which Mr. Tilden could lawfully or properly take the oath of office as President. I have dwelt upon the matter at some length because of its future as well as past importance. The idea that Mr. Tilden ever thought of taking the oath of office illegally is in my judgment quite as preposterous as is the other idea that would have omitted to take to take it if any contingency had arisen in which it was his right or duty to take it, or that any menace would have had the slightest influence his performing his whole obligation to the people. I will venture to say that if it had been his right and duty to take the oath he would have done so at the City hall in New York, surrounded by the forces which, according to Mr. Mines General Woodford pictured to his imagination, but at the federal capitol, even though he had known he would be kidnapped or subjected to a drumhead court-martial five minutes afterwards. It is doubtless true that revolutionary ideas were entertained by the hierarchy of office-holders in possession of the government. General Grant did utter menaces in published interviews and did make a display of military force in Washington to overawe Congress. I presume this was a part of the system of intimidation for which he allowed himself to be used by the office-holders, and which was intended to act upon public opinion through fear of disturbance, as well as upon Congress. But it is safe to say that whatever the effects they produced, they did not prevent Mr. Tilden form taking the oath of office. The feat that he would do so, which induced the Republicans to swear their candidate into office privately on the Saturday previous to the commencement of his term of office , besides repeating the ceremony at the inauguration, was born of that consciousness which causes the wicked to fell when no man pursueth. I was aware that about that time Mr. Tilden's house was besieged by emissaries of the press and the telegraph to know if the rumors to that effect which prevailed in Washington were true. This was a species of curiosity which I believe Mr. Tilden did not consider it any part of his duty to relieve.

To conclude: So the action of the Electoral Commission has conferred upon Mr. Tilden the unique distinction of being the first – let us hope the last – President-elect of the United States feloniously excluded from the chief magistracy; a distinction which, like the banishment of Aristides, the assassinations of Caesar, of Henry IV of France, of Lincoln, and of Carnot, makes it one of the conspicuous and indestructible landmarks of history."

Mary pauses for a moment, reflecting upon what she had just read. She then looks up from the letter and says to Samuel, "It's very good." Samuel smiles and nods his head in agreement. The wear of the election dispute has taken a toll on his health and Mary and Bigelow are concerned about him. Telegrams were still coming in from all over the country with thousands of his supporters pledging to take up arms for him. People were willing to do anything he asked of them but Samuel, after all of violence endured by the country before the recent close of the Civil War, did not want any blood shed in his name. He wanted peace.

CHAPTER TWENTY-FOUR

Your Fraudulency—Old 7 to 8

At close to midnight, the train that Hayes is a passenger on, along with his wife Lucy, stops at the Harrisburg, Pennsylvania train station. On this day, he is silent to any others about his feelings and how humiliated he feels by the actions taking place in Congress on his behalf. He considers himself to be an honorable man and realizes that the Republicans have commandeered the Oval Office with their dirty tricks, doing it more for themselves than they did for him.

When his train arrives in Washington that Friday morning, Senator Sherman is waiting, along with a few Federal soldiers, to escort him to his new position as President elect. Instead of accepting President Grant's invitation to go directly to the White House, Hayes has decided to be low key for the time being and thinks it is best to accept Senator Sherman's invitation to stay at his home.

Soldiers have been provided to follow the Hayes' carriage to protect him from the many disenchanted and unruly Tilden supporters. With all that has gone on, Hayes is not sure, himself, if he and Lucy will be safe. He considered the thought that someone might try to assassinate him before he is even sworn into office.

The following morning, after breakfast at the Sherman's home, Hayes meets with President Grant at the White House. In line with his earlier decision to be low key about the whole event, he requests that there be no large ceremony for his swearing in under the tense circumstances. Grant agrees and later that evening, at around 5 p.m., Hayes is sworn into the Presidency, with his wife Lucy at his side. It is a very quiet event without the usual pomp and formal ceremony.

In the days that follow, after Hayes is sworn in, several newspapers across the country protest to the public. The *New York Sun* puts a Black Border around its front page declaring the death of democracy. Another headline; *"It is done and fitly done in the dark by the grace of Justice Bradley."* Tilden supporters from New Orleans wire a telegram to Tilden's home, *"Will the Democrats see an usurper in the chair of Washington...Say, no! Never!! In tones that will resound from ocean to ocean. If you say the word, 50,000 Louisianans will take up guns for you."* Tilden receives hundreds of similar telegrams and letters protesting the election outcome from disappointed supporters around the country stating that they will do whatever he asks of them to secure his stolen presidency. Tilden is honored and appreciative by this outpouring of support.

On Wednesday June 13, 1877, a few weeks before departing on the ship *Scythia* for a long overdue holiday to Europe, Tilden makes a speech at the Manhattan Club. The crowd, mostly made up of his supporters, is huge and fills the area with hardly a space left to stand.

Samuel Tilden, duly elected by the voters is the true 19th President of the United States. Though he never formally concedes the election, he makes a speech in front of a large gathering addressing the President of the Manhattan Club and other Officers. He begins:

"Mr. President and Gentlemen of the Manhattan Club. I accepted your invitation under the idea that this was to be a merely social meeting, the special occasion of which was the presence in this city of Mr. Hendricks and of Governor Robinson and Lieutenant Governor Dorsheimer. One of your guests, Mr. Hendricks, embarks tomorrow on a foreign excursion for rest and recreation. He will carry with him our best wishes for a prosperous voyage, pleasant visit and a safe return, and for the health and happiness of himself and family. I have been availing myself, for similar purposes, of a brief interval, and find myself now, with some reluctance, drawn away from those private pursuits. But the occasion and the apparent general expectation seem to require that I should say a word in respect to public affairs, and especially that I should allude to the transaction which, in my judgment, is the most portentous in our political history."

Samuel takes a moment to clear his throat. His voice is not as strong as it was a few months earlier, but none-the-less he wants to thank everyone that supported him. He starts again.

"Everybody knows that, after the recent election, the men who were elected by the people President and Vice President of the United States were "counted out," and men who were not elected were "counted in" and seated."

Immediately, there are some sneers and booing. Samuel waits for them to settle down.

"I disclaim any thought of the personal wrong involved in this transaction. Not by any act or word of mine shall that be dwarfed or degraded into a personal grievance, which is, in truth, the greatest wrong that has stained our national annals. To every man of the four and a quarter millions who were defrauded of the fruits of their elective franchise, it is as great a wrong as it is to me. And no less to every man of the minority will the ultimate consequences extend. Evils in government grow by success and by impunity. They do not arrest their own progress. They can never be limited except by external forces. If the men in possession of the government can, in one instance, maintain themselves in power against an adverse decision at the elections, such an example will be imitated. Temptation exists always. Devices to give the color of law, and false pretences on which to found fraudulent decisions, will not be wanting. The wrong will grow into a practice, if condoned-if once condoned. In the world's history changes in the succession of governments have usually been the result of fraud or force. It has been our faith and our pride that we had established a mode of peaceful change to be worked out by the agency of the ballot box. The question now is whether our elective system, in its substance as well as its form, is to be maintained. This is the question of questions. Until it is finally settled there can be no politics founded on interior questions of administrative policy. It involves the fundamental right of the people. It involves the elective principle. It involves the whole system of popular government. The people must signally condemn the great wrong which has been done to them. They must strip the example of everything that can attract imitators. They must refuse a prosperous immunity to crime. This is not all. The people will not be able to trust the authors or beneficiaries of the wrong to devise remedies. But when those who condemn the wrong shall have the power they must devise the measure which shall render a repetition of the wrong forever impossible."

Samuel stops for a moment then continues with a lot of emotion and new found inner-strength.

"If my voice could reach throughout our country and be heard in its remotest hamlet I would say be of good cheer. The Republic will live. The institutions of our fathers are not to expire in shame. The sovereignty of the people shall be rescued from this peril and be re-established. Successful wrong never appears so triumphant as on the very eve of its fall. Seven years ago a corrupt dynasty culminated in its power over the million of people who live in the city of New York. It has conquered or bribed, or flattered and won almost everybody into acquiescence. It appeared to be invincible. A year or two later its members were in the penitentiaries or in exile. History abounds in similar examples. We must believe in the right and in the future. A great and noble nation will not sever its political from its moral life."

A thunderous applause and cheers ring out through crowd. These people want him to run again in the 1880 election. But at this time, Samuel has one mission on mind and that is to take a break from the rigorous duties of politics. He will deal with whatever his party wants or needs from him after he returns from his excursion to Europe. For now, he just needs to rest up and get his health back on track. He has a few brief moments of laughter when he hears that people have tagged President Hayes with the names "Old 7 to 8 and Your Fraudulency."

<hr />

After a long rest and a visit to Europe, Samuel is on the ship *Scythia* returning to his home in New York. He is standing by the rail looking out at the quiet, serene ocean and starlit night sky. He turns and smiles when he sees John Bigelow walking toward him. Accompanying his best friend is a young beautiful woman with long dark hair. Something about her is familiar and he's not sure, but he thinks he has seen this woman before.

"Well good evening, John," he says and then turns to the young lady. "I see you've found a friend."

The young woman extends her hand into his and says, "A pleasure to meet you too, Mr. President." While they are shaking hands, Bigelow introduces her. "Samuel, this is Marie Celeste Stauffer from New Orleans.

It was she, along with her mother, whom I assisted with their fallen packages that day in front of the Fifth Avenue hotel. And, by all accounts, the same lady that rode by us like the wind on that day in Central Park!"

Amused by the coincidence, "That was you?" Samuel asks Celeste, astounded. As the two begin to talk, Bigelow can see that Samuel is smitten by her southern charms. He listens for a few minutes to their conversation, then quietly walks away, leaving the two of them alone on the ship's deck.

A few days later, the *Scythia* docks in New York Harbor. A huge crowd of Tilden supporters and dignitaries wait to welcome Samuel home. There is a marching band playing loud music and the atmosphere is one of celebration. The people are waving Tilden campaign signs and some even have "President Tilden" signs.

As the passengers begin to disembark, Samuel walks down the gangplank with Marie Stauffer on his arm. Marie's mother and John Bigelow follow. Samuel stops when he is mid way, looking over the crowd and enjoying the welcoming party. The band stops playing.

One of Samuel's admirers shouts out, "You were robbed of the Presidency!"

Samuel smiles and calls out, "I did not get robbed," he says, opening his arms wide, "The people got robbed. Robbed of the dearest rights of American citizens. Young men, we who have guarded the sacred traditions of our free government will soon leave that work to you. Whether our institutions shall be preserved will depend on you. Will you accomplish that duty, and mark the wrongdoers of 1876 with the indignation of a betrayed, wronged and sacrificed people? I swear in the presence of all of you and I call upon you to bear witness to the oath, to watch, during the remainder of my life, over the rights of the citizens of our country with jealous care. Such usurpation must never occur again." The crowd roars with thunderous applause and cheers expressing their admiration for the man they believe is the real 19th President of the United States.

Mary is standing near the front of the crowd with her granddaughter and her son, William Pelton. Several dignitaries, including Honest John Kelly cheer with the crowd to welcome the man they believe is the greatest democrat ever. As the band starts to play again, Samuel catches Mary's eye and he waves to her. She waves back. Samuel looks at her and takes his hand and places it under his suit jacket to his heart and thumps it.

Mary nods her head and smiles, realizing that the young lady who is holding her brothers' arm, is the one making his heart thump.

The Proposed Tilden Trust Library
On the site of the Reservoir between 40th and 42nd Streets.

PART TWO

The Life of
Samuel J. Tilden

Written by John Bigelow

CHAPTER ONE

Presidential canvas of 1876 – Assailable points of Grant administration- Popular
majority for Tilden and Hendricks – Inception of the conspiracy to defeat the popular
choice – Senator Barnum, John C. Reid, and the "New York Times:—William E. Chandler's break of the day dispatches – Troops ordered to Florida – President Grant's
dispatch to General Sherman – Foul operations of conspirators in Florida – How
rewarded by President Hayes – General Barlow.

The presidential canvass of 1876 was one of exceptional bitterness.
The public officers of the party in control of the federal government had
been charged by the press on the platform, by prominent and responsible Republicans as well as by the opposition, not only with gross
neglect of official duty, but with official conduct for much of which the
laws provided the most degrading penalties. They charged, among other
things that during the whole eight years of General Grant's administration the ordinary expenses of the government, exclusive of pensions and
interest on the public debt, had been increased at the inordinate rate of
$75,000,000 a year.

That its influence had been exerted to procure its insertion on the bill
that was to double the President's salary, and, as an inducement for its
passage, a provision that the increase of pay which Congress had already
awarded the members should date back to the beginning of their term,
by which means they were to receive about $1,000,000 of back pay.

That in a single month in 1874 one million gallons of whiskey
were sold in St. Louis which has not paid the lawful tax, amounting to
$700,000, through the collusion of officials attached to the Treasury
Department, who were tried and convicted of sharing in the plunder.
As St. Louis was but one, and by no means the most considerable, of the
cities in which large distilleries were in operation, it was estimated and
charged that from these frauds alone, which had been going on for many
years, the loss to the treasury had been not less than $15,000,000 a year.

O. C. Babcock, the President's private secretary, and the one Avery, the chief clerk of the treasury, were both indicted for participating in these robberies. Avery was convicted, but to save the President's private secretary from the State prison, and for other reasons which it is too painful to even suggest, Mr. Henderson, the lawyer selected by the Attorney General for the prosecution of these rogues, was displaced at the special instance of the President, as was publicly charged, and, so far as I know, never denied.

That financial agency of our government abroad was taken from the old and responsible banking-house of the Barings, of London, who had held it through a long succession of administrations, and was given to the house of Clews and Co., of which one partner was an Englishman, but then residing in New York, and the other Swede, who at one time was Swedish consul in New York, form which position he had been relieved at the instance of our government for blockade-running during the war. To secure their appointment it was charged the Clews and Co. agreed, in writing to give a quarter, or some other portion, of their profits to one Cheever, a notorious familiar at the White House; another quarter to one James A. Van Buren, which name subsequently proved to be a pseudonym, and the appropriation to it was understood to represent a gratification to some personage too important to be named; and the eight to a brother-in-law of the President. It is not surprising that, with so many divisions, the dividends of Clews and Co. were disappointing, and that they soon failed and went into bankruptcy, debtors to the government for a large amount.

That the soldiers of the United States were ordered to take possession of the legislative halls of Louisiana in 1874, and drive from the House of Representatives who were opposed to the usurpation of the executive chair by William Pitt Kellogg, the Jonathan Wild of Louisiana politics, who had been placed in it by the aid of a drunken and corrupt judge of the federal court.

The books of the State department show that the indebtedness to the government of Clews, Habicht, & Co. on the 24th of September, 1872, when they went into liquidation amounted to $145,451.47. Up to November 29, 1887, the company had paid off $38,718.77 of this indebtedness. In 1882 the State department comprised with Henry Clews for his individual share of the indebtedness for the $12,500, leaving the sum of $94,232.70 still standing charged to Clews, Habicht, & Co. on the books of the Register of the Treasury

That George Williams Curtis was compelled to retire from Civil Service Commission, because "the circumstances under which several important appointments had been made seemed to him to show an abandonment both of the letter and the spirit of civil service regulations," and because "he was unwilling to be held responsible for acts which he considered nothing more nor less than a disregard of public pledges and a mockery of the public faith."

That Mr. Bristow, the Secretary of the Treasury, and Mr. Cox, the Secretary of the Interior, who where the only friends of a reformed civil service in the cabinet, were expelled from it because they were its friends.

That one vice-president, one speaker of the House of Representatives, three senators, and five chairman of congressional committees, all partisans of the executive, dishonored themselves, the government and the nation by marketing their influence as legislators; that a secretary of the treasury did the like by forcing balances in the public accounts; that an attorney general did the like by appropriating public funds to his own use; that a secretary of the navy did the like by enriching himself and his confederates out of percentages levied upon contractors with his department; while secretary of war was impeached for high crimes and misdemeanors.

Then there was the Emma mine swindle, in which one of our ministers to England was understood to be implicated; enormous frauds in the Indian and printing departments and in the New York customhouse; extravagant and corrupt expenditures for post-offices and public structures of various kinds, which, during fifteen years, had amounted to $51,164,978, while for the same purposes during the seventy-two previous years of our national existence the corresponding expenditures had been less than twenty-nine millions. There was the Venezuela scandal, the San Domingo scheme, the Credit Mobilier scandal, and defalcations of public offers so numerous as almost to constitute the rule rather than the exception in the public service; so numerous, indeed, that the Secretary of the Treasury persistently refused to comply with the law which required him annually to report them to Congress.

Bigelow states, "I will not swell these pages with more of these unsavory charges, which, to be compete and explicit, would alone fill a volume. It will be for the historian, in due time, to deal with this saturnalia of crime and political prostitution, which few Americans even now can recall with a blush.

Most of these charges were established by congressional or by judicial inquiry, many by both. They of course placed many thousands individuals – indeed, it would be no exaggeration to say hundreds of thousands- on the defensive, who, if deprived of the protection of sympathetic administration, would be personally as well as politically ruined. They naturally dreaded the accession of a Democratic administration, from which they could expect little indulgence; but the prospect of having their operations reviewed by an administration Tilden at its head made them desperate. His name had more terrors for them than that of any other man in the Republic, and when his nomination with such practical unanimity by the St. Louis convention transpired, they realized at once that *vae victis* (woe to the vanquished) was to be the battle cry of the campaign, and that Tilden must be beaten or they be ruined. They were in the condition of rats assailed in a room which offered no hole for escape. The situation gave them the courage and the recklessness of despair. The situation gave them the courage and the recklessness of despair. They took up the cry of the furious goddess, maddened by the unsuccessfulness of her malice.

"Flectere si nequeo superos Archeronta Movebo" "If I cannot move heaven I will raise hell."

They did not undertake to defend themselves, for that, they knew, was useless. Their crimes were of record, and suspected, if not known, of all men. Their plan of battle was to assail Tilden with charges bred of their own foul imaginings; in the language of Voltaire, *"faire la guerre des pots de chambre, (English translation—make war with your pots)* , in the hope of persuading the people that he was no better than they, and that they, and that nothing was to be gained by admitting him and his party to power. They denounced him as a railroad wrecker, because he had employed his extraordinary talents as a lawyer and an organizer in rescuing a number of railways from bankruptcy and converting them into productive properties. They charged him with extorting excessive fees for his professional services, though he had never had a bill for services successfully questioned, nor had he ever accepted a contingent fee in his life. They charged him with rebel sympathies during the war, though he was one of the leaders of the revolt against the administration which was proposing to legalize slavery in the free Territories; though he supported Van Buren and Adams for President in 18748-9; thought he refused his consent to repeal the Missouri Compromise in 1854;

though he attended and his name figured in the list of officers of the
Union meeting held in New York immediately after the attack on Fort
Sumter, and also attended another meeting of the bar, held for the same
purpose; and though he was during the war in more or less continuous
consultation with every member of President Lincoln's cabinet, the only
two surviving members of which were then on the stump advocating
his election.

They charged him with intending, if elected, to indemnify the South
for their losses during the rebellion and to assume the rebel debt – a
charge for which there was only the flimsy foundation that the Southern
States favored his nomination and were expected to vote for him at
the election. Though the prospect of the payment of such losses had
not been regarded of sufficient magnitude to deserve the notice of the
nomination convention of either party, Mr. Tilden waived his right to
disregard the charge, and in reply to a letter from the Honorable A.
S. Hewitt, who then represented in Congress the district in which Mr.
Tilden resided, gave these charges a most explicit and satisfactory denial.
Even the "Tribune," which had already quite forgotten Mr. Tilden's oft-
acknowledged claims to its respect as a man, and its admiration as a
statesman, confessed that the charge which it had not thought unworthy
of the hospitality of its columns had been fully disposed of by this
letter.

It was further charged that his health was too feeble to endure the
fatigues of the presidential office, especially when increased as they
would be enormously by the restoration of a party which had been
excluded from the administration of government for some fourteen
years, and by such changes of men and measures as would be the inevi-
table consequences of such restoration.

It was not the Governor's health about which they were solicitous.
They could have borne his clinical sufferings and even his demise with
Christian fortitude, and aided perhaps in imposing the burden which
would have contributed to it.

*"If the assassination could trammel up the consequence and catch with his
surcease success."*

But there was Hendricks quite ready to leap into the saddle. He was
no "reformer," it is true, but he was before all things a thorough party
man of the most unadulterated strain, who they knew full well would
neglect no partisan advantage or leave one stone upon another of the

administration party that could be thrown down. There was no alternative left them but to defeat Tilden, and as it could not be done by fair means, it was too late for them to scruple about a resort to foul.

The most unequivocal evidence of their having reached this stage of desperation was exhibited in the report put into circulation soon after the Governor's nomination, that he had failed to make full and fair returns of his income to the tax assessors. Because on one occasion he had received the sum of $20,000 as compensation for professional service which did not seem to correspond with his tax returns for that year, it was assumed that his return was false, concealing or ignoring the fact that the fee in question was his compensation for eight or nine successive years of severe professional toil. I shall have occasion to deal this subject more at length later, when the aid of the federal jurisdiction was invoked to assist, with this weapon in its hands, in defeating his renomination to the presidency in 1880 and in 1884.

But all their efforts proved unavailing. The Governor had lived too long in the public eye; his service had been too considerable; his character had sunk its roots too deep into the confidence of his countrymen, and its branches covered too large a territory to be seriously disturbed by such a storm as could be provoked be the reckless misrepresentations of a crowd of rogues whom the people were bent on haling to judgment.

At the election, on 7th of November, 1876 the total vote for Tilden electors in the United States was, 4,300,316 – for Hayes – 4,036,016 – a majority for Tilden of 264,300 – Tilden's majority over Grant majority in 1872 – 703,574 – Tilden's majority over Grant's majority in 1868 – 1,287,128.

He was the choice of the people and with a larger majority by some 700,000 than had ever been cast by the people of the United States for any other person. But all this majority did not make him President. The Constitution provides that the people of the several States shall choose electors whose votes are to decide to be counted, or for which candidate, are problems which henceforth, as we shall now proceed to demonstrate, there is no calculus of variations that is competent to solve.

As a necessary preliminary to this demonstration the reader is requested to imagine himself in the editorial rooms of the "New York Times" at ten o'clock on the night of the 7th of November; present John Foord, then editor in chief; John C. Reid, editor of the news department; and Charles H. Miller, the present editor of the "Times," but then occupying a subordinate position. Sufficient returns from the election had been received to extinguish all hope of electing Hayes, and to warrant the preparation of an editor.al article to that effect which appeared in the first edition of the "Times" on the 8th. The article commences as follows:

The New York Times set to ink this editorial for the morning paper dated November 8, 1876: "A Doubtful Election" At the time of going to press the result of the presidential election is still in doubt. Enough has been leaned to show that the vote has been unprecedentedly heavy. Both parties have exhausted their full legitimate strength, while the peculiar Democratic policy, for which such extensive preparations were made in the large registry of this city, and in the enormous registry in Brooklyn, have had its effect.

Conceding New York to Mr. Tilden, he will receive the electoral votes of the following states:

Alabama	10	Arkansas	6	Connecticut	6
Delaware	3	Georgia	11	Indiana	15
Kentucky	12	Maryland	8	Mississippi	8
Missouri	15	New Jersey	9	New York	35
North Carolina	10	Tennessee	12	Texas	8
Virginia	11	West Virginia	5		
				Total	**184**

"General Hayes will receive the votes of the following States:

California	6	Colorado	3	Illinois	21
Iowa	11	Kansas	5	Louisiana	8
Maine	7	Massachusetts	13	Michigan	11
Minnesota	5	Nebraska	3	Nevada	3
New Hampshire	5	Ohio	3	Oregon	22
Pennsylvania	29	Rhode Island	4	Vermont	5
Wisconsin	10	South Carolina	7		
				Total	**181**

"This leaves Florida *alone* still in doubt. *If the Republicans have carried that State, as they claim, they will have 185 votes* – a majority of one."

It will be observed that the desponding words which I have italicized in the first article are eliminated from the second, and all the doubtful States, including Florida, claimed for Hayes, assuring him a majority of one in the Electoral College.

What was it in Mr. Reid's mind in setting up a formal claim to all these States, on receiving the impression from Senator Barnum's inquiry that they were "close," we need not speculate about; for we have his own testimony upon the subject.

Not satisfied with the share which William E. Chandler had been appropriating to himself of the credit for securing the election of Hayes, Mr. Reid published in the "Times" of June 15, 1887, an account of what followed the operations in the "Times" office, which have already been disclosed.

Mr. Reid informs us that before daylight on the morning of the day succeeding that of the election, William E. Chandler, a personage who, as my reader of this generation at least are aware, was already renowned beyond the boundaries of his native State of New Hampshire for what the French call les petites politques (small politics) arrived at the Fifth avenue hotel in New York. Soon after his arrival, and between six and half-past six in the morning, Mr. Reid, who in this communication does not give his name, but uniform describes himself as an editor of the "New York Times," also entered the Fifth Avenue hotel. He went at once to the rooms of the national committee, and found them occupied only by a number of servants of the hotel who were in engaged in cleaning and setting the rooms to rights. He was informed that everybody had gone home or to bed a couple hours before. He left the room sand started for the clerks' desk to ascertain the number of Mr. Zachariah Chandler's room.

On his way to the office of the hotel he came in collision with a small man wearing an immense pair of goggles, his hat drawn down over his ears, a greatcoat with a heavy military cloak, and carrying a gripsack and a newspaper in his hand. The newspaper was the "New York Tribune." The stranger cried out, "Why Mr. Blank, is that you?" The gentleman knew the voice and said, "Is that you, Mr. Chandler?" He answered, "Yes I have just arrived from New Hampshire by train. Damn the men who

Note: Mr. Zachariah Chandler was then a member of the United States Senate form Michigan, and also chairman of the Republican National Committee.

have brought this disaster upon the Republican Party!" The gentleman replied, *"The Republican party has sustained no disaster. If you will only keep your heads up here, there is no question of the election of President Hayes.* He has been fairly and honestly elected.

Mr. Reid and Mr. Chandler then proceeded to the latter's room in the hotel.

The visitor went over the ground carefully, State by State, from Maine to Oregon, counting the electoral vote in each State, and showing the vote as it was finally counted for Hayes and Tilden. After he had finished, William E. Chandler said, "Well what do you think should be done?"

The gentleman replied, "Telegraph immediately to leading Republicans, men in authority, in South Carolina, Florida, Louisiana, California, Oregon, and Nevada."

Mr. Chandler made no reply to this proposition, but said, "We must go and see Zach."

After some difficulty, Mr. Reid and William E. Chandler succeeded in finding Zach Chandler's room.

The door was shortly opened, and Mr. Zachariah Chandler was discovered standing in his night-dress. William E. Chandler then said, closing the door," Here is a gentleman who has more news than you have, and he has some suggestions to make."

To which Zach Chandler replied, "Yes, I know him. What is it?" with which he seated himself on the edge of the bed.

William E. Chandler then said, "The gentleman will tell you the story himself. He understands it better than I do."

The gentleman then went over the details of the election, and added the recommendations he had made to William E. Chandler. The chairman of the national committee lay down and said, "Very well, go ahead and do what you think necessary."

Mr. Reid and William E. Chandler then rushed in company to the telegraph office in the hotel. It was not yet open for business. It would not be open for an hour or more.

The gentleman said, "I'll have to take these messages to the main office of the Western Union."

Chandler called a servant and directed him to have a carriage brought to the Twenty-third street entrance. Then Chandler said," Well, what do you want to do?"

The gentleman replied, "We'll first telegraph to Governor Chamberlain, of South Carolina." The gentleman dictated the dispatch, as follows; "To D.H. Chamberlain, S.C: Hayes is elected if we have carried South Carolina, Florida and Louisiana. Can you hold your State? Answer immediately."

Mr. Chandler took the dispatch in shorthand, as dictated. The following dispatch was then dictated to S.B. Conover, Tallahassee. Florida, "The presidential election depends on the vote of Florida, and the Democrats will try to wrest it form us. Watch it and hasten returns. Answer immediately. Do not be cheated in returns. Answer when sure."

To S.B. Packard, of Louisiana, the following dispatch was sent: "The presidential election depends on the vote of Louisiana, and the Democrats will try and wrest it from you."

Mr. Reid says dispatches of like import were sent to Oregon and California. He then adds: "William E. Chandler signed with his own name the dispatches to Oregon and to Gorman, of San Francisco. To the dispatches sent to Conver, Packard, and Chamberlain the narrator's recollection is he signed the name of Zachariah Chandler. William E. Chandler at one took the telegraph blanks and wrote from his stenographic notes the dispatches above printed, the gentleman standing by him taking every dispatch as he finished, and carefully reading it. When the last dispatch was transcribed, Chandler handed it over to the gentleman and said, "Are they all right?" He was informed that they were.

The gentleman jumped into the carriage waiting and told the driver to go to the main office of the Western Union with all possible speed. Probably the quickest time ever made by a carriage from the Fifth Avenue hotel to the Western Union was made that morning. Arriving at the Western Union office, the gentleman went to the receiver's desk and handed in the dispatches. The receiver replied, "The national committee has no account here, and we can't do it. Whey not charge them to the New York Times account?"

The gentleman replied, "All right," and the receiver immediately handed them back to him to be countersigned. This was promptly done. The gentleman returned to his carriage and was driven back to the Fifth Avenue hotel. There was still nobody stirring connected with the national committee.

The New York Times has never to this day, June 15, 1887 been reimbursed by the national committee or William E. Chandler; nor has William E. Chandler, or any national committee ever offered to repay the "Times" for the telegraph tolls or for any of the expense incurred on that morning.

Here we have, upon the most authentic possible testimony a quasi official account of the first stage in the erection of the complicated structure of fraud by which the choice of the American people was to be defeated and their executive government delivered over to a usurper.

That the Tilden and Hendricks ticket was entitled to 184 electoral votes was undisputed. That the Hayes and Wheeler ticket was entitled to 165 electoral votes was also undisputed. There were 369 electors in all. The Tilden ticket, therefore with 184 votes, needed by one more to give it the majority required for an election. The Hayes ticket, having only 166 electoral votes assured required 19 more votes to ensure the election.

The four votes of Florida, the eight of Louisiana, and the seven of South Carolina made just nineteen. To get one of these votes was sufficient to elect Tilden and Hendricks. To elect Hayes and Wheeler it was necessary to get the whole nineteen.

The "Times" of the 9th followed up the operations initiated in its columns the previous morning by boldly claiming to have returns which gave the election to Hayes, though it could have had nothing of the kind. If it had any returns of such import, they were of course simply the partisan reverberations of Chandler's dispatches.

THE BATTLE WON
"A REPUBLICAN VICOTORY IN THE NATION – GOV. HAYES ELECTED PRESIDENT AND WILLIAM A. WHEELER VICE PRESIDENT – THE REPUBLICANS CARRY TWENTY-ONE STATES CASTING 185 ELECTORAL VOTES- A REPUBLICAN MAJORITY IN THE NEXT CONGRESS."

The dispatches received since our last issue confirm the reports on which the "Times" yesterday claimed 181 electoral votes for Governor Hayes. On Wednesday the following States were put down as surely Republican: Colorado, California, Illinois, Iowa, Kansas, Maine, Massachusetts, Michigan, Minnesota, Nevada, Nebraska, New Hampshire, Oregon, Ohio, Pennsylvania, Rhode Island, Vermont, Wisconsin,

Louisiana, and South Carolina. Some of these States were claimed by Democrats; but all intelligence, thus far received, not only shows that the above estimate was correct, but Florida, which was left in doubt, has gone Republican by at least 1,500 majority,—our latest dispatches say 2,000,—and that the two Republican Congressmen are also elected. Encouraging reports were received from Oregon early yesterday morning, and in the afternoon came the decisive news that the Democrats conceded the State, which had given a Republican majority of over one thousand, and gained a Republican Congressman. In Nebraska the same condition of affairs was shown. There the Republican majority rose to 8,000. Dispatches from Nevada made it certain that the State had gone for Hayes. The latest news form South Carolina shows a Republican victory, the Democrats conceding the State to Hayes and the Republicans claiming 5,000 majority. Louisiana is one of the States which the Democrats have claimed; but our dispatches, coming from various sources in the State, show that it has gone Republican. The latest intelligence points to the certain election of Gov. Rutherford B. Hayes to the presidency, and a Republican victory in the nation.

In no other newspaper in New York City or elsewhere, I believe, was a serious doubt expressed of Tilden's election. It was conceded in the "Times" office, and but for the inquiry of Barnum I am assured, upon the best authority, that the question of his election would never have been raised. The evidence which that inquiry furnished of the closeness of the voted operated like an open basement window at night to a burglariously disposed passer-by. If the vote was so close as this inquiry warranted the suspicion that it was, what was easier for the administration, with its control of the army, of all the federal offices, including the judiciary, and with all the patronage of the federal government in reserve, to warp the Tilden vote sufficiently to give Hayes the nineteen votes which he lacked; and how few are active in politics anywhere who are not ready to reason like the tyrant of Thebes:

"Be just, unless a kingdom tempts usurpation; For that, sovereignty only is adequate temptation."

The scheme of the Fifth Avenue conspirators spread through the party as rapidly as the poison form the bite of an adder. Republican leaders all over the country were signaled at once to claim all the disputed States and persist in claiming them. At the same time it was arranged to send men, "who could be depended upon" to each of the States whose electoral vote was to be tampered with; to provide ample means for such contingencies as might arise; and finally to open communication with the President and Secretary of War to secure for the Returning Boards such protection for the work expected of them as they might require.

Senator Zachariah Chandler, chairman of the National Republican Committee, proposed to take charge of Florida, and a credit was opened for him at the Centennial Bank in Philadelphia, whose officers were his friends. William E. Chandler, the man with "the immense pair of goggles" also went to Florida, and the Department of Justice ordered it detectives to report to him in Tallahassee. Thomas J. Brady, with a force of special agents of the Post Office Department, followed the Chandler's with money for immediate use. William A. Cook, of Washington, was sent to Columbia, S.C. The election took place on Tuesday, the 7th, and before Thursday night the 9th, these men were all on their way to their posts.

On the same day, or night rather, the following orders were issued to General W. T. Sherman by J.S. Cameron, Secretary of War, all dated from Philadelphia:

10 P.M. "Order four companies of soldiers to Tallahassee, Fla., at once. Take them from the nearest points, not from Louisiana or Mississippi, and direct that they be moved with as little delay as possible.

11 P.M. "In addition to the four companies ordered to Tallahassee, order all troops in Florida to the same point, and if you haven't more than the companies named, draw from Alabama and South Carolina. Advise of the receipt of this and your action.

11:15 P.M. "Telegraph General Ruger to proceed once to Tallahassee, Fla., and upon his arrival there to communicate with Governor Sterns. Say to him to leave affairs in South Carolina in hands of an eminently discreet and reliable officer."

Note: George W. Childs in his Reminiscences reports that a Republican Senator and other leading Republicans were early at his office the day after the election to meet General Grant, who was then at Philadelphia attending the closing exercises of the Centennial Exposition, and the guest of Mr. and Mrs. Childs. These gentlemen insisted that Hayes was elected, "notwithstanding the returns." Mr. Childs tells us that Grant did not agree with them, but contented himself with merely expressing a negative opinion.

General Grant, who evidently had not yet been let fully into the scheme mapped out in the early morn of the day after the election, and who was satisfied that Tilden had been duly elected, did not quite comprehend the motive for all these military preparations for securing a fair election which had been held three days before. He evidently had suspicions was afoot, the nature and purpose of which there was a manifest disposition to disguise, if not altogether to conceal, from him. He concluded therefore, to do a little telegraphing on his own account and without the intermediation of his guileless Secretary of War. Persuaded in his own mind that Tilden and Hendricks were elected, he seems to have been getting suspicious that some of the people about him, with the connivance of Hayes, were plotting something for which he himself did not care to be responsible, and for that reason sent the following telegram to General Sherman, and gave it simultaneously to the press:

"To General W.T. Sherman, Washington, D.C.:

Instruct General Auger, in Louisiana, and General Ruger, in Florida, to be vigilant with the force at their command to preserve peace and good order, and to see that the proper and legal Boards of Canvassers are unmolested in the performance of their duties. Should there be any grounds of suspicion of fraudulent counting on either side, it should be reported and denounced at once. No man worthy of the office of President would be willing to hold office if counted in, placed their by fraud; either party can afford to be disappointed in the result, but the country cannot afford to have the result tainted by the suspicion of illegal or false returns. *Signed*: "U.S. Grant."

Two weeks before the election the federal troops in South Carolina had been increased to thirty-three companies, taking for that purpose every available on the Atlantic seaboard form Fortress Monroe northward.

The President's telegram, whatever the motive that inspired it, was not in accordance with the plans of the conspirators. The direction, "to see that the proper and legal Boards of Canvassers are unmolested in the performance of their duties" was easy to execute, for there was no danger whatever if the Boards of Canvassers being molested in the performance of their duties; and it was entirely within the scope of the executive authority, if lawfully invited, to direct the generals in command in the several States, in the event of an outbreak, to cooperate with the local authorities "to preserve peace and good order." No other interference of federal troops within a State was lawful, nor could even such and order by lawfully enforced until the governors of the respective States had reported that they were unable to preserve the peace, a condition of things which could not have been honestly affirmed to exist in any State of the Union at that time. But how were commanding generals to comply with the second term Grant's last telegram, and see whether there were any grounds for suspicion of fraudulent counting on either side? And to whom were they to report and denounce it? In Louisiana the canvassers all, without exception, were Republicans. And in Florida all but one were Republicans. Was it false counting by his own party the President wished his soldiers to guard against? If so, he did not send enough, or at least enough of the right kind. How, too, could the commanding generals ascertain whether there were any grounds of suspicion of fraudulent counting, unless they had been directed to supervise the reception, as well as the canvassing, of the returns? But this was equivalent to an impeachment of the integrity of the Returning Boards.

Besides, a "fair count of the votes actually cast" was precisely what the conspirators did not want. Two days before President Grant stepped between his Secretary of War and the people, with those memorable dispatches, the polls had been closed, and the returns "of the votes actually cast," save form remote counties and parishes in Florida and Louisiana had been turned in. There was no possibility then of fraudulent counting, except by the Returning Boards. When President Grant sent those dispatches of the 10th of November it is evident that if he really meant what he said he was not aiming his gun at any Democratic influences at work in the disputed States, but at the reckless crowd about him who were tampering with the Returning Boards.

Believing, as we now know he did, that Tilden was elected, he might very naturally have suspected that all the forces of the federal government were being rallied by his political staff for the single purpose of defeating him. Grant, with all his limitations, as a President, is generally believed to have been too direct a man to let fly the Parthian shaft with which he concluded his telegram to Sherman, of her were merely "playing the galleries."

The Returning Boards of South Carolina and Louisiana could be depended upon to return Republican electors, for the character of the Republican officials of those States were known to be equal to the emergency if properly, "protected" and adequately "encouraged." The "encouragement" was on its way, and the action of the Secretary of War left no doubt that the "protection" also was at hand. Of Florida the managers were not so certain, as there were doubts about the powers of the Returning Boards in that State, and also about the degree of dependence to be placed upon its members. W.E. Chandler telegraphed from Tallahassee in cipher on the 13th of November, "Send $2,000 to Centennial Bank of Philadelphia so I can draw for it. Have Arthur send Republicans acting with Democrats." On the 15th he telegraphed again," Florida needs eminent counsel and help. Can you send $3,000 and $2,000, making it $5,000? Danger great here."

Which of these sums was used for counsel and which for help has never transpired.

On the arrival of W.E. Chandler in Tallahassee, the 13th, telegrams were sent to the local Republican managers telling them that the "State is close and you must make an effort to render every possible assistance," and that "funds from Washington would be on hand to meet every requirement."

Chandler's promise that "counsel" and "protection" should not be wanting, and that the "funds" from Washington were on their way, were very well as far as they went; but Chandler was not the candidate for the presidency, and there was no satisfactory evidence that Hayes, if elected, would feel under any obligation to take up Chandler's paper. In fact, the business he was engaged in, and the means by which he and his confederates were carrying it on, were not calculated to inspire the utmost confidence in his promises, nor indeed a sufficient degree of confidence in his promises, nor indeed a sufficient degree of confidence to induce the average politician to disgrace himself for such an indefinite consideration. He felt too, probably, that for the security of his own share in the harvest for which he was ploughing, as well as to strengthen his credit with the Florida officials, he must be able to show the existence of more direct relations between himself and the candidate for whose election he was toiling. For this or some other reason he telegraphed to the private Secretary of Hayes, "to send Stanley Matthews and others of high character."

It so happened that when this note reached Columbus, Stanley Matthews, ex-Governor E.F. Noyes, and Attorney General Little, all of Ohio, Senator John Sherman and James A. Garfield, had already left for New Orleans "to fix" the electors of Louisiana. Chandler's request was promptly forwarded to them, and in response Noyes accompanied by John A. Kasson, of Iowa, and Lew Wallace, of Indiana started forthwith fir Tallahassee, where they arrive November 20th. Now the magnetic circuit was complete. Noyes came direct from Hayes, and whatever engagements he endorsed, it was correctly understood that Hayes in the fullness of time would execute. Up to this time Chandler had received $15,000, besides what he took with him. In one of his dispatches November 28th, he asks for "$3,000 in large bills; probably shall not need it,—majority about twenty,—but be ready for any emergency."

With a practically unlimited credit at Washington, and the prospective patronage of the federal government hypothecated to the conspirators, the fate of the electoral vote cf Florida was not difficult to forecast.

Note: Subsequently Samuel B. McLin, Secretary of State of Florida, and one of the members of the Returning Board, testified before a congressional committee to prevalent opinion amount the Florida Republicans that Mr. Noyes represented Hayes. He said, "Looking back now to that time (of the canvass) I feel that there was a combination of influences that must have operated most powerfully in blinding my judgment and swaying my action." What the combination of if influences were he in part disclosed. "I was shown numerous telegrams addressed to Governor Sterns and other from the trusted leaders of the Republican party in the North, insisting that the salvation of the country depended upon the vote of Florida being cast for Hayes. These telegrams also gave assurances of the forthcoming of money and troops if necessary in securing the victory for Mr. Hayes. Following these telegrams trusted Northern Republicans, party leaders, and personal friends of Mr. Hayes arrive in Florida as rapidly as the railroads could bring them. I was surrounded by these men, who were ardent Republicans, and especially by friends of Governor Hayes. One gentleman particularly Governor Noyes of Ohio, was understood to represent him and speak with the authority of a warm personal friend, commissioned with power to act in his behalf. These men referred to the general destruction of the country should Mr. Tilden be elected, the intense anxiety of the Republican party of the North, and their full sympathy with us. I cannot say how far my action may have influenced by the intense excitement that prevailed around me, or how far my partisan zeal may have led me into error; neither can I say how far my course was influenced by the promises made by Governor Noyes, that if Mr. Hayes became President I should be rewarded. Certainly their influences must have had a strong control over my judgment and actions."

L.D. Dennis, the Republican boss in Alachua county, also testified that Noyes "often spoke of Mr. Hayes and referred to him as his intimate friend, and gave us assurances of Mr. Hayes fidelity to the Republican cause, and of his special desire to take care of Southern Republicans."

When asked if Noyes was generally regarded by the people there as the personal representative of Hayes, Dennis answered, "We regarded him as such. I cannot state by what means I arrive at that conclusion, but he was regarded by the people there as the special representative of Mr. Hayes. It was generally understood that he was there at the request of Hayes."

Those who wish to know in ample detail to what foul uses all these vast and complex resources were devoted for the purpose of wresting from the State of Florida its right to a voice in the choice for the presidency, I must refer to the voluminous records of the forty-fourth and forty-fifth Congresses. Even a concise detail of it would occupy more space that I can venture to devote to the entire career of the most conspicuous individual victim of the conspiracy which is there laid bare. I must content myself with the briefest possible summary of some of the transactions to which the power and dignity of the federal government, and to a large extent the honor of the nation, were deliberately prostituted.

The returns of the county canvassers in Florida when footed up showed a majority for the Tilden electors,—24,441 votes for Tilden and Hendricks, and 24,350 for Hayes and Wheeler. By the law of Florida and by a decision of its Supreme Court the county returns were final, and the Canvassing Board had merely the ministerial duty of tabulating the votes and declaring the result. There was no resource fro the conspirators but to disregard the law and doctor the returns to the extent necessary to meet the emergency. This they unhesitatingly proceeded to do.

The votes of one precinct in Hamilton County, which gave Tilden electors a majority of 31, were all thrown out on the affidavits of two Republican inspectors that they had absented themselves at different times during the day of the election form the polls, and without any pretense of fraud of illegal voting.

The other votes of another precinct of Jackson county, Florida which gave the Tilden electors 291 votes and the Hayes electors 77, were thrown out because the inspectors went to dinner after locking the ballot-box in a secure place and leaving the key with the Republican inspector, who certified to the returns and testified that there was no fraud nor wrong about the election.

The entire votes of Manatee County – 262 for the Tilden electors to 26 for the Hayes electors – were thrown out on the ground that there had been no registration, when the fact was that Governor Stearns would not appoint a county clerk, that there might be no registration in this strong Democratic county. There was no pretense of fraud, or that any illegal vote had been cast. Governor Stearns was rewarded with the appointment of Commissioner of Hot Springs, Arkansas at $10 a day, within thirty days after the Hayes' inauguration.

The votes of Key West – 401 for Tilden and 59 for Hayes – were all rejected because the election officers failed to complete the certificate of their returns on the day of the election, without any imputation or pretence of fraudulent voting. The ballots had been counted after the close of the poll on the night of the election, the result announced, and the certificate partly made out, when a bottle of ink was upset and a new certificate had to be made. This was postponed until the following morning when the ballots were recounted and found to tally exactly with the count of the previous day, except that one more ballot was found for the Republican electors.

While no pretext was too flimsy to procure the rejection of votes for a Democratic elector, no crime was so flagitious as to exclude a vote for a Republican elector. The negro clerk and negro inspector of Alachua County brought with them L.G. Dennis, the Republican boss of that county, a blank for the returns of the election *already signed and sealed*, the figures not yet filled in. When asked by Dennis for the vote of their precinct, they said 178 Republican and 141 Democratic. At this Dennis expressed great indignation and said the business had not been properly managed. The blacks expressed contrition and were sent to an upper room, supplied with printed list of voters of the county, and from this proceeded to add 219 names to the poll list and as many votes for the Republican candidates. Notwithstanding that one of the inspectors made an affidavit that the return was forged and false, it was counted and allowed by State canvassers. Dennis procured one of the Democratic inspectors to corroborate the returns of the negro inspector and clerk by a bribe of $100, and another affidavit of the same character from on Floyd Dukes was procured at the price of $25.

When the *alter ego* of Mr. Hayes, ex-Governor Noyes, to whom was assigned the defense of this fraud before the State canvassers, wanted Dennis subsequently to support the transaction by his testimony before a Congressional committee, Dennis gave him to understand that he did not propose to do any swearing. His own testimony upon this point is worthy of reproduction.

Q.   Did Mr. Noyes ask you to become a witness yourself in regard to the precinct?

A.   Yes, Sir.

Q.   Were you a witness or had you made an affidavit with reference to box No. 2 of Archer precinct which affidavit was to be used before the Returning Board?

A. No, sir; I never made any statement whatever for that purpose.

Q. State the conversation which took place between you and Mr. Noyes in regard to your appearing as witness before the Returning Board in reference to box No. 2 at Archer precinct?

A. He did express that desire several times. I do not know that he ever spoke of it but once as though he intended to put me on the stand, and then I advised him not to do it.

Q. What did you say to him, and what did he say to you?

A. I do not recollect the exact words, but I think he said in a familiar sort of way that he should put me on the stand that day. I suggested to him that I should be a detriment to his case if he did, and that I thought he had better not do it.

Q. Can you repeat the exact words which you used in reference to your being a detriment to his case.

A. I cannot, but I made it strong. I may have said that unless he was ready to abandon his case, he had better not put me on the stand. I nay have made it as strong as that. I wanted to give him to understand that I did not want to go on the stand to make any statement under oath. I cannot repeat the exact words; but it was said with sufficient force to have the desired effect.

Q. Did Governor Noyes, after you told him in form of words that it would be inconvenient to his case to put you on the stand, ever refer to that refusal on your part to go on the stand in any form of words?

A. I think he jocosely said one day that I was not very forward about swearing, of something of that kind.

Q. Wasn't it something like this: You talk very well enough Dennis, but you don't swear?

A. Something to that effect.

For his services in maintaining the validity of this return, Noyes was rewarded soon after Hayes inauguration, with the mission to France.

The county judge and clerk of the Election Board of the seventh precinct of Jefferson County stole a bundle of one hundred Democratic tickets, which the inspectors had tied up as they were counting the ballots, and left in their place one hundred Republican tickets. The clerk confessed his crime and fled the State to avoid prosecution. Though the facts were all proven before the Returning Board, the return was accepted and counted. The county judge and clerk were rewarded with clerkships in the Land Office at Washington, with a salary of $1,200 each per annum.

In the Monticello precinct of Jefferson County all but five of the Democratic ballots were stolen and Republican ballots substituted and counted.

Joseph Bowes, who was the inspector at Precinct No. 13, Leon County, "procured a lot of small Republican tickets to be printed in very fine type, and on thin paper. These tickets, spoken of in Florida as "little jokers," he had printed at the official Republican printing-office. Before the election he showed them to Mr. McLin, and stated his purpose in using them. The plan was to fold them up inside the ballots that were voted, and have them surreptitiously cast, or otherwise smuggle them into the ballot boxes, which their small size easily admitted of. McLin advised Bowes not to use them. After the election Bowes stated that he had managed to smuggle seventy-three of them into the boxes of his precinct, and he told McLin, after the State had been awarded to the Democrats, and it was known. Drew was to be governor, that he was in a scrape on this account, and that he had to clear out for stuffing the boxes.

The evidence establishing this fraud of ballot-box-stuffing was before the Returning Board, but the return for Precinct No.13, Leon County was accepted.

General Francis C. Barlow, ex-Attorney-General of New York, was one of the visiting statesmen who went to Florida at President Grant's request to witness a fair count of the ballots actually cast. Dennis and Chandler soon discovered that Barlow was not the sort of man they required to deal with the Alachua case, and Noyes was assigned in his place. Barlow continued, however, to take an active part in making up the Republican case; but when the returns were all in, he became satisfied that, applying the same tests to the Republican votes as the Republicans insisted upon applying to Democratic votes, the result would be a majority for Tilden. He endeavored to impress this view upon one of the State canvassers,— Cowgill by name, -whom he believed to be an honest man. Why he did not lay it before the Board, unhappily for Barlow, if not for the country, does not appear. Barlow sears that after a full discussion of the case Cowgill said," I agree with you. I cannot conscientiously vote the other way. I cannot conscientiously vote to give the State to the Hayes electors."

Governor Stearns, learning that Cowgill was closeted with Barlow, joined them to learn what might be going on, and was told by Barlow what he had been saying to Cowgill. Cowgill left with Stearns. Barlow and he never met again. Cowgill came to Washington soon after the inauguration, confident of recognition. He had been promised and auditorship in the treasury, was tendered the position of special agent in the internal revenue service. This did not accord with his estimate of his services, and he returned to Florida, a wiser if not a better man.

When McLin, who was Secretary of State of Florida, and ex-officio member of the Returning Board, was subsequently asked by a congressional committee, "what promises these visiting statesmen from the North made to the Republican leaders and the Returning Board, if the State should go for Mr. Hayes, he replied: "Well General Wallace told me on several occasions that if Mr. Hayes should be elected, that the members of the Returning Board should be taken care of, and no doubt about that; that Governor Noyes represented Mr. Hayes and spoke with him and was in favor of it. Then on one occasion William E. Chandler came to me and stated that he didn't like to say it to me, but he would say it to me, and he spoke for General Wallace, also that if the State went and was canvassed for Mr. Hayes, that the members of the Returning Board,—at least he referred to a majority of the board,—Dr. Cowgill and myself, would be well taken care of, and there would be no doubt of it; he said he was authorized to say that."

McLin further testified that Dr. Cowgill told him that in March 1877, he was in Washington and saw Hayes frequently; that he was received very kindly by the President, and given free admission to the White House at all times, and that he had expressed himself as being under great obligations to him and me in the canvass, and that he felt not only under political obligations, but personal obligations, that he would certainly pay at an early day.

McLin was appointed justice of the Supreme Court of New Mexico *ad interim,* and failed confirmation because Senator Conover, of Florida, opposed it.

F.C. Humphreys, elector at large on the Republican ticket, was appointed collector of customs at Pensacola.

Dennis Eagan, chairman of the Republican State Committee, was appointed collector of internal revenue.

Governor Stearns was appointed commissioner of the Hot Springs, Arkansas.

J.M. Howell, the deputy clerk of Baker county, who assisted the county judge Driggers I getting up the fraudulent return from that county, was appointed collector of customs at Fernandina.

Dennis was appointed to a sinecure position in the supervising architect's office at Washington as a salary of seven dollars a day.

One of the negroes who assisted Dennis in making up the spurious returns for Alachua county, and swore to affidavits for him, was appointed night inspector in the Philadelphia custom house.

The other negro who rendered Dennis the same service was appointed a clerk to the auditor of the treasury of Post-Office Department.

.Joseph Bowes, who had the "little jokers" printed, and voted seventy-three of them himself, and who was one the busiest manufacturers of affidavits, and who had to fell the State to escape the legal penalties of his iniquity, took refuge in Washington, where he was rewarded with a clerk-ship in the Treasury Department, on a salary of $1,600 per annum.

W.K. Cessna, county judge of Alachua County, who assisted Dennis in procuring Green R Moore to make his $100 affidavit, was appointed postmaster at Gainesville, Fla.

Lewis A. Barnes, another of Dennis' assistants, was appointed register of the Land Office at Gainesville, Fla.

Moses J. Taylor, the clerk of Jefferson county and inspector of one of the polls of the Monticello precinct, who got away with all but five of the Democratic tickets and substituted Republican tickets was also made a clerk in the General Land Office at Washington.

John Varnum, an affidavit maker and assistant general of militia, was appointed receiver of the United States Land Office.

Manual Govin, a postmaster at Jacksonville, and an assistant affidavit manufacturer, was sent to consul to Leghorn.

M. Martin, acting chairman of the Republican State Committee, was made surveyor-general of Florida.

George H. DeLeon, secretary to Governor Stearns, was appointed a clerk in the Second Auditor's Office at Washington.

George D. Mills, telegrapher at Tallahassee and one of the clerks of the State canvassers was appointed clerk in the Pension Office at Washington.

John A. Kasson, who accompanied Noyes to Florida to vouch for Hayes' gratitude for favors expected, was appointed envoy extraordinary to Austria.

Lew Wallace, for like service, was appointed Governor of New Mexico, declining which, he was sent to Constantinople as minister-resident.

F.N. Wicker, the collector of customs at Key West, upon whose testimony the State canvassers rejected the poll No. 3 of that town, was continued in office.

Thomas J. Brady, Second Assistant Postmaster-General, who carried the money to Chandler, accompanied by H. Clay Hopkins, agent of the postal division of New York city, William T. Henderson, L.L. Tilball, B.H. Camp, Alfred Morton, all post-office inspectors, were retained in office by President Hayes. Tilball was subsequently promoted to the Unites Sates marshalship of Arizona.

William E. Chandler, not receiving a prompt reward for his services, turned upon the chromo President he had hung up in the White House for deserting his Louisiana and South Carolina coefficients, and practically acknowledged that Hayes had never been elected President by the people.

General Barlow, the only one of the visiting statesmen who seems to have believed that Grant and Hayes were in earnest in professing a desire for a fair count, was the only other one of the whole array whom Hayes failed to recognize. He was charged with disloyalty to the party, and put into Coventry, where it has since left him to chew the cud of sweet and bitter fancies. Had he the same duty committed to him again, I venture to doubt whether he would not, by a timely disclosure of his convictions, have assisted Tilden to take the oath of office to which the people had chosen him, instead of permitting that great office to be sequestered to the base uses of a partisan conspiracy by his forbearance.

NOTE: It is just to Mr. Barlow to say that his support if Hayes for President, in 1876 was not from any distrust of Mr. Tilden personally, nor form any doubt of his superior fitness for the duties of chief magistrate, but form a distrust of the party which nominated him.

The apprehensions here expressed may have had its weight in determining him to assume the passive attitude which he occupied after he had satisfied himself that the electoral vote of Florida was wrested from Tilden by fraud.

The general here, as Mr. William C. Bryant and many other distinguished patriots had done before him, make the capital mistake of underestimating the numbers and power of the Democratic party who supported the Union during the war, whose sacrifices in its behalf were not made nor to be estimated by any partisan measure. Mr. Lincoln in selecting for his cabinet advisers a majority of life-long Democrats, to say nothing of his generals, of whom by far the larger proportion who distinguished themselves were of the same party, displayed, in my judgment, a wiser appreciation of the political forces upon which he had to depend for the preservation of the Union.

CHAPTER TWO

Note: The conspirators' operations in Louisiana – William Pitt Kellogg – Visiting statesmen in New Orleans – The composition and operations of the Louisiana Returning Board – Garfield – Sherman – Anderson – Jewett – Eliza Pinkston – Fraudulent registration – The reward of the conspirators.

The methods by which Hayes electors were secured from Louisiana were, if possible, more shameless and indefensible than those employed for the like purpose in Florida.

William Pitt Kellogg, then Governor of Louisiana by virtue of an illegal order of Judge Durell of the United States District Court, enforced by federal troops under orders from President Grant, enjoys the credit of having concocted the measures by which the people of that State were deprived of their choice of presidential electors. His objective point was a seat in the United States Senate for himself. He had already managed to subject all the elective machinery of the State to his personal control. He had the appointment of the supervisors and assistant supervisors of registration for every parish and ward in the State; he dictated the appointments of all the commissioners of election, the State register of voters and his clerks.

Events subsequently disclosed a deliberate purpose on the part of Kellogg and his Republican confederates to invalidate the election in seven parishes where they found they could not control the negro vote, and by fictitious registration of names to make up whatever number of votes might be needed to secure a majority. To understand how this was to be accomplished it is necessary to notice some of the peculiarities of the Louisiana election laws.

The Returning Board in Louisiana had no power to reject the vote of any precinct unless the certificate from such precinct came to them accompanied by a sworn protest signed by the supervisors, that intimidation had been practiced. The Commissioners of Elections in each parish were required by law to make out their returns on the day of the election, and if anything happened to affect "the purity and freedom" of the election, they were to make a statement thereof under oath and have three citizens vouch for its truth, and forward this statement with their returns, the tally sheets, registration lists, all made out in duplicate, one to the supervisor and one to the clerk of the Parish Court.

These returns from the commissioners the supervisors were required by law to consolidate in duplicate; have them certified as correct by the clerk of the District Court, according to the returns in his office; to deposit one copy of the consolidate statement with the said clerk and *"forward the other mail, enclosed in an envelope of strong paper or cloth securely,"* to the Returning Board, with all the returns made by the commissioners, including their statement, if any, in regard to occurrences affecting the "purity and freedom" of the voting. They had no authority to reject the returns from any poll or to refuse to compile them in their consolidated statements.

When these consolidated returns reached the Retuning Board, its duty was first to compile the vote from those polls where there was presented no evidence that there had not been "fair, free and peaceable registration and election." That done, they were to take up the cases where the commissioners had reported that there had not been a fair, free, and peaceable registration and election.

The law required this Returning Board to meet in New Orleans "within ten days after the closing of the election, to canvass and compile the statements of the votes made by the Commissioners of Election," and to continue in session till "such returns have been compiled." The law also required that this board should consist of *"five persons to be elected by the Senate from all political parties."* The Senate pretended to have complied with this law by appointing four Republicans and one Democrat. The Democrat that was appointed resigned. The law provided that in case of any vacancy by death, registration, or otherwise, by either of the board, then the vacancy *shall be filled* by the residue of the returning officers." It was very certain that the presence of a Democrat to witness the work they had in hand would prove most inconvenient, and therefore they refused to fill the vacancy.

The scheme upon which Kellogg finally settled for invalidating the election was by alleging intimidation of voters, and upon that pretext throwing out enough Democratic votes to give the electoral vote of the State to Hayes.

During the two weeks succeeding the election, visiting statesmen of both the great political parties had flocked to New Orleans. Several of the more conspicuous representatives of the Democratic party there lost no time in addressing a note to Stanley Matthews, James A. Garfield, John A. Logan, William D. Kelly, John A. Kasson, William M. Evarts, E.W. Stoughton, and John A. Dix, each and all whom claimed to represent either the President *in esse* (In being; actually existing) or the President *in posse* (In potential but not in actuality). In this note they stated that having understood that the gentlemen that they addressed were there at the request of President Grant, to see that the Board of Canvassers make a fair count of the votes actually cast, they invited a conference in order that such influence as they possessed might be "exerted in behalf of such a canvass of the votes actually cast as by its fairness and impartiality shall command the respect and acquiescence of the American people of all parties."

This invitation was declined by the Republican "visiting statesman" on the ground that they were indisposed to reduce the function of the Returning Board "to the mere clerical duty of counting the votes actually cast, irrespective of the question whether they were fraudulently and violently cast or otherwise vitiated." They further stated that, "it is, in our judgment, vital to the preservation of constitutional liberty that the habit of obedience to the forms of law should be sedulously (Persevering and constant in effort or application) inculcated (To teach (others) by frequent instruction or repetition; indoctrinate) and cultivated, and that the resort to extra-constitutional mode of redress (To set right; remedy or rectify), for even actual grievances should be avoided and condemned as revolutionary, disorganizing, and tending to disorder and anarchy."

Such a plea in avoidance might be successfully demurred to in any court of justice of competent jurisdiction. How the habit of obedience to the forms of law was to be compromised by the proposed conference, even though at the worst it failed to secure concert of action, is not quite clear. Be that, however, as it may, if "obedience to the forms of law" was the motive of their long journey to New Orleans and their protracted detention there, it proved a singular waste of energy, for every one of the provisions of the election laws we have cited was systematically and repeatedly violated, not only with the knowledge of these political purists, with the undisguised cooperation of most of them. We shall presently see that these traveling statesmen took a very different view of their duty when canvassing the votes of the States in the Electoral Commission.

The election was entirely peaceable throughout the state. In the volumes of testimony subsequently taken by Congress there was not a particle of evidence that on the day of election there was any riot, tumult, or intimidation at a single polling place in the State. The election officers were all Republicans, and in accordance with the programme of the Fifth-avenue conspirators they had been all given to understand that their political future depended entirely upon their faithful execution of their party behests.

There were fifty-six parishes, exclusive of New Orleans,, in the entire State, and nearly one thousand polling places. There were seventy-four supervisors and assistant supervisors or registration, and three commissioners of election for each poll, all selected by the Republican managers, practically by Governor Kellogg.

And yet when the returns came to the supervisors, were consolidated, and made ready for transmission to the Returning Board, only two supervisors had made any protests affecting the fairness of the registration or the peaceable and honest character of the election. In but one instance was intimidation alleged. The exception was in the eleventh ward of New Orleans, where two custom-house dependants refused to sign the returns, alleging intimidation. This was for disfranchising four hundred

Note: The nature of these assurances may be gathered from the following circular issued by the Secretary of the Republican State Committee:

HEADQUARTES REPUBLICAN PARTY OF LOUISIANA,

ROOMS JOINT COMMITTEE OF CANVASSING AND REGISTRATION,

MECHANICS' INSTITUTE, Sept. 25, 1876

SUPERVISIOR OF REGISTRATION, PARISH OR ASSUMPTION, LA:

DEAR SIR: It is well known to this committee that, from examination of the census of 1875, the Republican vote in your parish is 2,200, and the Republican majority is 900.

You are expected to register and vote the full strength of the Republican party in your parish.

Your recognition by the next State administration will depend upon your ding your full duty on the premises and you will not be held to have done your full duty unless the Republican registration in your parish reaches 2,200, and the Republican vote is at least 2,100.

All local candidates and committees are directed to aid you to the utmost in obtaining the result, and every facility is and will be afforded you; but you must obtain the results called for herein without fail. Once obtained, your recognition will be ample and generous.

Very respectfully, your obedient servant,

D.J. M.A. Jewett,

   Secretary.

and twelve respectable citizens living in the best portion of the residence quarter of the city. The poll was surrounded all day by deputy marshals and metropolitan police, every one a Republican; and the United States supervisor, also a Republican, was present in the room where the votes were received.

Of the two instances in which the returns of the supervisors stated objections to the votes of their parishes in conformity with the law, one affected only the votes for justices of the peace and constables, and the other was a case where the supervisor declined to incorporate the votes of two polls where he had established but one, and the commissioners without authority had established two,

For one entire week after the election the Republican managers in New Orleans were confident that their plans had succeeded, and that they had carried the State. They so assured their friends at Washington. But to make assurance double sure, they instructed their supervisors of registration to send their returns to New Orleans by mail. The law required them to bring their returns in person. As they cam in, the supervisors deposited them at the custom-house instead of delivering, as the law required, to the returning officers. Only seventeen supervisors of registration sent their packages, as the law required, by mail; and the registered packages containing these returns, instead of being delivered to the returning officers as the law required, were stopped at the post-office, and retained there or handed over to the Republican managers.

Had there been intimidation, of course it could only been expected from the Democrats; but what had the Democrats to gain by intimidation? They knew that the Returning Board had been established expressly to "annual votes so secured and provide for votes so prevented." They knew, too, that the Returning Board in 1876 consisted of the same white members as in 1874, when in the parish of Rapids, where Wells, the president of the board resided the whole vote of the parish was thrown out and four Republican members of the Legislature seated, upon a secret affidavit of Wells as to occurrences in that parish on the day of the election, *when he was not there*. The members so seated had not claimed to have been elected, and subsequently, upon the recommendation of the congressional committee, were unseated, and the conduct of Wells was officially denounced.

The most and the best the Democrats could hope for was to offer the Returning Board no pretext whatever for setting aside the election because of intimidation, knowing as they did full well by experience that such pretext would be used against them without scruple or remorse.

The Returning Board consisted of J. Madison Wells, chairman, Thomas C, Anderson, Louis M. Kenner, and G. Cassanave, the last two colored.

The Returning Board should have begun their labors by the express terms of the law on the 17th of November, and should have remained in session until the returns had been complied. The first open meeting for business was not held until the 20th. The interval seems to have been industriously utilized in ascertaining how many votes were to be through out to save the Hayes electors, and from what parishes the votes should be taken. Hence the direction to the supervisors of registration to bring their returns in person, instead of sending them, as the law required, by mail. The returns were opened and read by Anderson. What had been going on between their delivery and their opening may be inferred from the following incident which occurred at the session on the 25th.

It had been remarked by the Democrats that very few of the returns came by mail, and it was also a subject of complaint that the returns from many parishes had not yet been received. The returns form De Soto, however, had come by mail. Anderson in submitting them to the Returning Board was quite emphatic in stating this fact. He read, "Consolidated statement of votes of the parish of De Soto," and, after a pause, adding, "with any quantity of affidavits attached." It happened that Mr. Burke and Mr. Glenn, members of the bar of Louisiana, and counsel for the Democrats, were in the room at this time, looking over

Note: Nine years before, General Sheridan had preferred charges against Wells, the president of the board, while he was provisional governor of Louisiana, for dishonesty, and subsequently – 1877 – Wells was indicted with his three colleagues by the grand jury of Louisiana for falsely and feloniously uttering and publishing as true a certain altered and forged and counterfeited public record; to wit, the consolidated statement of votes of the parish of Vernon, made by the supervisor of registration for said parish, whereby falsely and feloniously 178 votes were added to the number of votes actually cast for the Republican electors, and 395 votes were deducted form the number of votes actually cast for the Democratic electors by the voters of said Parish.

Wells took refuge in the swamps of New Orleans to escape arrest; the two negroes were held to bail in $5,000 each; and Anderson was brought to trial, convicted, and sentenced to two years at hard labor in the penitentiary, and to pay the costs of prosecution. An appeal was taken by his counsel to the Supreme Court, where he was finally acquitted, not on the ground that he had not been guilty of all the forgeries and falsifications alleged, but on the technical ground that the consolidated statement "made, such as was required to be made, by a supervisor of registration, was not the election return" contemplated by the Constitution, and therefore its alteration was not the forgery and falsification of "a legal record."

some papers in parishes laid aside as contested. Mr. Burke asked," When
was that package mailed?" Anderson replied that it was mailed at Mansfield, La., and received on the 18th. "What is the date of the first affidavit?"
asked Burke. Anderson with some hesitation, replied "November 25th"
– "How does it happen," asked Mr. Gloin, "that affidavits made on the
25th were in a package mailed on the 18th?" After considerable confusion
and hesitation, Abell, the secretary to the Returning Board, bethought
him to suggest that there were two packages, one received on the 18th
and the other that day; that the first contained the consolidated statement and the other the affidavits. Visiting statesman Stoughton came
to Abell's rescue.

Stoughton, "What return is this received today?"

Abell, "The return before the board now. I also received a small
package on the 18th, which I presume was a consolidated statement."

Stoughton, "Was the evidence in the package you received today?"

Abell, "Yes, Sir."

Stoughton, "Oh that settles it – merely a clerical error."

It did settle it, for it showed conclusively that the returns had been
tampered with; that the package Anderson had opened, and which had
been receipted for on the 18th, was one from which he took the consolidated statement, "with any quantity of affidavits attached." The evening
before this exposure occurred there had been a meeting of certain
persons specially interested in the vote of De Soto and tow or three
other parishes. Among them were George L. Smith, the candidate for
Congress from the De Soto district; the supervisors of De Soto, Bossier,
and Webster parishes; and D. D. Smith, the cashier of the post-office;
and D.J.M.A. Jewett, secretary of the Republican committee, who had
made himself conspicuous by recommending the Governor to appoint
no supervisors of registration in New Orleans, and thus threw out the
entire vote on the principal city of the State. At this gathering, the cashier,
Smith, unlocked the post-office vault and took out the returns from
De Soto, Bossier, Caddo, and Webster. Those from Bossier, Caddo, and
Webster had been brought by the supervisors or the parishes respectively,
or by some one selected by them for that purpose, and deposited at the
post-office for safe keeping until they were "fixed: for the uses of the
Returning Board.

The Returns from De Soto, though they had come by mail, instead
of going to the Returning Board as they should have done, were also in

the post-office vault and under the absolute control of the men most immediately interested in tampering with the vote of that parish. The purpose of this gathering is fully set forth in the following statement made by D.J.M.A. Jewett, one of the witnesses to its proceedings:

C.L. Ferguson, supervisor, mailed his returns per registered package to New Orleans from Mansfield, November 14th; he reached New Orleans in person about the 23rd; on the 24th I received from George L. Smith, in person, or from some person in his interest, a notice that my presence in the private office of the post-office would be desirable about 9 or 10 P.M. that night. On my arrival I found there George L. Smith candidate for Congress, fourth district; D.D. Smith, cashier post-office; C.L. Ferguson, supervisor De Soto parish; T.H. Hutton, supervisor Bosier parish; John S. Morrow, supervisor; Fred E. Heath, candidate for House of Representatives; and Samuel Gardner, citizen of Webster parish, with one or two others, I think, whom I do not now remember. I had detailed Mr. McArdle to attend, and he was there, but on account of objections on the part of George L. Smith he was sent away. The fact whether protest had been made or not, etc., having been considered, D.D, Smith unlocked the post office vault and produced there from the returns of De Soto, Bossier, Caddo, and Webster. Caddo, it was stated, he had brought down himself. Bossier and Webster he had, as I understood. On the De Soto package I noticed the post-mark of Mansfield and that it bore evidence of registration. It was however, already open. It was unrolled and examined by Smith and myself. *It was not possible to create a Republican majority except by throwing out polls, 1, 3, 5, 7 and 8. These were selected for protest, and Ferguson was asked for facts.* I draughted a protest based on such facts as he had knowledge of, either personally or from information received, or as was suggested by George L. Smith, or by the well known conditions of the parish. This Ferguson copied, and was directed to take the same before F.A. Woolfley for administration of the oath.

It was suggested to me, that of course it was not possible to attach this protest and various affidavits in hand affecting the same parish (taken before Commissioner Levissee, in Shreveport) to the consolidated state of votes, this having come forward by mail, and there being a disagreement of dates, but they should be handed or sent in under section 43, as per my circular letter of instructions.

Not withstanding, the unbounded stupidity of somebody rolled these up in the original package, which, restored apparently to its original condition, went forward by carrier to the board, November 25.

Such was Visiting Statesman Stoughton's notion of a *clerical error* which deprived Tilden of his majorities at five different polls in a single parish.

The returns from ten other parishes were doctored at the same time and in like manner.

"The returns from Bossier," say Jewett, "were handed by Captain Hutton, the supervisor, George L. Smith (the aforesaid candidate for Congress) *for safe keeping*, upon his, Hutton's, arrival in the city, and were by Smith placed in the vault of the post-office.

T.H. Hutton had, on November 13 (the day that he started from Bellevue for New Orleans), sworn his consolidated statement of votes (popularly known as the returns) before George B. Abercrombie, clerk of the court, and had deposited with said clerk a copy, as required by law, at the date named, and when the returns were examined by me in the post-office, this document bore in the space for remarks a protest of the Atkins Landing box (No. 1) and no other.

In my presence, in the private office if the post office, the supervisor interpolated in the same space under the protest noted above, and above the jurat, a second protest, affecting the Red Land box (No. 3). There is no question in my mind but that the protest and exclusion of this box was an afterthought which first took shape at this time (November 24)."

F.M. Grant, who brought the returns from Morehouse parish about a week before the 25th of November, to which there was no protest attached, declined, says Jewett, "the solicitations of Blanchard to make one."

Jewett proceeds:

"The evening of that or the following day, at the Governor's request, Blanchard and myself drove him out to the Governor's residence, where we had a conference respecting his parish and testimony. This being without effect, the Governor took him apart, into an adjoining room, and they conferred together some time. The next day he was again interviewed by Kellogg at the custom-house, and was (as I was informed) taken to see the visiting statesmen. Blanchard informed me that Grant was bulldozed by these and other partied for several days before he make the protest which he made November 18.

At this time I purposely avoided even seeing the visiting statesmen except as I met them casually at Kellogg's, and it was arranged between myself and Mr. Blanchard that he should do everything which would require the slightest connection with them.

This was done because it was not proposed that Mr. Blanchard should testify before either committee of Congress when they came, as was expected, and I desired to be, myself, incapable of answering any inconvenient questions which might be propounded to me touching these gentlemen and their connection with out affairs."

Grady, the supervisor of Ouachita parish, was unwilling to protest the election. "I am informed by Blanchard," says Jewett, "that Mr. Grady was bulldozed by Kellogg, Sherman, Garfield, and others for a week before he would sign the protest. He admitted to myself that he could not stand the pressure. I do not charge cr believe that any fact stated by Grady was untrue or unknown to him, at least by common report. The evidence was simply obtained in a manner which deprived it of any legal value."

Clover, the supervisor of East Baton Rouge, refused to compile the statements of votes cast at six different polls, through a willful disregard or ignorance of his duty, He was "sustained in his refusal," says Jewett, "by Kellogg, Campbell, and others, to whose advice he would have yielded. Mr. Clover undoubtedly did this with the promise or expectation of reward."

"It may be said," Jewett continues, "that I ought to have corrected him. This it would have been useless for me to do against the influence of those named, and, while Mr. Blanchard and myself were practically in control of the State registrar's office, and while Govern Hahn would have undoubtedly signed an order (drawn by either of us) to Mr. Clover, the law expressly excepted supervisors from obedience to the rulings or orders of the State registrar of voters, who is at the same time deemed their administrative chief."

Similar refusals of the supervisors of Orleans and Lafourche were attended with similar results.

How another *"clerical error"* in East Feliciana was corrected is thus state by Jewett:

"James E. Anderson, supervisor, refused, upon his arrival in New Orleans, to make any protest, alleging as a reason his fear of being murdered if he did so. This, in his case, I did not believe, having been convinced by his then secret conduct that he was a corrupt scoundrel, who would protest or not, betray one party of the other (he was unquestionably in the employ of both), as he might conceive to be for his interest.

"As Governor Kellogg was responsible for his being in his parish to go through the farce of an election, I abandoned to Governor Kellogg the task of getting him to testify to notorious facts unquestionably within his knowledge, and washed my hands of him and of his affairs. I was present on two occasions at Kellogg's house, when Anderson and the Governor were in conference respecting his testimony.

"On the 10th of November, immediately after his arrival, Anderson had signed a protest drawn by Hugh J. Campbell, which the following day he distinctly repudiated, and which he stated to be at least in part untrue. This protest was not finally accepted by him again until, as I was informed, Anderson had been promised the position of deputy naval officer, or something that should be a full equivalent. Anderson himself informed me while under the influence of liquor (about November 20) that 'he had got what he was after,' by which remark and its context I understood that he had received pledges of reward for his testimony. I have also been informed that Messrs. Sherman and Garfield assisted in bringing Mr. Anderson 'to listen to reason.'"

Jewett says, in conclusion, that "protests and evidence, such as it was, which had been received and filed up to November 27, excluded votes for Packard 1,620 and for Nichols 9,700. leaving Mr. Packard elected by a clear majority, with a Republican majority in the Senate and House, and also elected three Hayes and five Tilden electors."

Jewett adds that, in pursuance of a "conspiracy to which he alleges that J.M. Wells, Thomas C. Anderson, John Sherman, and J.A. Garfield, and others, were parties, polls were excluded in the parishes of Caldwell,

Natchitoches, Richland, Catahoula, Iberia, Livingston, and Tangipahoa, with the result, and for the purpose, of the returning as elected five Hayes electors who were otherwise defeated; that the consideration of this conspiracy was the absolute control of the federal patronage within the State of Louisiana by the said Wells and Anderson; that the evidence used to effect the object of the conspiracy was manufactured without regard to actual facts and with the knowledge of the several conspirators and that the consideration to be give to said Wells and Anderson had been delivered up to date."

But the Returning Board did not rely entirely upon the flexible consciences of supervisors. On the 28th of November Eliza Pinkston, a disreputable negress, no notorious in three States for mendacity and beastliness, was borne into the presence of the board and of "the distinguished gentlemen of national reputation: who were there helping to cultivate and inculcate the sanctities of the law. She swore that her husband had been taken from his house in the night, shot seven times, run through and through with knives, and mutilated in various ways her child's throat cut while in her arms; that she was twice shot and her person violated more times than she could remember and that all these outrages were committed by young white men of the neighborhood, many whom she professed to know and identify – one of them a well known and highly respected physician. She also admitted that this medical monster came the day following all these outrages, when sent for, and dressed her wounds and ministered to her wants.

There were scores of reputable gentlemen present who could have exposed this preposterous story, but they were not allowed to testify. The story would answer the concoctors of it better as it stood. Eliza Pinkston lived in Ouachita parish, which gave a large Democratic majority. The board wanted a pretext for throwing it out, and here they had it in a dramatic and thrilling piece of evidence to which the telegraph and the press would delight in giving the widest circulation. Absurd as the story was, it was deemed of sufficient importance for a committee of the House of Representatives to be sent down to Louisiana to investigate it. It was ascertained that her statement that her husband had been shot or mutilated was a fabrication; that the throat of her child had not been cut, and that there was no mark of violence on its body except a slight contusion on its head; that the men whom she charged with these outrages could not possibly have been in her neighborhood on the night in question; that she had made an affidavit in Monroe county for use before the Returning Board, in which she charged the crime of murder and other outrages on other persons, which was sent by the supervisor of Ouachita to the Returning Board November 23, but it was suppressed and withdrawn, and the another made in New Orleans, December 2, was substituted for it.

It was also ascertained that the Returning Board had falsified its own record of the receipt of the returns form Ouachita. The secretary announced that they had been received November 24, but when opened, a letter was found addressed to Mr. Abell, saying,

"Enclosed please find an affidavit of Eliza Pinkston, which I received too late to file with my returns. Please see that it is brought in with other evidence filed with my returns."

This letter was dated November 23rd.

The character of this woman whose testimony was invoked "to inculcate and cultivate obedience to law" as thus summarized by the congressional committee:

"The character of Eliza Pinkston, as developed before your sub-committee to the fullest extent, was such as to render her a fit instrument in the hands of designing men. She had been charged with the murder of the child of persons with whom she had but recently quarreled. The child died of poison. Eliza Pinkston, then know as Lizzie Finch, in Morehouse parish, was arrested, and acquitted only because the main witness to the crime was too young to understand the nature of the oath. The general impression was that she was guilty. When residing in Union parish, she had shamefully beaten an old woman living with her, death ensuing in a few days after. She had abandoned one of her young children, leaving it to starve to death in a fence corner. Another she made way with shortly after its birth. She was an habitual abortionist. She was in perpetual quarrel. Her testimony had been so effectually impeached in the counts of Morehouse parish that the Republican district attorney refused to call her as a witness. Everybody who knew her considered her a desperate character. Eye-witnesses proved that she live with her husband on very bad terms. She was about to kill him at one time when she supposed him asleep. Upon another occasion she assaulted him with an axe, intending to kill him. He was in perpetual dread of harm, as witnesses testified. She was ugly, vulgar, indecent, and lewd beyond the worst."

The rest of this description I am obliged to suppress as too indecent for these pages.

According to this poor wretch's story, which Sherman, Garfield, Stoughton, and Matthews professed to believe, as number of malefactors had been guilty of a series of hideous crimes, not only against the laws of the State of Louisiana, but against the laws of the United States. Why were not steps taken by either jurisdiction to arrest or punish any one of the alleged criminals? The arrest, trial, and hanging of a half-dozen of these murderers, if there were any would have been an object-lesson far more efficacious for cultivating and inculcating obedience to law in Louisiana, than employing the testimony of such an outcast to compass the usurpation of the presidency.

Towards the end of November the Returning Board thought they had rid themselves of enough Democratic votes, by the methods of which we have given only a comparatively few examples, to ensure the election of Hayes, of Packard for governor, and a Legislature that would be shameless enough to send Governor Kellogg to the United States Senate. But when they came to figure up the returns they found that they were still astray in their calculations and that guillotine must again be set to work; that they must throw out the polls in nine other parishes, and the entire vote of East Feliciana and Grant parish. They threw out, in addition, sixty-nine polls from twenty-two other parishes, and refused to include the polls which the supervisors of East Baton Rouge, Lafayette, Lafourche, and the assistant supervisors of three wards in New Orleans had, without any warrant of law, wantonly refused to compile.

In all, 13,214 Democratic electors were disfranchised and 2,415 Republican. The highest number of votes "actually cast" for a Democratic elector was 83,817, and for a Republican elector, 77,332. Five of the Republican electors' rand behind the vote of their colleagues 1,141. The average majority for the Democratic electors was 7,116.

NOTE: Report 156, Part 1 House of Rep. 44th Congress. 2d Sess. Page 45-6 & H.R. Misc. Doc No 34, part 2 44th Congress 2d Sess pp. 790-794

The extent to which the people of Louisiana were defrauded by the Returning Board and their accomplices can be determined by another and very simple test, which no amount of perjury not partisanship can assail.

We have seen that the pretext for throwing out the returns from most of the disfranchised parishes was intimidation of the negroes, by which they were prevented from registering and voting. The rejections from other causes were insignificant in number, and, in their influence upon the result, without importance.

The names of the registered voters for the entire State in 1876, according to the statistics of the State's register's office, were 207,622. of which there were of:

Colored – 115,268 – White – 92,354 – with a total of 23,914 colored voters in the majority.

According to the census of 1870, the colored males of twenty-one years and upwards were 86,913, and white makes of like ages, 87,066.

The colored class included Chinese and Indians, who had no votes.

In 1880 the white males of twenty-one years and over numbered – 108,810, Color makes of like age, 107,970 which showed that both classes had increased in about the same proportion, and their relative proportion could not have materially varied in 1876. If from colored makes the Chinese Indians, and foreign-born negroes are deducted, manifestly the colored voters could not have exceeded the white. Professor Chaille', who had made a special study of vital statistics in Louisiana, expressed the opinion that there was a small majority of white voters in the State. But, as we have seen, there were 22,914 more colored than white voters registered in the State in 1876. Five years after, and five years before, the white voters were in an undisputed majority, Where did these 22,914 colored votes come from, and what had become of the army of negroes who were alleged to have been afraid to register> These figures prove beyond a reasonable doubt that the names of over 20,000 names were registered that had only this nominal existence.

Again, by the census of 1870 the white population of the parish of New Orleans was 140,923 – of the negro – 50,456 with Whites over Negroes equaling 90,467.

By the census of 1880 the white population was 158,369 and the negro – 57619 – with White over colored by 100,750.

When the registration was completed in 1876, the 57,619 negro population was found to yield 23,495 voters, and 140,923 whites, only 34,913 voters.

Again the State census of 1875 gives an excess of 7,210 colored females over colored males in the parish of New Orleans, that is, in all, 36,013 females. Deducting these from the total of 57,619, there remained by 21,597 colored voters in the whole state in 1880. The number was doubtless somewhat less in 1876, and yet here were at least 2,891 more colored names registered that there could have been colored voters in the parish.

But not content with fraudulently registering nearly if not quite three thousand fictitious names, the Kellogg managers deliberately struck off from the registration lists the name names of 7,738 white voters. And this was the way it was done:

With the cooperation of Marshall, Pitkin, and the employees in the post-office, some 30,000 circulars were sent out by the letter-carriers, with instructions to return all not personally served. All 11,000 were so returned. The registration lists were then secretly taken to the custom-house, where the supervisors were directed to strike off the names of all not personally served.

Professor Chaille', after a careful study of all available data, has expressed his conviction that an honest and complete registration of the voters of New Orleans would have given about 40,584 white and 13,500 negro voters, instead of 22,495; and allowing for reasonable contingencies, such as absence, sickness, etc., there ought not to have been of these more than 12,000 registered.

But why accumulate further evidence of the nefarious processes by which this foul conspiracy against the rights of a sovereign State were consummated?

It is enough to have shown that the Tilden and Hendricks electors were chosen in Louisiana and Florida by large popular majorities.

That many thousands of Democratic voters were fraudulently disfranchised.

That in no single instance had the commissioners of election shown or even alleged intimidation of voters.

That there was not from a single polling-place in the State a statement of the vote returned in the form required by law.

Note" H.R. Misc. Doc No 34, Part 2, 44th Congress 2d Sess. Pp 1031-1032

That no one of the supervisors of registration had made objections to the registration of voters for a single voting place in the form required by law, nor had any of them reported intimidation or violence.

That four supervisors had assumed judicial powers, which the law conferred only upon the returning officers, and by refusing to compile had thus rejected the commissioners' returns from twelve polling-places; while three assistant supervisors for wards in New Orleans had illegally refused to consolidate returns from three polls.

The distinguished statesmen who had assisted at this carnival of lawlessness not only found nothing in the proceedings to rebuke, but did not scruple to share in the loot, presumably in proportion to the importance of their respective services securing it.

Senator Sherman was made Secretary of the Treasury, then quite the most important office in the President's gift.

Stanley Matthews was nominated to a seat on the bench of the Supreme Court of the United States. The Senate declined to confirm him. He was renominated, in 1881, by President Garfield, who had been one of his coadjutors in New Orleans, and through the influence common to all new administrations, with all its federal patronage in reserve, the opposition to him in the Senate was overcome, and he was confirmed.

James A. Garfield, who had his headquarters in the custom-house, where the affidavits were manufactured during the sessions of the Returning Board, was elected to the United States Senate by an arrangement with Stanley Matthews, and subsequently succeeded Hayes as the Republican candidate for the presidency.

William M. Evarts, who in 1875 had denounced the illegal organization for the Louisiana House of Representatives with the aid of the military, and all the proceedings and acts of that body as well as of the Returning Board of 1874, went to New Orleans in 1876, and lent the weight if his personal and professional influence to assist – unconsciously, I fain believe – the men who were harvesting the crop of crime he had denounced that planting. He subsequently was the leading counsel for Hayes before the Electoral Commission. He received the office of Secretary of State.

NOTE: Those who may desire to probe this iniquity to it profoundest deep are referred to the investigations made by committee on the 43rd, 44th and 45th Congresses, and to the more convenient compendium of A.M. Gibson, entitled, "A Political Crime," to which I have been greatly indebted in making this synopsis of the evidence submitted to Congress.

E.W. Stoughton, who prepared the report to the President justifying the conduct and fulsomely eulogizing the character of the worthless creatures who constituted the Returning Board, was rewarded with the mission to Russia.

It required the disfranchisement of a less number of the citizens of Louisiana to count in Packard as governor than to count Hayes electors; but ten a governor has less patronage than a president to bestow, and it became necessary to abandon Packard to secure a sufficient number of Southern Democratic votes in the House of Representatives, to ensure the ratification of the decision of the Electoral Commission, of which I shall have to speak presently. Packard was reconciled to his fate by receiving the consulate at Liverpool, a place which, whether it was worth fifteen or thirty thousand dollars a year, depended mainly upon the character of the man who held it.

Kellogg was rewarded for his services with a seat in the United States Senate,—by what means may be inferred from the fact that of the members of the Legislature who voted for him, eight senators, three officers of the Senate, thirty-two members of the House, and four officers of the House, and four officers of the House, making forty-seven in all, received lucrative appointments from the federal government, and, curiously enough, all of these patriots received their appointments from the department of which John Sherman was the chief.

If the persons connected with the canvass, election, and negotiations in Louisiana, sixty-nine were appointed to offices, and all but sixteen of these were treasury appointments.

Wells, the president of the Retuning Board, had one son appointed deputy surveyor at New Orleans; another son and son-in-law, to clerkships in the same institution, on salaries ranging from $1,400 to $1,600 per annum.

Anderson, Wells' white colleague on the Returning Board, was made deputy collector of the port of New Orleans; his son, C.B. Anderson, was made a clerk in the custom-house, on a salary of $1,400; his sons father-in-law, auditor, on a salary of $2,500; and his son's brother-in-law, clerk on a salary of $1,200.

Kenner, one of the negroes on the Returning Board, was appointed deputy naval officer of the same port; one of his brothers was appointed to a $1,600 clerkship, and another brother, a laborer, at a salary of $600.

Cassanave, the other colored member of the board, had a brother who was an undertaker appointed to a place in the custom-house. His own expenses, incurred in defending himself and colleagues in New Orleans against criminal charges, were defrayed in part by President Hayes and Secretary Sherman.

Woodward, clerk of the Returning Board, who assisted in falsifying the election returns, was appointed to a $1,400 clerkship, and was subsequently promoted to an assistant deputy surveyorship, at a salary of $1,600.

Abell, the secretary of the Retuning Board, was appointed to a $1,600 clerkship in the custom-house.

Judge G.B. Davis, a clerk of the Returning Board, and another man of equally easy virtue with any of his associates, also found an asylum in the custom-house.

Green, a colored minute clerk of the board, in due time reached the same port, and afterwards was appointed an inspector at $3 per day.

Charles Hill, another clerk of the Returning Board, and therefore possessed of perilous secrets, was appointed store-keeper, at a salary of $1460.

It is a fact not without significance that none of President Hayes cabinet ministers, save his Secretary of the Treasury, availed themselves the privilege of rewarding any of the members of the Returning Board or of their zealous subordinates.

Whether these dignitaries and emoluments were worth what they cost; whether the honors for which they were beholden to the frauds and forgeries of the four pied and speckled knaves who constituted the Louisiana Returning Board in 1876 are such as their offspring and friends will take pride in; and whether their names will be cherished by their countrymen for their active and passive parts in placing a man in the presidential chair who was not elected to the office by the people,—are questions which may be safely left to the final arbitrament of history.

"How far," said the Hon. Clarkson N. Potter, in his admirable and temperate report,—the most admirable because so temperate,—the controlling visiting statesmen like Mr. Sherman really believed there was any justification for the rejection of Democratic votes by the Returning Board, men will never agree. We are apt to believe in the right of what we earnestly desire. Men who thought the welfare of the country depended upon the continuation in power of the Republican party would naturally have been disposed to consider almost anything justified to retain it there. To us it seems impossible that the flagrant and atrocious conduct of the Returning Board was not realized above all by the men of most political experience, or that the most dangerous and outrageous political fraud of the age was not assisted and advised by those who next proceeded to take possession of its best fruits."

NOTE: Chairman of the select committee appointed by the House of Representatives, "to inquire into the alleged fraudulent canvass and return of votes at the last presidential election in the States of Louisiana and Florida."

CHAPTER THREE

NOTE: The electoral count of 1877- Senator Morton's scheme – Tilden's history of the presidential counts – President Grant concedes Tilden's election- Electoral commission created – Disapproved by Tilden – Refuses to raffle for the presidency – Horatio Seymour's speech before the New York electors – Dr. Franklin's advice to his son – the Florida case – the Louisiana case – The Oregon case – Conflicting decisions of the commission – The commission for sale – the forged certificates from Louisiana – Decision of the commission condemned by the House of Representatives-Letter of Charles Frances Adams – The Fraud Blazon – Tilden's reply – Protest of the Democratic minority of the electoral commission – Thurman and Bayard – James Russell Lowell.

At the meeting of Congress in December the absorbing question was the counting of the electoral vote. It had been usual for Congress to define in advance the manner in which this duty should be discharged. In the session of 1864-5 Congress provided that no electoral vote objected to by either House of Congress should be counted except by the concurrent votes of both Houses. This became notorious as "the 22nd rule." It as re-adopted at the three successive electoral counts of 1865,1869, and 1873. This rule, after having been in force fro three successive elections, was abandoned by a resolution of the Senate in December 1875, on motion of Senator Edmunds, at whiles instance the Senate adopted, "the rules of that body and the joint rules of the two Houses *except the 22nd joint rule heretofore in use.*" The House of Representatives was at this time largely Democratic, and, had the 22nd joint rule continued in force, any electoral votes which it refused to count would have been rejected. The rule, which was doubtful constitutionality, had been originally adopted, and subsequently renewed, for partisan ends; for partisan ends it was now dispensed with by the Senate, thus leaving the two Houses without any rule to govern them for counting the electoral votes in February, 1877.

Prior to 1865 and before the adoption of the 22nd joint rule above referred to, it had been the practice of two Houses of Congress, a little in advance of the day fixed by the Act of 1792 for counting the votes,—the second Wednesday of February,—to agree upon the place of meeting for the discharge of this duty and the order of procedure. Various efforts had been made from time to time, by one House or the other, previous to the adoption of the 22nds rule, to appropriated to itself the power to determine the validity of electoral votes; but all had, for one reason or another, proved abortive. The 22nd joint rule, adopted by the Republicans in 1865, assumed for the first time the right to reject electoral votes, as the prerogative of either House.

When the certificates of the electors of the several States came to be opened at Washington in 1877, it appeared that the certificates of thirty-four States were uncontested, but that the remaining four were to be contested. These were the certificates from the States of South Carolina, Florida, Louisiana, and Oregon. The electoral vote of the uncontested States was so distributed that the fate of the presidential candidates depended upon the electoral vote of the four contested States.

Congress having failed to make any provision beforehand, the mode of procedure in counting the electoral vote was the first question to be dealt with,

The Republicans had the control of the Senate, the Democrats of the House. The Constitution provided that "the President of the Senate shall, in the presence of the Senate and House of Representatives, open all the certificates, and the votes shall then be counted." Senator Morton took the ground that the President of the Senate should be invested with the plenary authority "to determine all disputes relative to certificates of the electoral votes; to count them and to declare the result, which declaration was to be accepted as final, conclusive and irrevocable." The President of the Senate at that time, Thomas W. Ferry, of Michigan, owed that position to his party subserviency rather than to his fame as a statesman. The adoption of such a rule would have been equivalent to pronouncing Hayes President and making the counting of the electoral vote an idle ceremony. To make it such was obviously the motive of those who advocated it.

The Constitution assigned to the President of the Senate no other specific duty but to open the certificates. Beyond that he was but one of three coordinate bodies authorized to count the votes, settle controversies, and declare the result, as had been virtually the unbroken practice from the foundation of the government. A year had not elapsed since the same Senator Norton had introduced an electoral-count bill which required that the affirmative action of both Houses of Congress should be required to reject *any* certificate of electoral votes, and if more than one return was made, only that one should," be counted, which the two Houses, acting separately, shall decide to be the true and valid return." Nothing had occurred to the Constitution which in the spring of 1876 required the concurrence of the two Houses, acting separately, to count an electoral vote, the President of the Senate to the contrary notwithstanding, that in the winter of the same year could transfer this power to the President of the Senate. That is nothing but a presidential election which begat the temptation to strike the House of Representatives with impotence for the purpose of ensuring the success of the Republican candidates, The inconsistency of the positions, and the absurdity of attempting to reconcile the Constitution with two modes of procedure so diametrically opposed to each other, did not prevent Morton's scheme finding favor with his partisans in Congress, who seemed to have reached the conviction that the end of defeating Tilden would sanctify any means necessary to accomplish it, and that the Constitution itself should yield to such an exigency. Such threatening proportions did this scheme assume that Mr. Tilden devoted more than a month to the preparation of a complete history of the electoral counts from the foundation of the government to show it to have been the unbroken usage of Congress, not of the President of the Senate, to count the electoral votes.

With influence, if any, this publication had upon the ultimate abandonment of Senator Morton's scheme it is difficult to say. Probably not much, for it taught the Senators nothing of which they were ignorant; but about this time the leaders of that body became aware that President Grant did not believe that Hayes was elected, and several prominent Republican members of Congress, among them Senator Conkling, of New York, were under the same impression, and could not be relied upon to assist in upsetting one of the most venerable traditions of the government, nor in becoming accomplices in the fraud to which it was intended to contributory.

President Grant seems at no time to have any doubt about the electoral vote of Louisiana belonging to Tilden and Hendricks, or if its being so ultimately decided. In some reminiscences of the late George. W. Child's, published first in the "Philadelphia Ledger" in 1885, and subsequently in a vole, that gentleman said,

" Just before General Grant started on his journey around the world, he was spending some days with me, and at dinner with Mr. A.J. Drexel, Col, A.K. McClure, and myself, General Grant reviewed the contest for the creation of the Electoral Commission, and the contest before and in the commission, very fully and with rare candor and the chief significance of his view was in the fact, as he stated it, that he expected from the beginning, until the final judgment, that the electoral vote of Louisiana would be awarded to Tilden. He spoke of South Carolina and Oregon as justly belonging to Hayes; of Florida, as reasonably doubtful and of Louisiana, as for Tilden."

Col. A.K. McClure and the late A.J. Drexel, who were also guest of Mr. Childs on this occasion, have confirmed his report of this conversation.

The plan, therefore of gagging the House of Representatives in the Electoral College received no encouragement from President Grant. Whether he would have ever made any serious opposition to such a consummation, or whether the Senate would have deferred to him if he had, it is now idle to speculate. Another more plausible, if no less unconstitutional, means of accomplishing the same result was devised for them, the authorship of which has been ascribed to President Grant.

On the 14th of December, 1876, the House of Representatives appointed a committee of seven of its members to act in conjunction with any similar committee of the Senate, "to prepare and report without delay a measure for the removal of differences of opinion as to the proper mode of counting the electoral votes for President and Vice President of the United States, and of determining questions which might arise as to the legality and validity of the returns of such votes made by the several States, to the end that the votes should be counted and the

NOTE: *The Presidential Counts; a complete official record of the proceedings at the counting of the electoral votes in all the elections of President and Vice President of the United States; together with all congressional debates incident thereto or to proposed legislation on that subject; with an analytical introduction. New York, D. Appleton & Co., 1877*

The first election of George Washington, in 1759, was only an apparent exception. The election was unanimous, the procedure a formality and with debate or deliberation. See *Presidential Counts;* also D.D. Fields. "The Electoral Vote of '76, pg. 5

result declared *by a tribunal whose authority none can question and whose decision all will accept."*

Four days later, and on the eighteenth of the same month, the Senate created a special committee of seven Senators with power," to prepare and report without unnecessary delay such a measure either of a legislative or other character as may in their judgment be best calculated to accomplish the lawful counting of the electoral votes and best disposition of all questions connected therewith, and the true declaration of the result, " and also, "to confer and act with the committee of the House of Representatives."

This joint committee consisted of Senators George F. Edmunds, of Vermont; Frederick T. Frelinghuysen, of New Jersey; Roscoe Conkling, of New York; Allen G. Thurman, of Ohio; Thomas F. Bayard, of Delaware; Matthew W. Ransom, of North Carolina; and Oliver P. Morton, of Indiana; and Representatives Henry B. Payne, of Ohio; Eppa Hunton, of Virginia; Abram S. Hewitt, of New York; William M. Springer, of Illinois; George W. McCrary, of Iowa; George F. Hoar, of Massachusetts; and George Willard, of Michigan. On the 18th of January this committee almost unanimously – Senator Morton only dissenting – reported a bill providing for the creation of a tribunal to be composed of five Senators, five Representatives, and five associate justices of the Supreme Court of the United States, four of the latter being designated by their districts in the bill itself, the fifth to be subsequently chosen by these four; to which tribunal should be referred the conflicting certificates and accompanying documents from the contested States, and all questions relating to the powers of Congress in the premises, with the authority to exercise the same powers in ascertaining the legal vote of such States. The bill further provided that the decisions of such tribunal in every case should stand, unless rejected *by the concurrent vote of both Houses.* Also those objections which might be made to any votes from States no presenting double certificates should be considered, not by the commission, but by the Houses separately, and *unless sustained by both,* should be of no effect.

The bill, after sharply contested debate in both Houses, passed the Senate January 25, and the House of Representatives January 26. In the former the vote was 47 yeas to 17 nays; the Republicans voting 24 yeas to 16 nays, and the Democrats, 23 yeas to 1 nay; absent or not voting, 9 Republicans and 1 Democrat. In the House there were 191 yeas to 86 nays, the Democrats voting 158 yeas to 18 nays, and the Republicans 33 yeas to 68 nays; absent or not voting, 7 Republicans and 7 Democrats.

How so large a number of the Democrats in Congress were induced to supersede the constitutional machinery for counting the electoral votes, for a device not only unknown to the Constitution, but in all its important bearings inconsistent with it, can only be explained as we explain most blunders which are woven into the web of every human life. Some yielded through ignorance, some for the want of reflection, some to quiet a controversy about the result of which they were indifferent or apprehensive, some to serve personal ends at home that seemed more important to them that the presidential issue, while upon others, many, if not all, these considerations may have been not without their influence.

Unfortunately for Mr. Tilden, the Senate swarmed with Democratic aspirants for the presidency; the two on the committee who negotiated the surrender having been strenuous competitors for that honor before the convention which nominated Mr. Tilden. Nor was the House of Representatives lacking in Democratic candidates who had not been able to regard with satisfaction the triumph of a candidate who had not been in the least indebted to Congress for his nomination, nor much for his success at the polls. Then again, there were perhaps no inconsiderable number who indulged the expectation that the proposed tribunal would elect their candidate. which was to them of more concern than the means by which it was accomplished. The latter class was recruited largely from among those who supported Senator Davis, of Illinois, who then occupied a seat on the bench of the Supreme Court, would be selected as the fifth member from that bench, and whose character and moral authority with his colleagues enough was known to quench any suspicion of his lending support to the fraudulent and unconstitutional devices upon which he would have had to sit in judgment.

Those who were seduced by this aleatory device were rewarded as they deserved. Just as the electoral commission bill became a law, the independent Republicans and the Democrats in the Illinois Legislature elected Judge Davis to the United States Senate. This afforded that gentleman an excuse, of which he naturally availed himself with a prompt alacrity, to decline the proffered place on the commission, and gave to the four judges, two selected from each party, the choice of the fifth, which resulted in the selection of Justice Bradley, a New Jersey

Republican, and in leaving the rival candidates entirely at the mercy of the Republican party. By whatever motive they were governed, by whatever temptations seduced, it is now but too evident that the representatives of the people in the lower House inexcusably abandoned their coign of vantage and shirked the most solemn and momentous of all their official responsibilities, in a few short weeks to be marched through the Caudine forks and take their seats of humiliation before the inexorable tribunal of history.

It is hardly necessary to say that Mr. Tilden was too large and experienced a statesman to approve of discharging any constitutional duty by any but constitutional methods. As soon as the action of the Returning Boards furnished a suitable provocation for his interference, he urged his

Note: It was supposed by many that Morton and others engineered the selection of Davis with a full knowledge that he would not serve. It is difficult to see why Davis did not serve on the commission in spite of his election to the Senate, unless his absence from the commission was one of the conditions of his election. However this may be, his retreat from the field in the presence of the enemy effectually disposed of whatever expectations of preferment he might have entertained from the Democratic Party.

This committee consisted of Sparks and Burchard, of Illinois; Tucker, of Virginia; Marsh, of Pennsylvania; Seelye, of Massachusetts; Monroe and Lawrence, of Ohio; and D.D. Field, of New York. The resolutions were as follows:

Resolved, First, That the Constitution does not confer upon the President of the Senate the power to examine and ascertain the votes to be counted as the electoral votes for President and Vice-President of the United States.

Second, That the only power which the Constitution of the United States confers upon the President of the Senate in respect to the electoral votes for President and Vice-President of the United States is to receive the sealed lists transmitted to him by the several electoral colleges, to keep the same safely, and to open all the certificates, or those purporting to be such, in the presence of the Senate and House of Representatives.

Third, That the Constitution of the United States does confer upon the Senate and the House of Representatives the power to examine and ascertain the votes to be counted as the electoral votes.

Fourth, That in execution of their power in respect to the counting of the electoral votes, the House of Representatives is at least equal with the Senate.

Fifth, That in the counting of the electoral votes, not vote can be counted against the judgment and determination of the House of Representatives.

Sixth, That the committee have leave to sit again and report hereafter further matter for the consideration of the House.

The Constitution of the United States, Art. 11, Sect. 111, provides: "The person having the greatest number of votes shall be the President, if such number be the majority of the whole number of electors appointed; and if there be more than one who have such majority, and have an equal number of votes, then the House of Representatives shall immediately choose, by ballot, one of them for President; and if no person have a majority, then from the highest on the list the said House shall in like manner choose the President.

friends in leadership of the House to expose and combat in full debate the threatened, unwarranted usurpation by the President of the Senate of the right to count the votes, and to take no further step until *in both Houses* the great but pacific constitutional battle had been fought on that issue. He was ready to accept all responsibility for the outcome. He assured them that if properly resisted the conspiracy must break down; that it must not be encouraged by the least symptom of concession, but fought inch by inch on the floors of Congress, until the real character of the proposed usurpation should become known throughout the country and the nation's opinion of it could reach Washington. Early in the session he prepared two resolutions which raised the issue upon which he wished that battle to be fought, and which, with some slight modifications by the House committee on "the privileges, powers, and duties of the House of Representatives in counting the electoral votes" that received his approval, were adopted by that committee and reported to the House.

Had the course there traced been followed, it is now apparent that the confirmation of Mr. Tilden's election would have been assured beyond a peradventure. The controlling voices of both parties in the Senate had over and over again, and within a few months, asserted and insisted upon the right of the two Houses to count the vote. They all knew, and many had repeatedly assisted in adding to, the imposing line of precedents under which a challenge of any electoral certificate by either House had sufficed to exclude its vote from the count. A challenge of a single one of the nineteen contested votes would have resulted in Tilden's election, either by the concurring vote of the two Houses, or, they failing to concur, in his election by the House of Representatives, to which the Constitution has confided the choice in such an emergency, and where the Democrats were in the majority, whether voting by themselves or by States.

Happily we do not depend upon rumor nor oral tradition for our knowledge of Mr. Tilden's views of this crisis and the proper mode of dealing with it.. They will be found most carefully and fully stated as early as the 1st of January, 1877, in the inaugural message of Governor Robinson, of which the portion which appears under the rubric of national affairs was written by Mr. Tilden. The forecast and wisdom of this statement, and its direct bearing upon what had occurred and upon what was to occur, time had only made more conspicuous. In the course of this statement he says:

TILDEN'S VIEWS OF THE CONSTITUTIONAL MODE OF COUNTING

ELECTORAL VOTES —NATIONAL AFFAIRS

'The recent presidential election threatens to prove an epoch of if solemn portent in our history. For the first time in the twenty-two elections which have been held for President and Vice-President of the United States, the result remains a subject of controversy after the canvass of the votes within the States had been made and announced. The two Houses of Congress have been heretofore repeatedly required to pass upon the authenticity and validity of electoral votes, but in no former instance had the election turned upon the questionable votes. In every former case the result has been determined by electoral votes which were not in controversy. In the present instance one candidate for President and one candidate for Vice-President have received 184 undisputed electoral votes, as well as a popular majority exceeding a quarter of a million. Another candidate for President and another for Vice-President have received 165 undisputed electoral votes. All the votes of three States,—four in Florida, eight in Louisiana, and seven in South Carolina,—making nineteen in all, are still in dispute; also one of the three in Oregon. In all these cases two sets of returns have been transmitted to the seat of government, directed to the President of the Senate,' to await the action of the two Houses of Congress, whose duty it is to verify, ascertain, and count the electoral votes.

In a situation involving such momentous results as the chief magistracy of this republic, all the baser as well as the better forces of society are naturally embattled to secure the prize. It is in such crises of history that the controlling force of cardinal principles is liable to be weakened, dangerous concessions to be made, perilous precedents established, sacred traditions violated, and the most important bulwarks of constitutional freedom rendered less secure.

In Louisiana we have seen a State government imposed on the people by the military force of the federal executive under color of a pretended order of a federal judge, which order in itself was void, and which led to the resignation of the judge who made it, to escape impeachment. We have seen the government thus imposed by military force condemned as illegal and a mere usurpation, by both Houses of Congress, and the electoral votes given under its auspices rejected in the counting of the presidential votes in 1873 by the concurrent judgment of the same tribunal. We have seen the government so imposed create 'a Retuning Board' practically vested with absolute power to revise and, if they please, to reverse the results of the election by the people of the State, and thus organize a political mechanism under which an oligarchy in temporary possession of the legislative power of a State might perpetuate their ascendancy indefinitely.

"I pause here in this statement to interpose, in behalf of the people of this great Commonwealth, a solemn denial of the power of any State government or of the federal government to vest such powers as are claimed by the Louisiana Returning Board in any Canvassing Board whatever.

"In the first place, such powers such powers in respect to the choice of presidential electors are not warranted by, but are repugnant to, the Constitution on the United States. The provision of section 1 of article 2 of that instrument, 'that each State shall appoint, in such manner as the Legislature thereof may direct, its presidential electors,' does not confer of the Legislation of a State an unlimited power over the subject. No one will pretend that a temporary majority in the Legislature of the State could grant to an individual, or, to a set of individuals, the power to appoint presidential electors; that it could make this grant for a period of years, or indefinitely, or to his or their heirs or assigns.

"What it cannot do in form it cannot do in substance; what it cannot do directly it cannot do indirectly. The choice which a Legislature is authorized to make for a State, in the mode of appointing presidential electors, is limited to a mere selection between certain known forms of action, recognized in the practice of popular government, and consistent with the nature of popular government. It is a choice of modes, but must not change or destroy the essential character of the thing itself. It is subject to the condition that 'the *State* shall appoint' the presidential electors. The State, that is, the political community knows in our jurisprudence and constitutional law by that name. must 'appoint,' and in doing so it must act by and through its known and rightful organs. At the time this provision of the federal Constitution was adopted, it was contemplated that the Legislature of a State possessing all the governmental powers not withdrawn by the provisions of the State Constitution, or transferred to the government of the Union, might itself choose the electors. And, indeed, that was the mode at first generally practiced by the States. The State Legislature at that time was regarded as the most natural and the legitimate organ of the State. The power to choose presidential electors might properly be conferred upon the people of the State by a general ticket, the voters throughout the State choosing all the electors; or they might be chosen by the people of the State voting in districts, each district choosing one elector. These were methods consonant with the principles of our system of government, and by either of which it could be properly said that the State did, in fact, 'appoint' the electors.

"It is historically certain that these different modes were in the contemplation of the convention which formed the Constitution. Experiencing some difficulty, however, in imposing this duty upon all the States by any one uniform system, it devolved upon the Legislatures of each State the authority to choose from among these methods, one for the exercise of that power which it granted in declaring that 'each State shall appoint.'

"While the Legislature of a State may provide that presidential electors shall be appointed by an election of the people, it cannot provide that that election shall not be a reality; that it shall be a sham, and that the actual power of determining the choice shall be invested in a packed committee, whether it be called a 'Retuning Board,' or by any other name.

"Neither can it invest a Board of Canvassers with indefinite or with arbitrary powers, nor with any authority which, by the principles and practice of our jurisprudence and the policy of our elective system, is not fairly incident to the function of ascertaining the votes of the people. This seems to me the obvious, the wide interpretation of the Constitution of the United States and of its laws. Any other doctrine will open the way to abuses, frauds, and usurpations, which must end in destroying popular elections. The moment we depart from a strict construction of grants of power in derogation of the integrity and efficiency of the elective system, we shall be able to find no rule that will protect the rights of the people. We shall tempt transient majorities to seek to prolong their power by tampering with the machinery of elections, and the easiest, most convenient, and most effectual method for such a purpose is by the contrivance of Returning Boards, which shall be packed and equipped with powers hitherto unknown to our laws and practically subversive of the will of the people.

"In the particular case of Louisiana, other equally grave illegalities are believed to exist. The powers vested in the Returning Board are inconsistent with the provision in the Constitution of that State, which guarantees the elective franchise to voters, and also with the provision which confers the judicial power upon the courts. It is probable that the powers of this board, by the law of Louisiana, do not apply to presidential electors; that the board itself was not constituted in accordance with the law under which it was created; and finally, that a condition, without which the Returning Board could not get jurisdiction in cases where it assumed to reject votes of whole districts, was no complied with. There is every reason to believe that the authority exercised by that Returning Board could not get jurisdiction in the cases where it assume to reject the votes of whole districts, was not complied with. There is every reason to believe, that the authority exercised by that Returning Board is void, as repugnant to the Constitution of the United States, and also to the Constitution and laws of Louisiana.

"In this state of the law, that Returning Board, according to public statements of conceded facts, by manipulations of the returns, have changed a majority for one set of presidential electors of about 9,000 to a majority for another set of about 4,000, which would be equivalent to a change of over 80,000 votes in the State of New York.

"In Florida we have seen a Board of State Canvassers, solemnly adjudged by the highest court in the State to possess none be ministerial powers, assume the authority to reverse the choice of electors as shown on the face of the returns made by the officers who conducted the elections and received the votes; and to do this in open disobedience and contempt of the judicial tribunal having jurisdiction in such matters, and vested with the right of final judgment.

"In South Carolina we have seen the Board of State Canvassers fabricating a canvass in like disobedience and contempt of the Supreme Court having jurisdiction and the right of final judgment; we have seen federal soldiery take possession of the capitol of the State, and a corporal at the door determining who were the elect of the people, and who were to be permitted to represent them as legislators. Notwithstanding some of these acts have been disavowed by the federal executive, no mark of disapprobation has been put upon the authors of the outrages; the officer in command goes still unrebuked, and when the Returning Board were committed to prison for contempt, by the highest court of the State, a judge of the United States District Court is sent down to South Carolina, and, without jurisdiction in the case, grants a writ of *habeas corpus*, and discharges the offenders.

These proceedings are the more extraordinary and alarming when we consider that such violations of law and of right have been resorted to, to overturn elections, all of the officers conducting which were of the same political party with the candidates in whose favor these acts have been committed; that the elections were held under the surveillance of troops of the United States without any constitutional warrant for their presence, and that the judicial decisions thus set at naught cannot be suspected of any partisan bias, for they were rendered both in Florida and South Carolina by judges, all of whom were of the same political party with the Retuning Board.

"These interferences of the military power have been committed in flagrant violation of the Constitution and laws. They were not provoked by domestic violence; they were not invited in the only way that would have made them constitutional, by the Legislature of the State; and they were continued after the election was over and during all the subsequent

---

NOTE: *habeas corpus*—One of a variety of writs that may be issued to bring a party before a court or judge, having as its function the release of the party from unlawful restraint.

proceeding of the Canvassing Board. Their tendency was to overawe the voters under the pretense of keeping the peace, though by measures in themselves unlawful, and to deliver dishonest officials from the natural sense of responsibility and the natural timidity in regard to the consequences of their acts, which are providential limitations to men's conception of the crimes upon which they venture.

"While these things were going on in the South a member of the cabinet at Washington was acting as chairman of a partisan national committee, and with the cooperation of some of his colleagues in the cabinet, counseling and systematically stimulating these desperate measures.

"The result which these proceedings seem designed to accomplish cannot be secured without one further step in the process of usurpation. The fabrication of electoral votes amounts to nothing unless they can be counted by the tribunal whose constitutional duty it is to verify and authenticate them. That inexorable necessity has given birth to a new device for counting the votes, not only unknown to the Constitution, but in conflict with the construction hitherto always accepted, and with the invariable practice and precedents. That device is for the President of the Senate to usurp the power if determining what votes shall be counted, and what shall not be counted, and to exercise that power in disregard of the orders of the two Houses. It would not be credible that so monstrous a claim as this could be seriously asserted if leading Senators had not publicly avowed it.

"Nothing could be more abhorrent to the spirit of our system of government that such a one-man power. The President of the Senate is elected by the Senators, and they in turn are elected by the State legislators. He is therefore, three removes from the people. If such a power were to have been vested in a single man, a depository would have been chosen not so far removed from popular accountability. But the people of this country will never vest such a power in any one many, however selected. They will never consent to a new construction of the Constitution and laws that bears such fruit. They will stand firmly in the ancient ways, and insist that the electoral votes in this emergency shall be counted as they have always been counted, by the two Houses of Congress, and by nobody else. They will look with just suspicion upon the purposes of any who would propose to depart form the precedents which have been hallowed by time, and the uniform practice of the Republic from its foundation.

REFERENCE U.S. SENATE WEBSITE:

NOTE: **1913:** The Constitution was amended (17th Amendment) to provide for <u>direct popular election of senators</u>, ending the system of election by individual state legislatures. Connecticut's approval gave the Seventeenth Amendment the required three-fourths majority, and it was added to the Constitution in 1913. The following year marked the first time all senatorial elections were held by popular vote.

The Seventeenth Amendment restates the first paragraph of Article I, section 3 of the Constitution and provides for the election of senators by replacing the phrase "chosen by the Legislature thereof" with "elected by the people thereof." In addition, it allows the governor or executive authority of each state, if authorized by that state's legislature, to appoint a senator in the event of a vacancy, until a general election occurs.

The 17th Amendment to the U.S. Constitution:

The Senate of the United States shall be composed of two Senators from each State, elected by the people thereof, for six years; and each Senator shall have one vote. The electors in each State shall have the qualifications requisite for electors of the most numerous branch of the State legislatures.

When vacancies happen in the representation of any State in the Senate, the executive authority of such State shall issue writs of election to fill such vacancies: Provided, That the legislature of any State may empower the executive thereof to make temporary appointments until the people fill the vacancies by election as the legislature may direct.

This amendment shall not be so construed as to affect the election or term of any Senator chosen before it becomes valid as part of the Constitution.

"The Constitution of the United States confers upon the President of the Senate no power whatever in respect to the counting of the electoral votes, except 'in presence of the Senate and House of Representatives,' to 'open' all the certificates which may be transmitted by the college to the seat of government, directed to him.

"The President of the Senate has ever claimed or exercised such a power at any of the twenty-one presidential elections that have occurred under our Constitution.

"The mode of procedure for the counting of electoral votes has been invariably regulated by the two Houses of Congress, by concurrent resolution or standing rules adopted before the count. Those resolutions or rules have prescribed every step in the whole process; every function of the tellers and of the President of the Senate, whenever any additional service, even of the most formal sort, has been required of him.

"In every instance the counting has been conducted in conformity with the procedure thus prescribed by the two Houses; by servants designated by the two Houses under instructions and in the presence of the two Houses, and with the entire concurrence and the implicit of obedience of every President of the Senate who has participated in these ceremonies.

"So often as any question arisen as to the authenticity or validity of an electoral vote, the two Houses have assumed and exercised the exclusive power to act upon and determine that question. They have, in contemplation of law, themselves made every count; they have from the first assumed exclusive jurisdiction to regulate and govern the whole transaction by temporary concurrent orders adopted for the occasion, by standing joint rules, and by the enactment of laws. Such has been the uniform and uninterrupted course of precedents, the invariable practice of the government, and the official exposition of the Constitution, which has been deliberately adopted, invariable acted upon, and universally accepted.

"*No filter repository of all such powers as are vested in or must of necessity be exercised by the government can be found that the two Houses of Congress. They are not only the general agents of the people under our representative system, but in case of the failure of a choice of President and Vice President by the electoral colleges, they are expressly charged by the Constitution with the duty of making the election.*

"*The people of the United States will never consent to have their Representatives in Congress stripped of these powers,* or tolerate this usurpation by a deputy of the Senate, or by any single person, and still less by an officer who is frequently interested as a candidate in the result of the count.

"In this sentiment and purpose the State of New York cordially concurs. Foremost among all our American commonwealths in population, in the variety and extent of her industries and interests, she has in every vicissitude of public affairs put forth all her strength, moral and physical, to maintain the existence and the just authorities of the Union, and she can never consent that the time-consecrated methods of the constitutional government shall be supplanted or overthrown by revolutionary expedients."

Why Mr. Tilden's advice, so simple, so wise, so logical. So sure sooner or later to enlist the sympathies and respect of every law-abiding citizen in the land, was not followed, is a question which I do not feel called to enter upon here. Besides, it involves the discussion of motives which can never be subjected to any undebatable test; and if they could be, the profit of such a discussion now is more than questionable. I shall discharge my duty as his biographer in reporting what Mr. Tilden did to save his party, without dwelling more than is necessary for that purpose upon what others did to wreck it.

The electoral commission scheme was not disclosed to Mr. Tilden until it was too late for any opposition on his part to be effective in prosecuting his method, which was only constitutional method of settling the questions in dispute. How it was first brought to his attention was thus set down in a carefully considered communication addressed by Mr. Manton Marble of the "New York Sun," on the 5th of August 1878. The tenor of this communication, as well as the circumstances under which it appeared, leave little doubt that before it was given to the public it passed under Mr. Tilden's eyes.

"On the evening of Saturday, January 13, the undersigned, calling upon Mr. Tilden, found him in receipt of the McCrary House bill with proposed amendments, and a letter from Mr. Hewitt advertising the Governor that his counsel thereon would be asked the next day. Mr. Tilden invited the undersigned to call on the morrow, when Mr. Hewitt should be there, to consider this bill – the supposed axis on which the deliberations of the House conference committee were revolving.

Additional note: The late James G. Blaine, serving as one of the visitors at the West Point Military Academy, a year or two after the inauguration of Hayes, expressed himself to me as greatly surprised when the Democrats in Congress assented to the plan of the electoral commission. He added that if the Democrats had been firm the Republicans had no alternative but to yield, and such was the result which he had anticipated.

"The undersigned thus came to be present January 14, the day and date when Mr. Tilden received from Mr. Hewitt's lips his first information that other measures had been abandoned.; that the Senate conference committee had just disclosed to the House conference committee and electoral commission bill it had privately preparing; that the House committee were pressed to accept and adopt the same, and that the subject he wished to confer upon was that.

"Mr. Hewitt explained as the Senate committee's reason for secrecy, that without it they could not carry the bill. It had been adopted by arrangement between the three Democratic and the four Republican members, and was so strictly observed that when Senator Kernan made inquiry of one of the former, he was told that nothing could be disclosed to him without violating an honorable understanding. So well was the secret kept, that Senator Barnum, now chairman of the national committee, passing through New York on Friday, the 12th, has expressed his conviction that a majority of the Senate, as Mr. Tilden's plan antici-pated, would concur in denying the right of Ferry to make the count.

"Before he read the new bill, Mr. Tilden was told by Mr. Hewitt that the Democratic members of the Senate committee were already absolutely committed to it, and would concur with their Republican associates in reporting it to the Senate, whether the House committee should concur or not, and whether Mr. Tilden approved of it or not.

"Is it not rather late, then," said Mr. Tilden, "to consult with me?"

"They do not consult you?" replied Mr. Hewitt. "They are public men, and have their own duties and responsibilities. I consult you."

In other words, as Mr. Tilden expressed himself to me at the time, the parents of this measure, "have sent Mr. Hewitt, not to consult with me about it, but to get my approval of it." This Mr. Tilden declined to give, and urged delay. When its friends pretended that tie pressed, he told them, "There is time enough. It is a month before the count. I had best be used, all of it, in making the people and their agents fully acquainted with their rights and duties."

To the statement that the Senate committee would not delay for this to present their bill, with the unanimous approval of its three Demo-cratic members, to the Republican Senate, Mr. Tilden replied: It is a panic of pacificators. They will act in haste and repent at leisure."

To representations of the danger of a collision of force with the execu-tive, Mr. Tilden replied," Nevertheless, this action is too precipitate. The fears of collision are exaggerated. And why surrender now? You can always surrender. That is all you have to do after being beaten. Why surrender before the battle for fear of having to surrender after the battle is over?"

Unfortunately, the course of procedure which Mr. Tilden had traced out and urged upon the party was no longer possible. Their line of battle had been broken. The two controlling Democratic Senators on the committee, by their negotiations had practically surrendered the Democratic fortress. The plain, square issue made by Mr. Tilden could not be revived after a willingness to negotiate and make concessions had once been manifested.

Even had it been still possible to defeat the proposed scheme of arbitration, that would not have restored the fortress; it would not have made it any longer practicable to resume Mr. Tilden's plan of battle. To that, as Mr. Marble justly remarks,

> "The conditions of success were an indomitable and untied Democracy and an unbroken favoring public opinion. But the mere proposal of the electoral arbitrament, back by great Democratic leaders, cause three illusions to prevail: the illusion that such an arbitrament was the only alternative to civil war; the illusion that such a tribunal must establish the truth in its decision and the people in their rights; the illusion of the business classes, oppressed by long-suffering under ruinous tariffs and fluctuating currencies, that is was the harbinger of new prosperity. So that the rand and file would have been resuming a contest abandoned by their familiar leasers as hopeless, and attempting recurrence to the earlier issue amidst a public opinion now reversed and hostile."

Note: This recalls the advice which Dr. Franklin gave to his son when Colonial Governor of New Jersey:

"Perhaps they may expect that your resentment of their treatment of me may induce you to resign and save them the shame of depriving you, when they ought to promote you. But this I would not advise you to do,. Let them take your place if they want it,—though in truth it is scarce worth your keeping,—since it has not afforded you sufficient to prevent your running every year behindhand with me. *One may make something of an injury, nothing of a resignation."*- Bigelow's "Life of Franklin," under date of Feb. 29, 1874.

Instead, therefore, of wasting his energies in useless criticism of what had been done, Mr. Tilden directed his attention to such modifications in the structure of this projected court of arbitration as he thought essential.

If an arbitration is to be adopted, he insisted that the members of the tribunal ought to be fixed in the bill itself, not left to chance or intrigue.

That the duty of the arbitrators to investigate and decide the case on its merits should be made mandatory, not left to their decision.

"With both these vital points left at loose ends," he said. "You cannot succeed. You cannot afford to concede, and you can exact, *first*, the selection of good men to compose the tribunal, which is the controlling point; and, *second*, define the nature of the function to be performed by the tribunal, which is next in importance.

"Fix these two points,—good men, explicit powers,—and you might possible get through. Leave them doubtful, and it is happy-go-luck,—the shake of the dice-box."

When pressed by suggestions of the improbability of the House insisting upon its independent constitutional rights without the support of the Democratic Senators who were committed to a compromise, he said,

"If you go into a conference with your adversary, and can't break off, because you feel you must agree to something, you cannot negotiate at all. Unless you are able to break off, you are not fit to negotiate. You will be beaten on every detail."

On the 15th of January Mr. Hewitt telegraphed from Washington to his brother-in-law, Edward Cooper, in New York:

"The Senate committee will probably reject five and report six judge plan immediately. Our Senators feel committed to concur. House committee will not concur, and for present will probably not report."

To this suggestion Mr. Tilden said, "I may lost the presidency, but I will not raffle for it.: To Mr. Hewitt he telegraphed through Mr. Cooper:

"Procrastinate to give few days for information and consultation. The six-judge proposition inadmissible."

The next day Mr. Hewitt telegraphed again to Mr. Cooper:

"Washington, Jan. 16, 1877 – After protracted negotiations Senate (committee) receded from six-judge (scheme), declined five-judge, and offered four senior associates justices, who are to choose the fifth judge, excluding chief justice. Our Senate friends earnestly favor acceptance, because they do not believe it possible to pass over. The Democrats on House committee believe this is the last chance of agreement. We cannot postpone beyond 11 tomorrow, and if we decline, Senate committee will report their original plan, to which our friends are committed. Telegraph your advice."

Mr. Tilden sent the following answer:

"New York, January 16. – Be firm and be cool. Four judge plan will not do. Perhaps worse than six. Complaints likely to arise of haste and want of consultation with members, and embarrassment in exercise of their judgment after plan is disclosed, by premature committal of their representatives. There should be more opportunity for deliberation and consultation. Secrecy dangerous. Probably mistake in itself, and if it results in disaster would involve great blame and infinite mischief."

The night of the day that the foregoing telegram was sent, the fore-going telegrams were canvassed by Mr. Tilden in the presence of several of his friends, at the conclusion of which he dictated the following tele-gram:

"No need of hot haste, but much danger in it. Some days' interval should be taken. The risk of publicity (is) harmless.

"No information here, nor any opportunity to get information which could justify abstinence from condemning such an abandonment of the Constitution and practice of the government, and of the rights of the two Houses and of the people.

"Nothing but great and certain public danger, not to be escaped in any other way, could excuse such a measure. We are over pressed by exag-gerated fears, and forget that the other side will have greater troubles than we, unless relieved by some agreement.

"They have no way out but by usurpation; (they) are bullying us with what they dare not do, or will break down in attempting.

"So long as we stand on the Constitution and settle practice, we know where we are. Consequence of new expedient not enough considered.

"Only was of getting accessions in the Senate is by House standing firm. And judicious friends believe in that case we will go safely through. Opportunity to consult such friends should be given, before even tacit acquiescence (by House committee), if that is contemplated, Though details nay be properly discussed, final committal by House committee should be firmly withheld."

Before this telegram had reached, or at least been seen by, Mr. Hewitt, the surrender had been consummated.

In no single particular from the beginning to the consummation of the transaction had the advice of Mr. Tilden been acted upon. He advised the House of Representatives, with a majority in sympathy with the majority of the people, to stand upon it constitutional rights, and leave to the Senate, if it dared, the responsibility of violating those rights.

Instead of exercising the rights and discharging the duties imposed upon it in the most unequivocal terms, it accepted a scheme for counting votes which originated with a body having no corresponding contingent authority, and in political sympathy with the majority of a commission recruited from and controlled by a bench every member of which had been appointed by Republican Presidents.

Mr. Tilden had urged publicity and discussion, insisting that secrecy in respect to any plan involving the rights and interests of the whole people was unwise, dangerous, and essentially undemocratic. The scheme adopted was conceived and begotten in a corner, and never exposed to the light of day until it had wrought irremediable mischief; still less was it submitted to such a discussion as befitted a measure involving the chief magistracy of fifty millions of people.

Mr. Tilden advised against the betrayal of any symptoms of a possibility of concession. "You can surrender at any time," he said. "It will be time enough to surrender when you are beaten." They began their deliberations by concession, and surrendered without an engagement, fully a month before the time for discussion and for the arrival of reinforcements of public opinion for their constituencies could have expired. They made indecent hast to precipitate themselves at the feet of their adversaries, as though they supposed their humiliation would be imputed to them for righteousness.

Mr. Tilden advised them to trust the people, to stand by them and the Constitution; and no one American statesman had ever a better right, from experience, to speak dogmatically on the subject.

Instead of trusting the people, they conducted all their negotiations in secret, and suppressed discussion until everything was surrendered worth saving, or that discussion might have saved.

When it was decided to submit the issue to arbitration, Mr. Tilden insisted that the law creating the arbitrators should require them to decide the issue on its merits, and not leave to them the determination of what were to be their duties. Firmness upon this point, to which the Republicans of the Senate, sooner or later, must have yielded, would most certainly have resulted in confirming the election of the candidate of the people's choice.

This wise advice was rejected, and rejected, too, for clowns' swords and Quaker guns. As the Honorable Henry Watterson most fitly said:

"Mr. Tilden was the one man who took in the whole case and provided a plan to compass it. That plan was for the House of Representatives to exercise its constitutional rights to share in the count of the vote, no State to be counted except by the concurrence of both Houses, precisely as had been done in all preceding elections, each State lacking the concurrence of the two Houses to be thrown out; in the event of a failure of either candidate by this process of throwing out to secure a majority of all the votes, the House to elect the President and the Senate to elect the Vice President. That was Mr. Tilden's plan, pure and simple. It sprang directly from the Constitution, the law and the practice. To overreach it, the conspirators much proceed openly to treason and usurpation. In that event, the House still had its right to elect, and, 'if it elects me,' said Mr. Tilden at the time, 'I will go to Washington and take the oath if I am shot for it the next day.'

"Mr. Tilden's plan embraced no shilly-shallying or foolishness. It meant business. He had to move either by force or by law. Force was out of the question. The country was not prepared for war, and the party would not follow him into war. All that a show of fight on his part could do would be to inflame a few excited spirits and play into the hands of the conspirators, who had the tools, and only wanted the pretext to come down upon the unorganized and helpless Democrats. Wisely he declined either to raffle or bluff for the presidency. He proposed to proceed by law,—the law of every preceding electoral count,—and to force the Republicans, if bent upon their work of usurpation, to resort to violence and treason. He believed they would break down before they got through it. Believing in the people, his idea was that the people needed only to be educated in their rights to maintain them. He presented a line of action. He prepared a magazine of instruction. These were set aside, and, in lieu of them, a bridge was constructed, over which the conspirators could, and did, walk in safety."

On the 31st January the commission was elected,—three Republicans and two Democrats being taken, by agreement, from the Senate, and three Democrats and two Republicans for the House.

- Republicans from the Senate:

George F. Edmunds, of Vermont – Frederick T. Frelinghuysen, of New Jersey and Oliver P. Morton, of Indiana.

- Democrats from the Senate:

Allen G. Thurman, of Ohio, and Thomas F. Bayard of Delaware.

- Democrats from the House:

Josiah G. Abbott, of Massachusetts, Henry B. Payne, of Ohio and Eppa Hunton, of Virginia

- Republicans from the House:

James A. Garfield, of Ohio and George F. Hoar, of Massachusetts

The justices of the Supreme Court designated in the bill were:

- Democrats:

Nathan Clifford, of Maine and Stephen J. Field, of California

- Republicans:

Samuel F. Miller, of Iowa and William Strong of Pennsylvania

The fifth justice elected by these was Joseph P. Bradley, of New Jersey.

In all seven Democrats, and eight Republicans.

It was determined by the Republicans in caucus to leave Senator Conkling off the Electoral Commission, though he had been more influential probably than any other Senator in securing the passage of the bill creating it.

Note: Mr. Childs says, "Grant was the originator of the plan. He sent for Mr. Conkling, and said with deep earnestness: "This matter is a serious one, and the people feel it deeply. I think this Electoral Commission ought to be appointed.' Conkling answered: Mr. President, Senator Morton is opposed to it and to your efforts. But if you wish the commission carried, I can do it.' He said, "I wish it done."

Tilden's popular majority over Hayes in the State of New York was 32,818, and the largest aggregate vote ever cast up to that time in that State. It exceeded Grant's vote in 1872 by 81,298, and Greeley's of the same year by 134,764.

Conkling was omitted because he was known to be in accord with the President in thinking that the vote of Louisiana rightfully belonged to Mr. Tilden. He was the only Republican Senator on the committee who was omitted from the commission. Conkling had agreed to address the Electoral Commission in opposition to its counting the electoral vote of Louisiana for Hayes. Various explanations of his failure to do so are in circulation. I have not been able to determine which of them all had the demerit of securing his silence.

On the 6th of December the electors of the State of New York assembled at the capitol at Albany, organized by the election of Horatio Seymour, president o the college, and proceeded to cast the electoral vote of the Sate of New York for Tilden and Hendricks for Vice President. On taking the chair Mr. Seymour became the interpreter of the profound concern which had been awakened among the people of all parties in Mr. Tilden's native State by the rumors which were coming from the South. Time has given Mr. Seymour's remarks a pertinence and an importance which was hardly accorded to them at the time of their utterance. After referring to the fact that the year in which were about to participate in the election of a new President of the United States was the hundredth anniversary of our existence as an independent people, he continued:

"At this moment of general congratulation the people were startled by the assertion that there had been discovered in remote Southern States the exact number of electoral votes which would be given to and would elect the presidential candidate who was not the choice of the majority of the American people. This surprise was greater because it was one of the charges made by the Republicans in the canvass to excite the minds of the men in the North, that the 'solid South' would support the Democratic ticket. It was also urged that every Southern State had a deep interest in doing this, because they meant to make demands upon the national treasury. While this charge was unjust, no reason can be given why South Carolina, Florida, and Louisiana should not act in accord with the overwhelming majorities of the adjoining States. The public excitement reached the highest point when it was learned that the men who proposed to give these electoral votes to the candidate of the minority had been for years past charged with grave crimes, and that their personal security against legal punishment depended upon their success if falsifying the returns of their States. To them an honest count meant just punishment. I cannot be charged with partisan prejudice for any terms of reproach I may use in regard to the officials of Louisiana. I have no words strong enough to describe their unworthiness as set forth in official reports made by their political friends. I cannot, if I would, paint the aversion shown in the halls of the capitol by honest Republicans, who shunned them as leprous men whose touch and presence was polluting. Yet a few such men, acting solely in reference to their personal interests, and who believe that the blackness of their crimes in strengthens their claims upon the gratitude of their party, have thus put in peril the interests, the honor, and the safety of the American people. We have not the poor satisfaction of feeling that the dangers that threaten us are even invested with the ordinary dignity of danger. The pride of our citizens is humiliated, and their feelings of security under our laws and Constitution are lessened, when they see that the solemn verdict of eight million voters may be reversed by less than eight infamous men – men who have been branded by the leading orators, statesmen, and journals of their own political party as vile and corrupt, in terms more vigorous that I can repeat. If, under our Constitution, the majority of the electoral votes of the States had been fairly given to the Republican candidates, although the popular majority is against them, all would have acquiesced in their election. Such results are to be regretted, as they do not give administrations the moral power they should have for their own dignity and the good of the country. To elect men to govern the Union against the will of the people by unfair methods is revolution. Such plots involve anarchy, distress, and dishonor. Those who engage in them, when they have taken the first steps, must go on at all hazards. They have staked their political fortunes – it may be their lives and liberties-upon success. Fear goads them on to darker acts of treason. The first false steps forced a reluctant South into rebellion. In the same way they now impel desperate politicians who upheld usurpation in Louisiana in the past, to stand by them now, regardless of the honor and safety of the American union. Will a free people trust such men with the reins of power? Will they consent to be dragged into danger and dishonor by men who are goaded on by fears which always haunt the guilty?

"The glory of this centennial year this fades away and darkens into this national shame and reproach. Aroused patriotism can crush resistance to law, but corruption kills honor, virtue, and patriotism, says the foundations of society, and brings down the structure of states and nations in ruin and dishonor.

"While we implore all classes of citizens to enter upon the duty of deciding what shall be done to avert threatened evils, we respectfully appeal to the great Republican party to see if the heaviest responsibility for a just decision does not rest upon them. And we make this appeal with confidence that a great organization, which had its full share of virtue and patriotism, will not, when it calmly reviews the events of the day, fail to do justice to us, to themselves, and to the country. We do not complain that under the excitement of the canvass, or that before the heat of the election should have passed away, you may for a moment grasp eagerly at a victory without seeing that such a victory may prove a curse to you as well as to others. But we beg you will reflect, now that you have had exerted in your behalf, not only the whole power of the national administration with its hosts of officials, but that the execution of all the laws relating to the election of the officers of the general government was entirely in the hands of your partisans. If we look at the provisions of these laws, we find that they contain features of a startling character, as they were framed before the passions excited by civil war had been allayed, and with reference to States still looked upon as hostile to our Union. The judicial officers of every grade who interpret these laws, almost without exception, belong to your party. The marshals who execute them are heated politicians, the very tenure of whose offices depends upon the success of your ticket. They can summon a vast array of deputies, and all of these may make arrests, in some cases without process, and by express enactment are places above the reach of the laws and the judiciary of the States. At the late election Republican officials, at the expense of the general government, could examine every registry in the principal towns and cities. They could and did arrest men for accidental clerical errors of others in giving the name or the number of a house. In only one instance under these laws was there recognition of the party in power. We do not complain of the enforcement of these laws. On the contrary, we point with satisfaction to the fact that they furnished the proof made by their partisan opponents, that the Democratic vote was an honest one. If fraud is suspected, it must be the work of others, not of the Democratic party. Even if these election laws had been in all cases fairly enforced, they still made a vast array of partisan forces and power, supported by the common treasury, but exerted against the party that carried with it a majority of the American people. We hear much of coercion, intimidation, and undue influences, but nothing approaching this in power can exist in any part of our country. There is no organization which could for a moment contend with it, backed up as it has been by the American army.

"We also appeal to the Republicans to see if it is not true that during the late election the officials at Washington overlooked the fact that they were the government of a country, and acted throughout merely as the administration of a party. Has one step been taken, or the army moved, save at the instance of their political friends? Has there been a recognition of or a consultation with a single citizen who was not allied to them in interest and feeling?

"There is a darker phase of the last election. The administration sent our cabinet officer to take charge of the canvass on behalf of the Republican Party. His very position at the head of its managing committee made a forced loan upon neatly one hundred thousand official dependents. It proclaimed to then in louder tones than words, "You must work. You must vote You must pay to aid the election of a candidate who declares himself in favor of civil-service reform." It told them that if, believing and acting upon his assurance, they followed their own convictions and votes for his opponents; they would be punished by the loss of their positions. They were forced, in thousands of cases, to submit to extortion with smiling faces, but with heavy hearts. If a like intimidation had been used in a Southern State, it would have been seized upon by the administration as a reason for decaling martial law, for arresting and imprisoning every suspected citizen. …

"I have too much respect for the characters of Messrs. Hayes and Wheeler to thing that they wish to be put at the head of this Union against the declared wishes of a majority of the American people. I do not doubt that if this is to be done by men in Louisiana, of whom they think as ill as we do, that they would feel that the highest offices of state would be for them not positions of honor and dignity, but political pillories, in which they would stand to be pointed at, now and hereafter, as the representatives of a foul fraud. One thing all men see: *The Republican party cannot decide its own case in its own favor against the majority of the American people, upon the certificate of branded men in Louisiana, without making the body of our citizens and the world at large feel that it is a corrupt and partisan decision.* Such judgment will

not only destroy our honor and credit for the day, but will be a precedent for wrongdoing in the future. We cannot have Mexican politics
without Mexican finances and Mexican disorders. The business of all
civilized countries have been taught by recent bankruptcies and disorders in governments, made unstable by agitations, to be watchful and
distrustful when they see the slightest deviation from political honor,
without which there can be no financial honor. On the other hand, let
the party now in power yield to the popular will, demand honest returns
in accordance with the Constitution, bow to the majesty of the law, and
then every citizen will feel a renewed confidence in our institutions and
the whole world will hold us in higher respect and honor."

The commission at Washington perfected it organization on the first
day of February, and the same day received the contested certificates of
the State of Florida.

I shall be brief in dealing with the deliberations of the Electoral
Commission, for the simple reason that the Republican members of
that tribunal controlled it; and upon every question, I believe without
a single exception, bearing upon the success of their candidate, voted
with their party. Whatever his success depended upon going behind
the returns; when his success depended upon treating the returns as
sacred and conclusive; and when his success depended upon treating
the returns as sacred and conclusive, they were treated as sacred and
conclusive; and when his success depended upon counting the vote of
a federal office-holder, though disqualified by the Constitution form
serving as an elector, his vote was counted. They adopted no rule of
law or constitutional construction which was not compelled to yield
promptly to party exigencies.

The Florida case involved two vital questions:

First, The legality of the proceedings of the Returning Board in
returning as duly chosen, and the Governor of Florida certifying, the
appointment of Republican electors from that State; and,

Second, Was Frederick C. Humphreys, one of the electors so returned
the certified, being at the time holder of an office under the federal
government, eligible under the Constitution, which provides that no
"person holding an office of trust or profit under the United States shall
be appointed an elector"?

The commission disposed of the first question by deciding by a strict party vote, eight to seven, "that it is not competent under the Constitution and the law as they existed at the passage of said act to go into evidence *aliunde (Defined:* From another source; from elsewhere; as, a case proved aliunde; evidence aliunde.) the papers opened by the President of the Senate in the presences of the two Houses, to prove that other persons than those regularly certified to by the Governor of the State of Florida, in according to the determination and declaration of their appointment by the Board of State Canvassers of said State prior to the time required for the performance of their duties, had been appointed electors, or by counter-proof to show that they had not; and that all proceedings of the courts of acts of the Legislature or of the executive of Florida, subsequent to the casting of the votes of the electors on the prescribed day, are inadmissible for any such purpose.

Here the rule is formally laid down that the commission has no legal nor constitutional competence to go behind the electoral certificates delivered to and opened by the President of the Senate.

This rule held good only so long as it served the purpose of the majority.

"As to the objection made to the eligibility of Mr. Humphreys, the commission if of the opinion that, without reference to the question of the effect of the vote of an ineligible elector, *the evidence does not show that he held the office of shipping commissioner on the day when the electors were appointed."*

Here is the distinct admission that they did take evidence *aliunde* (From another source; from elsewhere; as, a case proved aliunde; evidence aliunde) the certificates, to prove that Mr. Humphreys was not ineligible.

The reader is requested to note that this decision in Humphrey's case is made "without reference to the question of the effect of the vote of an ineligible elector." They declined to pronounce against the validity of such a vote, for they already had reasons for apprehending that other cases would come before them in which the electors would appear ineligible on the face of the certificates; and as the loss of a single electoral vote would have been fatal to their candidate, they did not mean to commit themselves against counting the vote of an ineligible elector if his vote should prove to be necessary. In other words, they had undertaken to count Mr. Tilden out and their candidate in, and they did not propose to deprive themselves of the liberty of so construing the Constitution as to accomplish their purpose.

When Louisiana case was reached, it appeared that two of the electors certified by the Returning Board were disqualified by the Constitution of the United States, and four others by the Constitution of Louisiana, which provides that, "no person shall at any time hold more than one office." A.B. Levissee when elected was a United States commissioner, and O.H. Brewster was surveyor of the United States Land Office. They resigned their federal offices temporarily, were substituted for themselves by their colleagues, and voted for Hayes and Wheeler. Both these men were promptly reappointed to their respective federal offices and resumed their duties. When their case was reached by the commission, it was manifest that the majority could not elect their candidate under the rule laid down in the Florida case. Accordingly they held,: that it is not competent to prove that any of said persons so appointed electors as aforesaid held an office of trust or profit under the United States at the time when they were appointed, or that they were ineligible under the laws of the State, or any matter offered to be proved *aliunde* the said certificates and papers."

The commission also decided "that the returning officers of elections who canvassed the votes at the election for electors in Louisiana were a legally constituted body, by virtue of a constitutional law, and that a vacancy in said body did not vitiate its proceedings." The constitution of Louisiana, article forty-eight, prescribes who the returning officers of elections shall be; to wit, the officers of elections at the different polling-places throughout the State. Senator Edmunds, on the 16th of March, 1875, declared in the Senate in unequivocal language that the election law creating the Returning Board was in conflict with the constitution of the State. And yet Mr. Commissioner Edmunds, on Feb. 16, 1877, voted

Note: During the count of the electoral votes in 1837 the question of the eligibility of the electors was considered by a Senate committee composed of Henry Clay, Silas Wright, and Felix Grundy, who reported that, "The committee are of opinion that the second section of the second article of the Constitution, which declares that 'no Senator or Representative, or person holding an office of trust or profit under the United States, shall be appointed and elector,' ought to be carried in its whole spirit into rigid execution… This provision of the Constitution, it is believed, *excludes* and disqualifies deputy postmasters from the *appointment* if electors; and the disqualification relates to the *time of appointment* and that a resignation of the office of deputy postmaster after his appointment as elector *would not entitle him to vote as elector, under the Constitution.*"

that the election law of Louisiana creating the Returning Board was not in conflict with the constitution of the State. Representative George F. Hoar made a report to the House of Representatives in 1875; in which he used the following language in regard to the Louisiana Returning Board's conduct in the election of 1874; "We are clearly of the opinion that the Returning Board had no right to do anything except to canvass and compile the returns which were lawfully made to them by the local officers, except in cases where they were accompanied by the certificates of the supervisor or commissioner provided in the third section." How much more grossly had the Returning Board violated the law in 1876 than in 1874; and yet Mr. Commissioner Hoar voted, Feb, 16, 1877, that the presidential electors returned as elected by that Returning Board were legally elected.

When the Oregon contested case came up before the commission, the electoral tribunal did not permit itself to be in the least embarrassed by its previous rulings. By the laws of Oregon its returning officers were the Governor and the Secretary of State. One of the Republican electors was a postmaster, and consequently disqualified by the Constitution for serving as an elector. The Secretary of State, therefore, gave the certificate to his opponent E. A. Cronin, a Democratic elector. Cronin voted for Tilden and Hendricks. One copy of a certificate of his vote as a Tilden elector in due form was forwarded by mail to the President of the Senate, a second was filed with the United States District Judge, and the third was borne by Cronin to himself to Washington and delivered to the President of the Senate. His vote, therefore, for Tilden and Hendricks was legally and regularly before the two Houses of Congress. Cronin had unnecessarily gone through the form of organizing an electoral college which neither the laws not the Constitution of the United States require, and for that purpose had appointed two persons to act with him. As one vote for Tilden in Oregon would be fatal to Hayes as one in Louisiana and Florida would have been, this vote had to be rescued as a brand from the burning. But how? Here was a Tilden elector regularly certified by the authorized returning officers. To reject him was to elect in his place a man certified to them to have been an officer of the federal government. Was it to be prepared for this emergency that they forbore in the Florida case to decide whether the holding of a feral office disqualified Humphreys as an elector? It was a very aggravating case for the Republican commissioners to deal with, but they rose to the level of the occasion; "the hope was not drunk wherein they had dressed themselves;" they did not weakly let, "I dare not" wait upon "I would," but boldly decided "that the Secretary of State did canvass the returns in the case of before us, and thereby ascertained that J.C. Cartwright, W.H. Odell, and J.W. Watts had a majority of the *votes given for electors*, and had the highest number of votes for that office, and by the express language of the stature are deemed elected." They further held, "that the refusal or failure of the Governor of Oregon to sing the certificate if the election of the persons so elected does not have the effect of defeating their appointment as such electors."

The commissioners made this decision in favor of Watts, the Republican, solely upon the ground that he had "the highest number of votes." But if the highest number of votes was sufficient for an elector in Oregon, why was it not sufficient in Florida where the electoral ticket had an incontestable majority of ninety-one, and in Louisiana where it had an incontestable majority of over 7,000. They altogether suppress the supreme fact that the Secretary of State had certified to the Governor that another person had been elected and that Watts had not been; and the further fact that the Secretary of State and Governor, and no one else, by law constituted the returning officers of Oregon. This suppression was necessary because in Louisiana they had held that an elector is not appointed according to the terms of the Constitution until he has received the certificate of such appointment from the returning officers. Therefore the decision which elected Watts in Oregon should have admitted all the Tilden and Hendricks electors in Louisiana and Florida, and the decisions in Louisiana and Florida should have elected a Tilden elector in Oregon, had the commission attached any importance to the virtue of consistency in their rulings, or felt that their appointment on that commission invested them with any other function or imposed upon them any other duty than to make Hayes President without violating any more nor any less of the ten commandments and the laws of their country than was necessary. Like Cassandra's lover, they adapted the ethics of the Pagan instead of the Christian code for their purpose:

"Mutemus clypeus, Danaumque insignia nobis Aptemus: dolus an Vritus, quis in hoste requirat?"

There were at least nine Republican electors who where disqualified by virtue of their holding offices under the federal government at the time of their election. Only in the cases of Florida, Louisiana, and Oregon, however, could the question of their eligibility be raised before the commission, and in no two of these cases were the decisions the same. And yet the members of this commission were severally sworn as the Holy Evangelists, "to impartially examine and consider all questions submitted,"… "and true judgment give thereon, agreeably to the Constitution and the laws."

It seem not appropriate to insert here an entry which I made in my diary of the 9th of February, 1877.

"On Thursday (the 8th) Tilden told me a man had called to say that commission was for sale. Whe I expressed an incredulous sort of astonishment, he said that one of the justices (Republican) was ready to give his vote for the Tilden electors for $200,000. I asked which one. He said he thought he would not tell me that at present. I told him it was improbable, for the judges were all well paid and had life terms of their office. He said the justice in question is reported to be embarrassed from old engagements and obligations…Tilden also told me that the Florida Returning Board was offered to him, and for the same money. 'That,' he said, 'seems to be the standard figure,'"

In a notable debate in the House of Representatives in February, 1879, the Hon. A. S. Hewitt, replying to a scurrilous allusion to Mr. Tilden which Mr. Garfield, who had been a member of the Electoral Commission, had been betrayed into making, confirmed the report that the presidency had been in the market. Time ahs only added significance and gravity to his many expostulation.

"I think, however, that I can account for this extraordinary proceeding. During the progress of this debate, a gallant soldier, an able lawyer who has been an attorney-general of my State, and who is a staunch Republican, General Francis C. Barlow, of New York, had given evidence on the lower floor of the capitol that the votes of the State of Florida had been unjustly counted for Mr. Hayes; the conclusion being that if it had been counted for Mr. Tilden, he to-day would have been occupying the White House instead of it present de facto and not de jure tenant. is an expression that means "based on ", as contrasted with, This evidence must have touched the gentleman from Ohio to the quick; it must have revived the memories of eight to seven; it must have reminded him how, when the electoral bill was pending in this House, for one whole evening he devoted himself to proving that the law creating the commission was unconstitutional, but that if it should be passed it would be the duty of the commission to take evidence of fraud and go behind the returns. And yet when he was made a judge, acting under a law which he had declared to be unconstitutional, and which as he had affirmed, required evidence to be taken; he consented to violate the Constitution and to deny the admission of the evidence which was necessary to arrive at the truth. When the great wrong thus done by the vote of the gentleman from Ohio-for it was his casting vote in every case that excluded the evidence – was thus made manifest by the testimony of General Barlow, did that feeling of remorse which is the attribute of great minds force him to attempt to drown the reproaches of conscience by alleging that the man who to-day is of right President of the United States was the 'author and finisher' of frauds and therefore should be excluded form the high office to which he had been elected by the people?

'High minds of native pride and force
Must deeply feel thy pangs, remorse!
Fear for their scourge mean villains have;
Thou art the torturer of the brave.'

"Gentlemen on the other side realize fully that a great wrong cannot be committed in this country without being finally redressed by the voice of the people, for they remember what took place in General Jackson's case in 1828, and they know that the voice of the people is the voice if God, who had declared, 'Vengeance is mine, I will repay, saith the Lord.' They see no refuge from the coming judgment but in destroying the character of the man whom they have robbed. For months an uninterrupted stream of abuse, misrepresentation, and calumny has been poured out upon his devoted head, but the testimony of the last few days has justified the assertion which I have never failed to make when Mr. Tilden's character and integrity have been attacked, that not one particle of dishonest action can be traced to him, but, on the contrary, it is now manifest to all men that he scorned to purchase *the presidency which found a ready market elsewhere.*"

Mr. Hewitt has more recently stated at a public meeting in New York that the electoral vote of one of the contested States had been offered to him for a price.

There is one more chapter in the history of this extraordinary tribunal, without which it would be incomplete.

..."*Longa est injura, longae ambiges.*"

When Anderson was selected to bring the certificates of the Louisiana Returning Board to Washington, he handed the package to Ferry, the President of the Senate, of the 24th of December. Instead of accepting it as he should have done, for better or worse, Ferry called Anderson's attention to the fact that the endorsement on the outside, setting forth the contents of each envelope, had not been signed by the electors as the law required, and recommended Anderson to examine the law and see whether the certificate had been made in accordance with it.

It was the duty of the President of the Senate to receive the package, to open it only in the presence of both Houses of Congress, and leave them to decided what to do with it. He had previously received the duplicate of the package handed to him by Anderson; and he knew that the electors were *functus offcii* and no more competent to repair any defect of omission or commission in their returns, weeks after their legal existence had ceased, then to recall the cloud which had shaded them the preceding day. Contrary to the Constitution, which required that the election return should be opened by the President of the Senate in the presence of both Houses of Congress, Anderson's package was opened in Washington by parties whose names have not officially transpired, when, to the consternation of the Hayes engineers, it was discovered that the lack of electors' signatures on the envelope was by no means the only, nor the most serious, defect of the return; that instead of voting separate ballots for President and Vice-President, as required by the Constitution, they had voted for both on one ballot, and had failed to make their return of the votes cast for each candidate on distinct lists with separate certificates, also express requirements of the Constitution.

There was but one course left for them to save their candidate. The certificates made out and signed by the electors in triplicate on the 6th of December must be suppressed, and the false ones purporting to comply with the provisions of the Constitution, must be substituted for them. Anderson left Washington the night of the day he reached there, arrived in New Orleans on the morning of December 28th, and repaired at once to the quarters of Governor Kellogg. The Governor sent for his private secretary, Clark, who at one set about the preparation of new certificates. There was no time to waste. The forged certificates must be on their way to Washington at 5:20 p.m. of the next day,—one set by the hand of a messenger, and another set by the mail;—in order to reach Washington within the time fixed by law fro their reception, the 3rd of January, 1877.

Kellogg and Clark, however, with the aid of Anderson, proved equal to the occasion. They had certificates printed to correspond – paper and impression – with the certificates of December 6th. The new certificates were spread out on a large table in the third floor of the State House, where they were to be signed. Such of the electors as could be found were taken up to this room, one at a time, in the order in which they had signed the original certificates. Two, Levisee and Joffroin, were away fully three days' journey from New Orleans. Their autograph signatures, therefore, could not be had. But when the electors who had originally signed below the signatures of these absentees, went up to affix their names to the new certificates, they found the names of the absentee electors in their place. Who forged these names is a question now of secondary importance. The accomplices in the fraud did not agree in their testimony as to the actual perpetrator of the forgery, though none pretended that the names had not been forged. It would have been idle to have done so, as the impossibility of either of the two electors being in New Orleans either on the 28th or 29th of December was a matter of common notoriety.

These forges certificates were not sent to Washington this time by Anderson, who had taken the former certificates, but by a clerk in the State auditor's office, named Hill, who on his arrival went first to Zachariah Chandler, the secretary of the treasury, and chairman of the Republican national committee, to whom he bore a letter also from Governor Kellogg. Chandler read Kellogg's letter, and then directed Hill to go to the capitol and deliver the forged electoral certificates to Mr. Ferry, the President of the Senate. Senator Sherman was invited by Mr. Ferry to come in and witness the delivery and receipt if the package. That ceremony over, Sherman took Hill into the room of the finance committee, and wrote a letter to Kellogg, which he delivered sealed to the messenger to be delivered to Kellogg in person. .

Thus far it seemed as though this *crevesse,* which at first threatened fall their elaborate fabric of Iniquity, had been closed up, or at least gotten under control.

It was still necessary, however, to obtain from the United States district judge in New Orleans the electoral certificates which, in accordance with the requirement of law, had been deposited with him on the 6th of December and replace it with one of the certificates forged on the 29th of December. The district judge declined to grant the application for this substitution, on the ground that he was the custodian of the package merely, and without authority to deliver it to any one except upon a requisition from the Speaker of the House. This respect for the law on the part of the judge seemed puerile to the Kellogg "combine," but it was none the less awkward.

When the two Houses of Congress in their call of the States reached Louisiana, Mr. Ferry, the presiding officer, first handed to the tellers the genuine Kellogg certificate, which had come to him by mail. Next the McEnery certificate, which had come to him in duplicate,—one copy by mail and the other by messenger; the next the forged Kellogg certificate, of which two copies - one by mail and the other by messenger; and the next the forged Kellogg certificate, of which two copies,—one by mail and other by the messenger Hill - had reached him; and finally a certificate signed by John Smith, declaring that the vote of Louisiana had been cast for Peter Cooper.

This burlesque certificate was read as the others had been, but the convention unanimously ordered it to be suppressed and no mention of it made in the record.

It is now generally understood that this burlesque certificate was sent in to create such a diversion of the attention of the convention as to enable the irregularity of the other certificates to escape observation. If so it was a complete success, for not one of the Democratic lawyers, managers, Senators, or Representatives remarked that there was one certificate made by the Republican electors of Louisiana which did not comply with the requirements of the Constitution, and the duplicates of another, form the same electors, which were in proper form, though forged,—a circumstance which could hardly have been possible but for the confusion and distraction which resulted form the reading of Peter Cooper certificate and the discussion which it provoked.

No trace of this paper remained after the recess of the joint convention of the day it was read. It was probably carried off by its author, who no doubt had more serious motives for sending it than to perpetrate a practical joke, and equally good motives for having it disappear when its purpose was accomplished. The papers in the contested case went to the Electoral Commission immediately after the joint convention adjourned. When the secretary began to read them, and before there had been an opportunity for any one to inspect them, one of the Democratic commissioners moved that the reading be dispensed with and the papers printed. The motion was not opposed. Thereupon the Hon. Nathan Clifford marked the certificates severally for identification as follows:

The first certificate of the Kellogg electors which did not meet the constitutional requirements was marked "No. 1 N.C.;" the Democratic certificate which was all right was marked, "No. 2, N.C.;" and the forged certificate was marked "No. 3, N.C." With these marks on the certificates, they were sent to the printer; but not to the public printer, not to the congressional printer, not to the government printer, in accordance with the invariable rule before and after this, but to a private job printer. When they came back printed the distinguishing marks put on the m by Judge Clifford were found to have been omitted; and what is even more extraordinary, this job printer, instead of sending back the originals with the printed copies to the secretary of the commission, who was their responsible custodian, sent only the originals to the secretary, and had two of his press boys distribute the printed copies among the members of the commission and the counsel.

It is no longer susceptible of demonstration that his job printer did not distribute copies of the genuine certificate marked, "No. 1, N.C.;" but if they were distributed, it seems unaccountable that neither of the Democratic commissioners, neither the Democratic lawyers,—some of them the ablest in the country,—nor any one of the two hundred Democratic members of Congress, each and every one whom was already sufficiently familiar with the means by which Republican electors had been returned in Louisiana to be misled by no presumptions in favor of anything they did,—it seems, I repeat, unaccountable that none of these gentlemen should have observed that the copies of certificate No. 1 did not correspond with the copies of the forged certificate No. 3.

Had printed copies of the genuine certificate "No. 1, N.C.," been distributed, it was practically impossible that its defective form should have escaped detection. Its comparison with the other forged certificate "No. 3, N.C.," must have been made, and the differences between them have exploded the whole plot. Nothing of this kind happened, however, and we are driven to the conclusion that two copies of the forged certificate were distributed by this job printer, instead of one copy of the genuine and defective certificate, and one copy of the formally correct but forged certificate.

This curious sequence of strange and unforeseen contraries which beset the final action of the Louisiana Returning Board from the day that action was reduced to writing, was destined to acquire additional proportion and consequence at the hands of Senator Morton. When the Electoral Commission had decided, by a strictly party vote of eight to seven, to count the electoral vote of Louisiana for Hayes and Wheeler, the Senator from Indiana was careful in his motion to that effect to specify "the electoral votes in the certificate 'No. 1, N.C.,'" the genuine but constitutionally defective one. This was done, so far as Mr. Morton was concerned, with full knowledge that the other set of electoral certificates from Louisiana, and the only ones made out in the form required by the Constitution, "were not to be depended on."

When later the record of the proceedings in Congress and of the Electoral Commission came to be made up, it was made to appear that there were before Congress and the commission the certificate of the Democratic electors and the genuine but defective certificate of the Republican electors, and no others: whereas there is every reason to believe that Congress and the commission had before them and considered only two copies of the forged certificates and no other Republican certificates, and that they never had an opportunity of considering the defects of the genuine certificate which was put unchallenged upon their record.

The decision of the Electoral Commission in the case of Oregon, the last disputed State, was communicated to the joint convention of the House of Congress on Thursday, the first day of March. The convention then proceeded with the count, which it prosecuted to its completion on the following Friday morning at ten minutes past four, at which hour the President of the Senate, Thomas W. Ferry, of Michigan, announced that Rutherford B. Hayes, of Ohio, had received 185 electoral votes, a majority of the whole number, and had been duly elected President of the United States; and that William A. Wheeler, of New York, had received the like majority, and had been duly elected Vice President of the United States.

There was a ghastly sort of fitness in selecting "hangman's day" on which to stain the annals of the great Republic with this ignominious record.

"Excidat illa dies aevo, neo postera credant
Saecula; nos certe tacamus, et obruta multa
Nocte tegi nostrae patiamur criminis gentis

"May that foul day be blotted in time's flight
And buried in oblivion's gloom of night
We will at least forbear the deed to name,
Nor let posterity believe our shame."

Republican institutions have never received a more serious blow, nor one from which they will be so long in recovering. If we do these things in the green tree, what may we be expected to do in the dry? We may go on for a while, perhaps indefinitely, "grinding on the gudgeons (_Slang._ One who is easily duped) but now to restore the faith in our institutions, once delivered to the fathers?

"I comprehend perfectly," said an eminent French journalist, with as much wit as justice, "how we may depantheonize Marat," but I cannot conceive how you will ever be able to demaratize the Pantheon."

I hereby dismiss the story of this the most ignominious (Deserving disgrace or shame; despicable) conspiracy of which modern history has preserved any record. I regret, for the readers sake as well as my own, to have felt compelled to dwell upon it as such length, though I have given only an imperfect summary, far from a complete list of the varieties of crime by which it was consummated. If there be any one who care to pursue the investigation further, they are referred to the congressional record of the investigations which those crimes provoked. I have deemed it my duty to penetrate so far only into these "corners of nastiness" as to satisfy all who may take the trouble to glance through these pages, that electors favorable to Tilden for President were chosen by the people of the United States in 1876, and that by a cumulative series of frauds and crimes, in which leading national statesmen, cabinet ministers, and persons occupying seats in the highest judicial tribunal in the land were, some in a greater, some in a lesser degree accomplices, that choice was defeated and a usurper put in his place. It is due to the memory of Mr. Tilden that these facts should be so stated that future historians shall have neither difficulty nor hesitation in taking note of them.

Why men occupying the most exalted and responsible positions in the country should have ventured to compromise their reputations by this deliberate consummation of a series of crimes which struck at the very foundations of the Republic, is a question which still puzzles many of all parties who have no charity for the crimes themselves. I have already referred to the terrors and desperation with which the prospect of Tilden's election inspired the great army of office-holders at the close of Grant's administration. That army, numerous and formidable as it was, was comparatively limited. There was a much larger and justly influential class who were apprehensive that the return of the Democratic party to

Note: On the day previous to the 3rd of March the House of Representatives, by a vote of 137 to 88 adopted a series of preambles introductory to the following resolution:

Resolved by the House of Representatives of the United States, "That it is the duty of the House to declare, ad this Houses does solemnly declare, that Samuel J. Tilden, of the State of New York, received 196 electoral votes for the office of President of the United States, all of which votes were cast and lists thereof signed, certified, and transmitted, to the seat of the government, directed to the President of the Senate, in conformity with the Constitution and laws of the United States, by electors legally eligible and qualified as such electors, each of whom had been duly appointed and elected in the manner directed by the Legislature of the State in and for which he cast his vote as aforesaid; and that said Samuel J. Tilden having thus received the votes of a majority of the electors appointed as aforesaid; her was thereby duly elected President of the United States of America, for the term of four years commencing on the 4th day of March, A.D. 1877; and this House further declares that Thomas A. Hendricks, having received the same number of electoral votes for the office of Vice President of the United States that were cast for Samuel J. Tilden for President as aforesaid, and at the same time and in the manner, it is the opinion of this House that that the said Thomas A. Hendricks, of the State of Indiana, was duly elected Vice President of the United States for the term of four years commencing on the 4th day of March A.D. 1877"

Note: The Democratic minority of the Electoral Commission directed the Honorable Josiah Gardner Abbott, on the of their colleagues from Massachusetts, to prepare an address to the American people, protesting against the decisions of the majority, in which he was to set forth the reason for their action which, under the laws establishing the commission, they had no opportunity of reporting to Congress. This address is a vigorous and compact statement of the wrongs with they and the country had sustained at the hands of the majority, but, for reasons which have not transpired, was never promulgated. It is understood however, that the result would not have been changed by protesting, and the minority did not wish to further weaken the respect for the government from which there was no refuge but in revolution. For a copy of this protest, which is an essential part of the history of the Electoral Commission, See Appendix A.

power threatened a reactionary policy at Washington, to the undoing of some or all important results of the war. These apprehensions were inflamed by the party press until they were confined to no class, but more or less pervaded all the Northern States. The election tribunal, consisting of mainly men appointed to their positions by Republican Presidents or elected from strong Republican States, felt the pressure of this feeling, and from motives compounded in more or less varying proportions of dread of the Democrats, personal ambition, zeal for their party, and respect for their constituents, reached the conclusion that the exclusion of Tilden from the White House was an end which justified whatever means were necessary to accomplish it. They regarded it like the emancipation of the slaves as a war measure. In that way they quieted their consciences for a time at least, and found a peace which passeth all understanding, by virtue of a course of reasoning which they might be suspected of having borrowed from one of Mr. Dickens' amiable heroes:

"I am glad to see you have so high a sense of your duties as a son, Sam," said Mr. Pickwick.

"I always had, sir," replied Mr. Weller.

"That's very gratifying reflection, Sam," said Mr. Pickwick approvingly.

"Werry, sir," replied Mr. Weller. "If ever I wanted anything o' my father, I always asked for it in a werry 'spectful and obliging manner. If he didn't give it me, I took it for fear I should be led to do anythin' wrong through not havin' it. I saved him a world o' trouble in that vay, sir."

"That's not precisely what I meant Sam," said Mr. Pickwick, shaking his head with a slight smile.

"All good feelin, sir, the werry best intentions, as the gen'lm'n said ven he run away from his wife 'cos she seemed unhappy with him," replied Mr. Weller.

The President and Vice President declared by the Electoral Commission to have been the choice of the electors were inaugurated on Sunday, the 4th of March. On the following day the Hon. Charles Francis Adams addressed to Mr. Tilden a letter which, though brief, produced a national sensation. It ran as follows:

Boston March 5, 1877

"Honorable S. J. Tilden, *New York:*

My Dear Sir: On this day, when you *ought* to have been the President of these United States, I seize the opportunity to bear my testimony to the calm and dignified manner in which you have passed through this great trial.

It is many years since I ceased to be a party man. Hence I have endeavored to judge of public affairs and men rather by their merits that by the names they take. It is a source of gratification to me to think that I made the right choice in the late election. I could never have been reconciled to the elevation, by the smallest aid of mine, of a person, however respectable in private life, who must forever carry upon his brow the stamp fraud, first triumphant in American history. No subsequent action, however meritorious, can was away the letters of that record.

Very respectfully yours,

Charles Francis Adams

The formal and public charge from the son of one President, the grandson of another President, himself in one important national crisis a candidate for the vice-presidency, and in another yet graver national crisis our minister to England, that the man who only the day previous had been formerly clothed with the chief magistracy of the nation, "must forever carry upon his brow the stamp of fraud," conveyed with it throughout the land something of the shock of the fire-bell rung in the night. Had such a letter from such a source appeared the day following the inauguration of any previous President of the United States, its author could hardly have expected immunity form personal outrage. The truth of the charge, however, was so indisputable, that, so far as I am aware, no one of Mr. Hayes's friends or partisans ever attempted to deal with its author, as would have been natural had it been questionable.

Among Mr. Tilden's papers the following fragment of what purports to have been intended as a reply to Mr. Adams' letter has been found. Though only a fragment and never communicated to Mr. Adams, it is interesting a revelation of the state of feeling which the letter had awakened, and of Mr. Tilden's deliberate view of the frauds by which the rights of the nation had been violated.

New York, April 1877

"My Dear Sir: The approving judgment expressed in your letter of
March 5th is esteemed by me as the best of testimonies. The circumstances you mentioned, which characterize it as a mere judgment, free
from bias of partisanship, passion, or interest, enhance its value. So
do also, I may be allowed to add, the large experience, long familiarity
with and habitual thoughtfulness concerning public affairs, and the high
standards of right and duty.

I should have had little excuse for any want of the qualities of personal
demeanor which you commend; for I have not been conscience, in the
vicissitudes (defined: One of the sudden or unexpected changes or shifts
often encountered in one's life, activities, or surroundings) of what you
speak of as the 'great trial,' of any feeling of desire or regret, separate form
the public cause I have represented.

That cause I do regard as the greatest that can interest the attention
of this generations of Americans.

In advocating the creation of the Union, our wise ancestors often
predicted that intestine wars – if unhappily we should fall into them
– would end in a subversion of constitutional government and civil
liberty. Those who thought, as you and I did, that the federal government should be maintained and carried through the armed conflicts in
which it had become inevitably involved, did not shut our eyes to the
peril that in the process our institutions, in their spirit and practical
working, might be greatly and injuriously affected. Changes in the ideal
standards that govern men administering the government and limit what
they dare or do, and limit also what the people will tolerate; changes
in the unwritten laws established by tradition and habit, often more
controlling than constitutions and statues; changes in the enormous
recent growth of perverting, abusive, and corrupting influences,—these
were evil tendencies, full of danger to everything really valuable in our
political system.

To curb and correct these evil tendencies; to restore to the barren
forms of government a spirit and substance and practice in accord with
the best ideals and original models which had been formed under
fortunate circumstances of our early history; to remove the fungus over-
growths engendered by civil war, while preserving what ever of good it
had saved or gained,—this was the first of objects. A general reform of

administration, reducing burdens upon the people and facilitating a revival of industries, would attend as incidents. A complete and cordial reconciliation between estranged populations and classes, the removal if unfounded distrust and fear of each other, the inspiration of mutual confidence, was a necessary condition.

Such was the work most needful to our country in its present condition, the most beneficent that could engage the efforts of patriotism or humanity,—such was that work as it appeared previous to the late election. The events which have happened since and to which you allude have added a new element to that work. Or, perhaps, they have disclosed how far we have drifted away in practice from the theory if our government, and shown that we have a more difficult task to get back than had been apparent. The immense powers which the corrupt influence of the government had to perpetuate itself was never so developed as in the late canvass. I was accustomed to say that it was necessary to start in August with a public opinion which would naturally give you two-thirds of the votes in order to receive a majority in November. The civil service was never so audaciously and so unscrupulously used for electioneering purposed as in the late canvass. The whole body of 100,000 office-holders were made to feel their accountability for partisan service, and a large part of them brought into great activity. The money contributions systematically exacted, and the sums drawn from contractors, jobbers, and persons having business relations with the general government, aggregated a large fund, while the machine was openly worked by a cabinet minister acting as the head of a partisan committee.

The army, likewise, was used as an electioneering instrument. In Louisiana, Florida, and South Carolina the carpet-bag governments –their robberies, oppressions, and crimes – had so repelled public opinion, had so antagonized all taxpayers, all men of business, property, social weight, and personal influence, that the element that remained was incapable of any cohesion, or any action on its own motion. The real object of the military display was not to keep up a police, which was unnecessary and was no part of the function of the federal army, but was to act on the imaginations of the ignorant, disintegrated social atoms and enable the agents of the administration to organize and lead them. It was as true as it is confessed now that without its aid added to the other support of the government, no Republican party could exist in those States.

But all these odds were overcome by the mere mortal force of public opinion demanding better government; and a popular majority of 260,000 votes and an electoral majority of twenty-three votes resulted.

This was not withstanding that California was carried by fraud now ascertained, and several of the new States by corrupt means.

Then came the after frauds: the change of the actual result declared at the polls, by governmental influence falsifying the returns of two States and falsifying the count of the electoral votes."

I was at Mr. Tilden's house when the news of his exclusion form the presidency was announced to him, and also on the 4th of March, when Mr. Hayes was inaugurated. I venture to quote the following contemporaneous entry from my diary, relating to his bearing on that occasion.

"It was impossible to remark any change in his manner, except, perhaps, that he was less absorbed than usual and more interested in current affairs. I spent a week at this time a guest in his house, and I could not see that he was much disappointed as most of the people about him. He had not been so cheerful at any time in the last three years as since the 4th inst. My explanation of this is satisfactory to me. His notion of being President meant a life of care, responsibility, and effort such as none of his predecessors ever encountered. He never contemplated the presidency except as a fearful struggle. When his election was out of the question he was naturally more sensible of his escape form the giants which he had seen in his path than of the honors which might have been his, but were to be worn by another. This sense of relief and the opportunity it offers of looking after his health, which is daily improving in consequence, have rather made him happier otherwise. When the giants shall have entirely disappeared, and his freedom form care and anxiety become familiar to him, it is probable that he will feel more keenly the loss he has sustained, He regards Thurman and Bayard as chiefly responsible for his miscarriage."

There have been occasional criticisms of Mr. Tilden, not only by those who wished an excuse for their own disloyalty to their party or for their personal pusillanimity (cowardice), but also by some of his faithful friends, that he did not take the oath of office and go on to

Washington and claim the presidency at all hazard and regardless of
the title conferred by congressional authority upon another. I believe
Mr. Charles O'Connor was one of these friends, and I also remember
how signally I failed in the effort of 1877 to make Victor Hugo comprehend Mr. Tilden's submission to the decision of the electoral tribunal.
He shook his head at the close of my exposition, as if to say, "That is
not the way we do things here in France," which was very true. But
Charles O'Connor, with all his prodigious (astonishing) abilities as a
jurist, was never successful in forming or leading a political party that
embraced more than one person; and Victor Hugo resigned his seat in
the only deliberative political assembly to which he was ever chosen
by his countrymen, from sheer reluctance to prolong the exhibition
to the world of his utter impotence and insignificant in a council of
statesman. Mr. Tilden had frequent applications from all parts of the
country, mainly from friends, for information bout his plans; which he
had done what he proposed to do, and what he expected his friends to
do towards reclaiming the office which had been wrongfully wrested
from him. These letters were, I believe, uniformly referred to me, and
I answered such as seemed entitles to an answer. A few days before
the fourth of March, when the new President was to be inaugurated, a
communication appeared in one of the morning papers, "The World,"
I believe,—affirming, upon the alleged authority of General Woodford,
the United States District Attorney for the Southern District of New York,
that Mr. Tilden was about to take the oath of office as President in New
York, and then to proclaim himself President of the United States. A
representative of one of the daily journals called upon me to ascertain
the truth of that statement. As the criticisms of Mr. Tilden's behavior,
after the members of his own party had, with comparative unanimity
and against his judgment, consented to refer the counting of the electoral vote to a special commission, still occasionally reappear where
they can be made to palliate or excuse other people's shortcomings, I
will here cite the substance of my reply to the inquires of the reporter,
in which is embraced all, I think, that needs further to be said on that
subject. After disposing of a few topics pertinent, I said:

"There were two contingencies in which it would have been lawful
and obligatory for Mr. Tilden to have taken the official oath as President.

"*First,* if Congress had performed its constitutional duty of counting the electoral votes and had declared that Mr. Tilden was chosen by the electoral colleges.

"The two Houses of Congress have all the powers for verifying the electoral votes which the Constitution of the laws confer or allow. Nobody else in the federal government has any such powers. This exclusive jurisdiction of the two Houses has been exercised without interruption form the beginning of the government. It is known to all those who came in contact with Mr. Tilden at this period that he concurred in this view of the powers and duties of the two Houses of Congress exclusively to count the electoral vote. He was perfectly free and unreserved in the expression of his opinions on this subject.

"This contingency, however, never presented itself. Congress, before the time fixed by the law for counting electoral votes, passed the electoral bill, wherein it substantially abdicated its powers and enacted that the Electoral Commission should, in the first instance, make a count, and that its count should stand unless overruled *by the concurrent action of the two Houses.* The electoral tribunal counted Mr. Tilden out, and counted in a man who was not elected. Congress did not overrule their count; consequently the false count stood as law under the act of Congress.

"*Secondly,* The other contingency, in which it would have been lawful and obligatory on Mr. Tilden to have taken the oath of office, was that House of Representatives on the failure of a choice of President by the electoral colleges had itself proceeded to make the election, voting by States in the manner prescribed by the Constitution.

"This contingency, like the first one, never occurred.

"The House of Representatives is required, by the express language of the Constitution, to elect the President when neither of the candidates can command a majority of the electoral votes.

"The right of the two Houses to count the electoral votes and to declare that any person has a majority is a matter of implication, precedent, and practice. But the right of the House of Representatives to supply the failure of a choice is a positive constitutional command. It is not only a right, but a duty. The provision is mandatory. The House is a witness at the opening of the certificates; it is an actor in counting the votes by its own tellers and in its own presence.

"Having such and the best means of knowing whether a choice has bee made by the elector colleges, it is also expressly vested with a power and duty to act exclusively and conclusively in the event that no person proves to have been chosen by a majority of the votes of those colleges. The House acquires jurisdiction by that fact. The assent of the Senate to the existence of that fact is nowhere prescribed or required. No judgment, certification, or act of any official body is interposed as a condition the assuming or jurisdiction by the House. When the House has once acted in such a case, no review of its action nor any appeal from its decision is provided for in the Constitution. It is difficult to see why the House in such a case, like all tribunals of original jurisdiction and subject to no appeal, did not insist upon its rights as the exclusive judge of the fact and the law from which it acquired jurisdiction. It was, I am told, a fear that the Senate might lead a resistance to the rightful judgment of the House, and that General Grant would sustain such a revolutionary policy with the army and navy and the militia of the great States in which the Republicans had possession of the governments, that deterred the House of Representatives from the assertion of its rights and induced it to abdicate in favor of the Electoral Commission.

"But without speculating upon causes or motives, one thing is certain: the House of Representatives did not elect Mr. Tilden in the manner prescribed by the Constitution On the other hand, it did concur with the Senate in anticipating and preventing the contingency in which it might have compelled to act, thus providing an expedient which disarmed it. It adopted the electoral law and went through all the forms required for the execution of the electoral scheme. True, it afterwards, passed a declaratory resolution condemning the action of that tribunal and asserting that Mr. Tilden had been duly elected; but the Constitution had not provided that a man should or could take office as President on a declaratory resolution of the House of Representatives merely. If that resolution could have had full effect to abrogate the electoral law which the House had assisted to enact, it would have created no warrant of authority to Mr. Tilden to take the oath of office. A vote by States that he should be the next President of the United States was still necessary to give Mr. Tilden any more title to the secession that Grant, and that vote the House of Representatives never gave him.

"I might have disposed of your question more briefly by simply saying that no contingency provided by the Constitution ever existed in which Mr. Tilden could have lawfully or properly take the oath of office as President. I have dwelt upon the matter at some length because of its future as well as past importance. The idea that Mr. Tilden ever thought of taking the oath of office illegally is in my judgment quite preposterous as is the other idea that he would have omitted to take it if any contingency had arisen in which it was his right or duty to take it, or that any menace would have had the slightest influence in preventing his performing his whole obligation to the people. I will venture to say that if it had been his right and duty to take the oath he would not have done so at the City Hall in New York, surrounded by the forces which, according to Mr. Mines, General Woodford pictured to his imagination, but at the federal capitol, even though he had know that he would be kidnapped or subjected to a drumhead court martial five minutes afterwards. It is doubtless true that revolutionary ideas were entertained by the hierarchy of office-holders in possession of the government. General Grant did utter menaces in published interviews and did make a display of military force in Washington to overawe Congress. I presume this was a part of the system of intimidation for which he allowed himself to be used by the office-holders, and which he intended to act upon public opinion through the fear of disturbance, as well as upon Congress. But it is safe to say that what-ever the effects they produced, they did not prevent Mr. Tilden from taking the oath of office. The fear that he would do so, which induced the Republicans to swear their candidate into office privately on the Saturday previous to the commencement of his term of office, besides repeating the ceremony at the inauguration, was born of that consciousness which causes the wicked to flee when no man pursueth. I was aware that about that time Mr. Tilden's house was besieged by emissaries of the press and the telegraph to know if the rumors to that effect which prevailed in Washington were true. This was a species of curiosity which I believe Mr. Tilden did not consider it any part of his duty to relieve."

The following lines from the austere muse of J. Russell Lowell in the satire entitled "Tempora Mutantur" were widely quoted in the columns of the Massachusetts press during the campaign of 1876:

The Ten Commandments had a meaning then,
Felt in their bones by least considerate men,
Because behind them in public consciences stood,
And without wincing made their mandates good,
But now that statesmanship is just a way,
To dodge the primal curse, and make it pay;

Since the office means a kind of patent drill,
To force an entrance to the nation's till;
And peculation something rather less
Risky than if you spelt it with an S;
Now that to steal by law is grown an art,
Whom rogues our sires, their milder sons call 'smart.'

"The public servant who has stolen or lied,
If called on may resign with honest pride.
An unjust favor put him in, why doubt
Disfavor as unjust has put him out?
Even if indicted, what is that but fudge,
To him who counted in the election judge"
Whitewashed, he quits the politician's strife,
At ease in mind, with pockets filled for life."

Mr. Lowell was one of the Republican presidential electors of Massachusetts, and from the lofty moral standard by which he had been in the habit of judging public men, the suspicion obtained the currency among his friends in the press that he would refuse to cast his vote for Hayes, which would have resulted in electing Tilden.

Note: President would not rhyme with "fudge."

In a letter to Leslie Stephen, written December 4, and nearly a month after the presidential election, Mr. Lowell thus excuses himself for casting his electoral vote for Hayes.

"There was a rumor, it seems, that I was going to vote for Tilden. But in my own judgment I have no choice, and am bound in honor to vote for Hayes, as the people who chose me expected me to do. They did not choose me because they had confidence in my judgment, but because they knew what that judgment would be. If I had told them that I should vote for Tilden They would never have nominated me. It is a plain question of trust. The provoking part of it is that I tried to escape nomination all I could, and only did not decline because I thought it would be making too much fuss over a trifle." "Letters of James Russell Lowell.

The frauds disclosed after the election, by which a majority of the electors was secured for Hayes, did not, however, prevent Mr. Lowell's acceptance of the mission to Spain at the hand of President Hayes; to prove, perhaps, that the allegation of his muse,

"That statesmanship is just a way

To doge the primal curse, and make it pay,"

has its honorable exceptions.

In further justice to Mr. Lowell it deserves to be recorded that he has a very respectable precedent for lending his name and reputation to bolster the administration of the only spurious President in our annals.

In an old life of Charles James Fox I have read the following entry:

"1781, June 20. Sold by auction, the library of Charles James Fox, which had been taken in execution. Amongst the books was Mr. Gibbon's first volume of Roman History, which appeared, by title-page, to have been given by the author to Mr. Fox, who had written the following anecdote:

"The author (Gibbon), at Brooke's, said there was no salvation for this country till six heads of the principal persons in the administration were laid on the table. Eleven days after, this gentleman accepted the place of Lord of Trade under those very ministers, and has acted with them ever since."

If fame for its own sake, if live long in the memory of man, be an end in itself worth toiling for, Tilden was to be congratulated upon the decision of the Electoral Commission, for it was the means of conferring upon him an historic prominence which the most successful administrations of the presidential office could not have assured him. The poet Martial tells us that the name of Mucius Scaevola, who had thrust his right arm in the fire to punish it for having taken the life of another by mistake for that of the royal invader of his country, would have found its way to the "wallet in which Time carries, on his back, alms for oblivion," had the avenging dagger reached the heart of King Porsenna, for whom it was intended.

"Major deceptae fama est et gloria dextrae

Si non errasesett, fecerat illa minus.

So the action of the Electoral Commission has conferred upon Mr. Tilden the unique distinction of being the first – let us hope the last – President elect of the United States feloniously excluded from the chief magistracy; a distinction which like the banishment of Aristides, the assassinations of Caesar, of Henry IV. Of France, of Lincoln, and of Carnot, makes it one of the conspicuous and indestructible landmarks of history.

"Greater the glory and eke the fame
Of Scaevola's hand deceived,
Had it not missed it patriot aim,
The less it had achieved."

Appendix A

DRAFT OF THE ADDRESS PREPARED FOR THE MINORITY OF THE ELECTORAL COMMISSION OF 1877 - In this instance the minority was the Democratic Party even though the Democratic Party controlled the House of Representative. There were seven Democrats and eight Republicans; which gave the deciding vote to Hayes to steal the election from Samuel Tilden by one electoral vote.

Address of and BY THE HONORABLE JOSIAH G. ABBOTT, L.L.D. – Massachusetts – House of Representatives and a member of the Electoral Commission.

To the People of the United States:

The minority of the joint commission established by the act of Congress of January 27, 1877, to decide questions arising in the count of the electoral votes, desire to address the people of the whole country on the subjects submitted to and decided by that commission.

No more important questions can ever come before any tribunal or people for consideration and determination. Upon their determination depends who shall be President of this country, whether he shall owe that great office to the free, hones choice of the people, or to bribery, forgery, and gross fraud.

The minority of that commission, by the law establishing it, had no opportunity of reporting the reasons for their action to the two Houses of Congress. The presence of a stenographer at these consultations was denied, so that record thereof exists. No way is open to those who did not join in, but on the contrary protested against, the decisions of the commission, to make public their protest except by this address. The returns of the electoral vote of four States – Florida, Louisiana, Oregon, and South Carolina – were submitted to and decided upon by the commission.

FLORIDA

In the case of Florida there were three certificates. The first, signed by the Governor, certified that the four Hayes electors were elected according to the law of Florida and the acts of Congress. The second was signed by the Attorney-General, and the third by the Governor elected on the seventh of November last; both certified the election of the Tilden electors. The Attorney General was one of the three persons first canvassing the votes.

To the third certificate were attached certified copies of all the returns of votes form every precinct in the State, which were originally made to the Secretary of the State, together with an act of the Legislature providing for a new canvass of the vote according to the law as it had been decided by the Supreme Court, and the result of the new canvass thus ordered.

It was offered to be proved, and it was not denied that such was the fact that by counting all the votes returned to the Secretary of State, according to law of Florida as expounded by the Supreme Court, the Tilden electors had been duly elected.

It was offered to be proved, and was not denied, that the Tilden electors commenced proceedings in *quo warranto* (noun : a hearing to determine by what authority someone has an office or franchise or liberty) against the Hayes electors in the court of that State having jurisdiction by its constitution, notice of which was served on the latter before they gave their votes, and as soon as they were declared elected, and which was prosecuted to this judgment – that the Hayes electors had not been elected and had no title to the office, but that the Tilden electors had legally elected and were entitled to the office.

It was offered to be proved, and was not denied, that the two canvassers who had made the certificate of election of the Hayes electors, which by the law of Florida was made on *prima facie (adv.* - At first sight; before closer inspection) evidence, had erred in their construction of the law and exceeded their jurisdiction by so doing, in their canvass of votes on which the certificate was based.

Thus if was offered to be proved, and the facts were not denied, that the Governor's certificate given to the Hayes electors was false, and that the determination and certificate of two of the three who made the Board of Canvassers was false in fact and in violation of the laws of Florida, and that in making it the two had exceeded their jurisdiction. It was offered to be proved that the Supreme Court of Florida had, in effect, decided that the two canvassers had made a false certificate and exceeded their jurisdiction, and that the Circuit Court had so decided. It was offered to be proved that both the Legislation and the executive of the State had so determined, and had attempted by all means in their power to prevent the State being defrauded of its true and real vote.

The majority of the commission decided that the determination and certificate of two of a board of three canvassers, with ministerial powers only, and which by law was prima facie, not conclusive, evidence must stand and decide the great question of the presidency, although it could clearly be proved to be false in fact, and that in making it the two canvassers had exceeded their jurisdiction and authority, as held by the Supreme Court of the State, and although the Legislature and Governor had both declared it false , and that by giving effect to it the State would be defrauded of its true and real vote; and although the electors, in whose favor it was made, had been declared by the courts not to have been elected. The injustice of the decision was the more marked and flagrant by contrast. All the State officers, from the Governor down, who were voted for on the same ticket with the Tilden electors, and been counted out by the same two canvassers, at the same time, and by the same canvass by which the latter were counted out, had been declared elected by the action of the highest court of the State, and are now and have been holding their several offices to the general contentment of the citizens of Florida. But the Hayes electors alone are permitted by this decision to consummate the wrong, and act in offices to they were never elected.

Against this decision of the commission the undersigned protested and now protest as wrong in law, bad in morals, and worse in the consequences which it entails on a great country.

It gives absolute power to two inferior ministerial (*Law.* Of, relating to, or being a mandatory act or duty admitting of no personal discretion or judgment in its performance officers) officers to withhold their determination till the day when the electoral vote is cast, as was done in this case, and then give the vote of a State to a candidate who has never received it, as was done in this case, and tells the people there is no redress (To set right; remedy or rectify) for such and outrage.

It is the decision admirably calculated to encourage fraud, and ensure its being perpetrated with success and impunity (Exemption from punishment, penalty, or harm).

It is a decision by which the people of a State may be defrauded and robbed of their dearest rights by a few unprincipled wretches, and be then compelled to acquiesce in the great wrong.

It is a decision claimed to be based on the doctrine of State rights, but, in fact, is in direct conflict with that great doctrine, for by it States and the people of States can be stripped of their rights and liberties, with no power to resist.

We protest against the Finally because by it the people f the whole United States are defrauded and cheated; because by it a person is put into it the great office of President, who has never been chosen according to the Constitution and law, and whose only title depends on the false and fraudulent certificate of two men in the State of Florida, instead of a majority of legal voices of the whole people, declared through and by their electoral college.

LOUISIANA

In the case of Louisiana, the decision of a majority of the commission is a stupendous wrong to the people of that State, and all the other States, and in defiance of all right, justice, law, and fair dealing among men.

The law of that State establishes a Returning Board to consist of five persons of different parties, with power to fill vacancies, and to canvass and compile returns of votes from the different parishes and precincts, and declare the result. The board is given power and jurisdiction – provided affidavits are annexed to and received with the return from any precinct or parish – to inquire whether intimidation has existed, and if it is established to throw out the return for such parish; but this jurisdiction is carefully confined to cases where affidavits are attached to and returned with the returns with the returns of the votes; in no other case whatsoever is the power to reject votes given.

It was offered to be proved, and was not denied, that the board giving the certificate to the Hayes electors consisted of four persons – all of the Republican party – instead of the five persons of different parties, as required by law; that these four members had been requested by Democrats to fill the vacancy with a Democrat, but had uniformly refused to do so.

It was offered to be proved, also, that this board of four persons- all of the Republican party- in order to perpetrate the frauds with ease and impunity, employed five disreputable persons as clerks and assistants, all of whom had been convicted, or were under indictment, for various offences, ranging from subornation of perjury up to murder. Indictment, at least, if not conviction, seemed the only admitted qualification of employment by that extraordinary board.

It was offered to be proved, and was not denied, that this board, in order to give the certificate of election to the Hayes electors, had rejected ten thousand votes, and this was done, although not a return thrown out had been accompanied by the requisite affidavit to give jurisdiction to act at all.

It was offered to be proved that the members of this Returning Board, in order to give the certificate to Hayes electors had resorted to and used affidavits known by them to be false and forged, had themselves been guilty of forgery, and had been paid for making their determination, thus adding bribery to the catalogue of their crimes.

Numerous other corrupt and fraudulent practices were offered to be proved against the members of this Returning Board, among the least of which was a wicked conspiracy to rob the people of Louisiana of their rights and liberties.

The decision of a majority of the commission rejected all this evidence and held that the certificate of election given to the Hayes electors must stand, and could not be inquired into, if all such offers of proof could be substantiated.

By that decision the people of the United States are told that the certificate of a board constituted in direct defiance of the law establishing it, and made by grasping a jurisdiction never granted to it, arrived at by forgery, perjury, wicked conspiracy, and the grossest frauds, and finally bought and paid for,

must stand, and cannot be set aside; although steeped in sin and iniquity, it
must make the chief magistrate of a great, free, and intelligent people.

The undersigned protest against this decision, also, as bad law, worse in morals, and absolutely ruinous in its consequences.

They denounce it in the presence of the people of the United States, and in the face of the world, because if intended and designed for such a purpose, it could not have been more cunningly contrived than it is to encourage the grossest frauds, conspiracies, and corruptions in the election of a President.

They denounce it, because it will debase the national character, deaden the public conscience, and encourage fraud and corruption in all public and private transactions and business of the people.

They denounce it, because for the first time it declares to the people by their organic law, the Constitution, it is ordained that a man may seek for, obtain, and hold this great office of chief magistrate of two and forty millions of freemen by fraud and cheating.

Nay, more , that he may openly buy the votes to elect himself, and pay down the price when the purchase is consummated by the count by the two Houses of Congress, and call them to witness the payment; and that there is no help for it but revolution.

They denounce it, because, in effect, it puts up the great office of President at auction, and says to the whole world that it may be bought in safety, and that there is no way known to man by which the title by purchase can be disputed or gainsaid (to declare false; deny).

OREGON

In the Oregon case, a certificate signed by the Governor and Secretary of State, and under the great seal of the State, certified to the election of two Hayes and one Tilden elector. The three Hayes electors produced no certificate of election signed by any person – only a certificate of certain results – from which it was claimed that it could be inferred who were elected. The law of Oregon required a list of the persons elected to be signed by the Governor and Secretary of State, under the great seal, and this requirement, as well as that of the acts of Congress, was fully met and satisfied by the fires certificate. There was no certificate in the second case in any manner complying with the laws of Oregon or the acts of Congress. Yet by the decision of the commission the first certificate was rejected and the second taken, although clearly neither in conformity with State or Federal law.

The undersigned voted against counting the vote of the Tilden elector, because, notwithstanding the certificate of the Governor and Secretary of State, they were satisfied he had not been elected by the people of Oregon, and that his vote would not have been the true vote of that State.

The majority of the commission decided to set aside and reject the certificate and return, precisely the same in character that they had holden to be conclusive against all evidence in the Florida and Louisiana cases. They adopted and acted on a certificate insufficient if they regarded their former rulings, under any law, State or National.

The undersigned denounce the Oregon decision as utterly at war with and reversing the rule established in the former two cases, and because it changes the law to meet the wants of the case, establishing different rules applicable to the same facts to bring about a desired result.

In the Florida case, where the evidence failed to establish the fact, the majority of the commission voted to receive evidence to prove one elector held an office of profit and trust under the United States when appointed.

In the Louisiana case, where there was no doubt that the two electors held such office when appointed, it was voted not to receive evidence of the fact, because it was not offered to be proved that they continued to hold such offices where they voted.

Apparently, the rules change as the requirements of the case change.

SOUTH CAROLINA

In South Carolina, the undersigned voted against the Tilden electors being declared elected, because they had not received a majority of the votes of the people.

In that case it was offered to be proved, in substance, that the United States troops in large numbers were sent to the State before the election, for the purpose of influencing and controlling the votes to be given thereat (Adv - At that place, there), by interfering with and overawing the people, and that the militia of the State was used for the same purpose; that the polls were surrounded by armed bands, who by violence and force prevented any exercise of the right of suffrage (Noun-The right or privilege of voting; franchise) except on one side; in fact, that the election was controlled by the armed forces of the State and Nation, and a resort to all manner of brutality, violence, and cruelty, and was not free.

The majority of the commission refuse to admit the evidence, on grounds that would fairly warrant a President of the United States in using the whole army to take possession of all the ballot-boxes in any State, and allow no voting except for himself if he was a candidate for re-election., or for his party, and which would require both Houses of Congress to recount the vote so obtained, and to give him the fruits of such a willful and wicked violation of all constitutional law and right.

If any decision better calculated to destroy the liberty of a free people, to destroy all faith in a Republican form of government, a government of the people by the people, could be devised and contrived, the under-signed have not been able to discover it.

They denounced the decision as an outrage upon the rights of all the people, and, if sustained, and acted on, as the utter ruin of our institu-tions and government.

The foregoing is a brief statement of the action of the commission. To defeat that action the undersigned have done all in their power. They protest against it before it was accomplished, and they protest against it now.

They know the commission was established to receive the evidence, not to shut it out.

They know the conscience of this great people was troubled by fear that any one should obtain the high office of President by fraud, cheating, and conspiracy, and that it demanded that the charges and counter-charges of corrupt practices in reference to the election in three States should be honestly investigated and inquired into, not established and sanctified, by refusing all inquiry and examination.

They know the conscience of the whole people approved the law estab-lishing the commission, nay, hailed it with joy, because it established, as all believed, a fair tribunal, to examine, to inquire into, and determine the charges of fraud and corruption in the election of three States; and they believe that this conscience has been terribly disappointed and shocked by the action of the commission, which establishes fraud and legalizes it perpetration, instead of inquiring into and condemning it.

The undersigned believe the action of the majority of the commission to be wrong, dangerous, nay, ruinous in its consequences and effects.

It tends to destroy the rights and liberties of the States and United States and the people thereof; because by it States may be robbed of their votes for President with impunity, and the people of the United States have foisted upon them a chief magistrate, not by their own free choice honestly expressed, but by practices too foul to be tolerated in a gambling hell.

By the action of the commission the American people are commanded to submit to one as their chief magistrate one who was never elected by their votes, whose only title depends on fraud, corruption, and conspiracy.

A person so holding that great office is a *usurper* (noun - one who seizes and holds (the power or rights of another, for example) by force and without legal authority) and should not be and will be so held by the people. As much as a usurper as if he had signed and held it by military force; in either case, he equally holds against the consent of the people.

Let the people rebuke and overrule the action of the commission. The only hope of the country rests on this being done, and done speedily and effectually, so it may never become a precedent to sustain wrong and fraud in the future.

It is the first and highest duty of all good citizens who love their country to right this foul wrong, as soon as it may be done under the Constitution and laws.

Let it be done so thoroughly, so signally, so effectually, that no encouragement shall be given to put a second time so foul a blot on our nation escutcheon (Noun - A shield or shield-shaped emblem bearing a coat of arms).

The Last Will and Testament of Samuel Jones Tilden

Died August 4, 1886

Mindful of the uncertainty of life, and beginning now in the full possession of all the faculties of mind and memory, I Samuel J. Tilden of Graystone, in the city of Yonkers, county of Westchester and State of New York, do hereby make, publish, and declare this my last Will and Testament, in the manner and form following, that is to say:

I.   I hereby expressly revoke and cancel any and all other wills heretofore made by me.

II.   I hereby nominate, constitute, and appoint John Bigelow, of Highland Falls, Andrew H. Greene, and George W. Smith, of the city of New York, Executors and Trustees under this my last Will and Testament.

III.   I direct that the compensation to be paid to and receive by my said Executors and Trustees shall be to each the yearly sum of Five-thousand dollars; but such annual compensation shall be in lieu of and a full satisfaction and discharge for any and all commissions and charges other than actual disbursements to which my Executors and Trustees might or would be entitled in capacity, under the laws of this State, in any and all trusts (including all services in the special Trusts to be constituted under this Will), if their compensation were not hereby fixed and agreed upon as aforesaid; that any sum which George W. Smith may receive as my private secretary or as an officer or servant of the York Mining Company or Delphic Iron Company be deducted from his compensation as Executor and Trustee. Such compensation of Five thousand dollars shall be so long as he shall be in performance of the duties of the special Trustee under this Will of my general estate, and as trustee, manager, or director of the corporation hereinafter provided. Such compensation shall be paid out of my general estate so long as it shall remain in the custody of my Executors and Trustees, and by the corporation hereinafter provided, after the residue of my general estate shall be vested in such corporation.

IV.   I will and direct that all the powers and authorities granted in and by this my last Will and Testament to my said Executors and Trustees shall and may be exercised by a majority of the persons or by the person who shall for the time being lawfully hold and be in the exercise of teh the functions of an Executor and Trustee hereunder.

V.   I request and direct that no bond or security shall be required by any Surrogate, Probate Court, or judge from my Executors and Trustees on account of the non-residence of such Executor and Trustee, or either of them, within the jurisdiction of such Surrogate, Probate Court, or judge, or for any reason whatsoever.

VI.   In case of the death, resignation, or incapacity of either of my said Executors and Trustees, the survivors of them shall immediately appoint a successor by and instrument in writing under their hands and seals; and upon such appointment being made, the person so appointed shall thereupon become and be invested with all the powers, rights, and authorities conferred upon an Executor and Trustee hereby appointed.

VII. I direct my said Executors and Trustees to pay and discharge all my just debts and liabilities out of my personal estate.

VIII. My said Executors and Trustees are directed to constitute the Trusts for specific persons hereinafter more particularly described and defined. My said Executors and Trustees shall be Trustees of the special Trusts by them so constituted; but the said Trusts shall be distinct and separate from the general Trust under this instrument. In their capacity of Trustees of Trusts for specific persons, they shall have power to manage the several Trusts; to collect the income thereof, and to apply the same as herein directed; to sell in their discretion the securities and to reinvest the proceeds thereof.

IX. I hereby direct my said Executors and Trustees to allow my sister, Mrs. Mary B. Pelton, during her natural life, the use of the house number thirty-eight West Thirty-eight Street in the city of New York. I also direct them to pay any mortgage to which the said premises may be now subject. I also direct my said Executors and Trustees to invest two several sums of Fifty thousand dollars each, in separate and distinct Trusts, and to apply the income of the said two Trusts to use of the said Mary B. Pelton during her natural life. Upon the decease of my said sister Mary B. Pelton, the house known as number thirty-eight West Thirty-eighth Street in the city of New York shall be applied to the use of my grand-niece Laura A. Pelton for the remainder of her natural life. Upon the decease of my sister Mary B. Pelton , one of the said Trusts of Fifty thousand dollars shall be applied to the use of my grand niece Laura B. Pelton, unless my said sister Mary B. Pelton shall by her last will and testament have made a different disposition of the same, which she is hereby empowered to do. Upon the decease of the said Laura A. Pelton, if she leave issue, the said house number thirty-eight-West Thirty-eighth Street designated as the first Trust, and the principal of the said second Trust, being Fifty thousand dollars, shall be paid over to the heirs of her body. If she leave no issue the principal of said first Trust, being of the said house number thirty-eight West Thirty-eighth

Street, shall be paid over as she may by her last will and testament direct, and the principal of the said second Trust shall be paid over to the Tilden Trust hereinafter mentioned, if the same shall have been authorized and constituted; or, if the said Tilden Trust shall not be capable of receiving the same, the principal of the said two Trusts shall be applied to such charitable objects as the Trustees for the time being. Of the two said Trusts, may designate. Upon the decease of my sister Mary B. Pelton, the principal of the third Trust, being for Fifty thousand dollars, shall be applied to the use of my niece Caroline B. Whittlesey, during her natural life, and upon her decease shall be paid over to the heirs of her body, if she leave any. If she leave no such heir, the same shall be paid over by her last will and testament she may direct. In addition to the foregoing provisions herein made for the benefit of my sister Mary B. Pelton, my Executors and Trustees shall invest such sum not exceeding fifty thousand dollars as I may hereinafter in writing instruct them to do, and hold the same as a distinct and separate Trust. The Trustees of the said special Trust shall apply the income thereof to the use of the said Mary B. Pelton during her natural life, and after her decease shall pay over the principal sum to the Tilden Trust thereinafter mentioned, if the same shall have authorized and constituted; or if the said Tilden Trust shall not be capable of receiving the same, the principal of the said Trust shall be applied to such charitable objects as the Trustees for the time being of the said Trust may designate.

X.   I direct my said Executors and Trustees to invest Fifty thousand dollars in two special and separate Trusts of Twenty-five thousand dollars each, and apply the income to the said two Trusts to the use of Lucy F. Tilden, widow of my late brother Moses Y. Tilden, during her natural life. Upon her decease, the income of one of the two said Trusts shall be applied to the use of her adopted daughter Adelaide E. Buchanan during her natural life, unless the said Lucy F. Tilden shall by her last will and testament have made a different disposition of the same, which she is hereby empowered to do. Upon the decease of the said Adelaide E. Buchanan, the principal of the said Trust of Twenty-five thousand dollars shall be paid over to the heirs of her body, if she leave any, unless the said Adelaide E. Buchanan shall by her last will and testament have made a different disposition of the same, where she is hereby empowered to do. If she leave no issue, the principal of the said Twenty-five thousand dollars shall be paid over to such person or persons as she may designate by her last will and testament. Upon the decease of the said Lucy F. Tilden, the principal of the other Trust of Twenty-five thousand dollars shall be disposed of as hereinafter directed. --My Executors and Trustees are directed to convey to Adelaide E. Buchanan the obligations of her husband for Five thousand dollars which I loaned to him some years ago. In addition to the other provisions made in this instrument for the benefit of the said Adelaide E. Buchanan, my Executors and Trustees are also directed to set apart Twenty thousand dollars in the First Mortgage bonds of the Oregon Short Line Railroad Company as a special Trust for the benefit of the said Adelaide E. Buchanan. The Trustees of said special Trust shall apply the income thereof to the use of the said Adelaide E. Buchanan during her natural life, and after her decease shall dispose of the same as in this instrument in hereafter directed.

XI. I hereby direct my said Executors and Trustees to invest the sum of Fifty thousand dollars, to be known as the Sixth Trust, and to apply the income of the same to the use of Susan G. Tilden, the widow of my brother Henry A. Tilden, during her natural life. Upon her decease the income of the same shall be applied to the use of my niece Henrietta A. Swan, during her natural life, unless that the said Susan G. Tilden shall by her last will and testament have made a different disposition of the same, which she is hereby empowered to do. Upon the decease of the said Henrietta A. Swan, the principal of the said Trust shall be paid over to the heirs of her body, if she leave any, unless the said Henrietta A. Swan shall by her last will and testament have made a different disposition of the same, which she is entitled to do. If she leave no issue, then the principal of the said Trust of Fifty thousand dollars shall be paid over as she may direct by her last will and testament, which she is hereby empowered to do.

XII.   I direct that my said Executors and Trustees shall vest in a special Trust for the benefit of my niece Caroline B. Whittlesey One hundred shares of the stock of the Cleveland & Pittsburg Railroad Company standing in my name as Trustee, but for which she holds the power of attorney from me to collect the income thereof. The Trustees of the said special Trust shall apply the income thereof to the use of the said Caroline B. Whittlesey during her natural life; and upon her decease they shall pay over the proceeds of the said stock to the heirs of the body of my said niece Caroline B. Whittlesey, if she leave any, and if she no such heir pay over or assign the same to such person as she may be her last will and testament direct.

XIII.   I also direct my said Executors and Trustees to assign to the said Caroline B. Whittlesey my interest in the Delphic Iron Company, whether consisting of stock or loans, counting the same at cost and interest, and also assign all sums her husband William A. Whittlesey may be owing to me at the time of my decease for loans or advances to him or for which he may be liable. I also direct my said Executors and Trustees to invest a sum sufficient to make with the stock in and loans to the Delphic Iron Company and the said loans and advances to the said William A. Whittlesey, or for which he may be liable the sum of Fifty thousand dollars in a special Trust for the benefit of the said Caroline B. Whittlesey. The Trustees of the said special Trust shall apply the income of the said special Trust to the use of the said Caroline B. Whittlesey during her natural life, and after her decease shall pay over the same to the heirs of her body, if she leaves any. If she leaves no such heirs then they shall pay over the same as she may by her last will and testament direct.

XIV.   I direct that my said Executors and Trustees shall vest in a special Trust for the benefit of my niece Henrietta A. Swan

One hundred shares of the stock of the Cleveland & Pittsburg Railroad Company standing in my name as Trustee, but for which she holds the power of attorney from me to collect the income thereof. The Trustees of the said special Trust shall apply the income thereof to the use of the said Henrietta A. Swan during her natural life; and upon her decease they shall pay over the proceeds of the said stock to the heirs of the body of my said niece Henrietta A. Swan, if she leave any, and if she no such heir pay over or assign the same to such person as she may be her last will and testament direct.--I also direct my said Executors and Trustees to invest the sum of Fifty thousand dollars as a special Trust for the use of my said niece Henrietta A. Swan during her natural life, and after her decease shall pay over the same to the heirs of her body, unless she in her last will and testament shall otherwise direct, which she is hereby empowered to do. If she leaves no such heir the said principal shall be disposed of as hereinafter provided.

XV.   I hereby request the heirs-at-law of my late brother Moses Y, Tilden to unite in conveying to Lucy F. Tilden his widow, for her use during her natural life, the dwelling house in which he formerly resided at New Lebanon, with about thirty acres of land adjacent thereto, and I direct my Executors and Trustees to join in such conveyance in my behalf.------ ------------------------------I hereby request the heirs of my late brother Moses Y. Tilden, and the heirs of my late brother Henry A. Tilden and my sister Mary B. Pelton or her heirs, to unite in conveying to my Executors and Trustees the residue of the lands formerly owned by my father, Elam Tilden, or subsequently acquired by my late brother Moses Y. Tilden other than the thirty acres, or acquired by my late brother Henry A. Tilden other than the lands adjacent to his dwelling- house or used in connection with his manufactories, and excepting also the land upon which a stone building heretofore uses as a school was erected by my late brother Henry A. Tilden. I hereby direct my Executors and Trustees to cause said conveyances to be executed as a condition precedent to the payment of the legacies hereby given. My object is to keep the landed property together and in the family, and I direct my Executors and Trustees to apply the same use of my nephews George H. Tilden and Samuel J. Tilden, second, during their natural loves. After their decease the same shall be disposed of as they or the survivor of them in their last will and testament direct.

XVI.   I authorize my said Executors and Trustees, at such time as they may deem judicious, to release to my said nephews George H. Tilden and Samuel J. Tilden, second, a debt which they owe to me for cash advances lately made by me to them in their business now amounting with interest to the sum of about Thirty-four thousand dollars, and also a mortgage which I hold against them now amounting with interest to about Thirty-three thousand dollars. ----------------- --I direct my said Executors and Trustees to pay certain notes given many years ago by my late brothers Moses Y. Tilden and Henry A. Tilden to Catherine H. Pierson, the principal of which I afterwards guaranteed to save my mother form endorsing the same, which said notes have been assumed by my nephews George H. Tilden and Samuel J. Tilden, second, who will be relieved by the payment thereof.

XVII.   I direct my said Executors and Trustees to set apart the sum of Seventy-five thousand dollars as a special Trust for the benefit of my nephew George H. Tilden. The income of the said special Trust shall be applied by the Trustees thereof to the use of the said George H. Tilden during his natural life. Upon his decease, the said Fund shall be paid over to the heirs of the body of the said George H. Tilden, if he leave any. If he leave no such heir, then my nephew Samuel J. Tilden, second, him survive, the said Fund shall be applied by the Trustees of the said Fund the use of the said Samuel J. Tilden, second, and upon his decease the said Fund shall be paid over to the heirs of his body, if he leave any. If he leave no such heir the said Fund shall be paid over as he in his last will and testament may direct.

XVIII.   I direct my said Executors and Trustees to set apart the sum of Seventy-five dollars as a special Trust for the benefit of my nephew Samuel J. Tilden, second. The income of the said special Trust shall be applied by the Trustees thereof to the use of the said Samuel J. Tilden, second during his natural life. Upon his decease the said Fund shall be paid over to the heirs of his body, if he leave any. If he leave no such heir, then if my nephew George H. Tilden survive him, the said Fund shall be applied by the Trustees of the said Fund to the use of the said George H. Tilden, and upon his decease the said Fund shall be paid over to heirs of his body, if he leave any. If he leave no such heir the aid Fund shall be paid over as he is his last will and testament may direct.

XIX. I direct my said Executors and Trustees to set apart the sum of One hundred and fifty thousand dollars as a special Trust for the benefit of my niece Ruby S. Tilden. The income of the said special Trust shall be applied by the Trustees thereof to the use of the said Ruby S. Tilden during her natural life. Upon her decease the said Fund shall be paid over to the heirs of her body, if she leave any. If she leave no such heir, then if my niece Susan G. Tilden her survive, the said Fund shall be applied by the Trustees of the said Fund to the use of Susan G. Tilden, and upon her decease the said Fund shall be paid over to the heirs of her body, if she leave any. If she leave no such heir the said Fund shall be paid over as she in her last will and testament may direct.

XX. I direct my said Executors and Trustees to set apart the sum of One hundred fifty thousand dollars as a special Trust for the benefit of my niece Susan G. Tilden. The income of the said special Trust shall be applied by the Trustees thereof to the use of the said Susan G. Tilden during her natural life. Upon her decease the said Fund shall be paid over to the heirs of her body, if she leave any. If she leave no such heir, then my niece Ruby S. Tilden her survive, the said Fund to the use of the said Ruby S. Tilden, and up her decease the said Fund shall be paid over to the heirs of her body, if she leave any. If she leave no such heir the said Fund shall be paid over as she in her last will and testament may direct.

XXI. I direct my said Executors and Trustees not to enforce against the estate of my brother, the late Henry A. Tilden, or against the estate of my late brother Moses Y. Tilden, loans which I heretofore made to them, amounting to about Three hundred thousand dollars; but to release and cancel the same wherever the said Executors and Trustees shall be requested in writing to do so by George H. Tilden and Samuel J. Tilden, the second sons of the late Henry A. Tilden, or by the survivor of them.

XXII. I direct my said Executors and Trustees to set apart a separate Trust the sum of Twenty-five thousand dollars for the benefit of Anna J. Gould during her natural life. In case she shall be with me exercising care over me during the rest of my life, I direct that the said sum of Twenty-five thousand dollars be increased to One hundred thousand dollars. The income of the said special Trust shall be applied by the Trustees thereof to the use of the said Anna J. Gould during her natural life. Upon her decease one-half of the said Fund shall be paid over as the said Anna J. Gould may by her last will and testament direct. The other half shall be paid over as herein directed.

XXIII. I direct my said Executors and Trustees to set apart Fifty thousand dollars of First Mortgage six per cent International and Great Northern Railroad Company bonds, and Fifty thousand dollars of the First Mortgage binds of the Oregon Short Line Railroad Company guaranteed by the Union Pacific Railway Company, as a special Trust fir the benefit if my friend Miss Marie Celeste Stauffer, daughter if Isaac Stauffer, Esquire, of New Orleans. The income of the said special Trust shall be applied by the Trustees thereof to the use of the said Marie Celeste Stauffer during her natural life; free form any interference or control of any husband she may have; and upon the decease of the said Marie Celeste Stauffer the Trustees of the said special Trust shall pay over the principal of the said bonds, or assign the same, to the devisees or heirs of the said Marie Celeste Stauffer.

XXIV. In all cases in which the special Trusts are herein directed to be created for the benefit of particular persons and the income directed to be applied by the Trustees of special Trusts. It is hereby declared that the said income shall be kept free form all pledges, incumberances, or anticipation thereof, and every such pledge, incumberance, or anticipation shall be void. The Trustees of the said special Trusts are hereby empowered and directed to suspend payment of such income during the existence of any such pretended pledge, incumberance, or anticipation. In all cases in which such special Trust shall be for the benefit of any female, the said income shall be kept free from the control or interference of any husband which the said female now has or may hereafter have; such income being intended to be sacredly devoted to the separate personal use of said female, and is not to be pledged, incumbered, or anticipated by her.

XXV. I direct my Executors and Trustees, in case any special Trust hereby directed to be constituted shall fail in whole or in whole or in part by depreciation of securities, to make the same good out of my general estate, so long as the general Trust to my Executors and Trustees shall continue; and in the case the said Executors and Trustees shall convey any portion of that estate to a corporation designated as the Tilden Trust, or shall vest the same in any Trust or Trusts for charitable purposes to do so on the express condition that the said conveyance shall be subjected to obligations to make good the funds devoted to the said special Trusts, and shall exact from the grantee in every such case an acknowledgement of such obligation and agreement to fulfil the same. This provision is made subject to the condition that the corporation shall be duly authorized by law, by a special act or otherwise, to accept the grant, subject to the obligations herein directed to be imposed upon or assumed by the said corporation. I also direct my said Executors and Trustees to obey such instructions as I may hereafter give them in respect to the allotment or selection of securities for the said special Trusts or any of them.

XXVI. I hereby authorize and direct my Executors and Trustees during the continuance of the trust of my general estate to apply any surplus income to or towards the several special Trusts hereby directed to be constituted in the same manner as they might apply the principal of my said estate to the said purposes.

XXVII. I direct my said Executors and Trustees to apply the use of Henrietta Jones, of Monticello, out of my general estate, a sum not exceeding Five hundred dollars per annum during her natural life, or so long as the Trust embracing my general estate shall continue.

XXVIII. In case John J. Cahill shall remain in my service the residue of my life, I authorize and direct my Executors and Trustees to pay over to him the sum of Five thousand dollars.

XXIX. The Trustees of the said special Trust are hereby authorized form time to time to change the investments hereby directed to be made for the use of specific persons, and to purchase other securities in lieu thereof, except in the cases where the securities are herein designated and appropriated to a specific purpose.

XXX. I authorize my Executors and Trustees to contribute out of my estate to Mrs. Maria Sinnott, for the purpose and the education of the children of her late husband, James P. Sinnott, such sum as they may deem sufficient, not exceeding, however, the sum of Five hundred dollars per annum for five years.

XXXI. I direct my said Executors and Trustees to pay over to such of the following persons as may be in my service at the time of my decease to wit, George Johansen, Henry Gilbert, Edward Riley, Catherine Burke, and Rosa Clark each the sum of One thousand dollars; and to John Lynch, Elizabeth Byrnes, Bridget Gettins, Dennis O'Hare, and Daniel Herr each the sum of Five hundred dollars.

XXXII. I direct to my Executors and Trustees to apply Ten thousand dollars, or such part of it as may be necessary, according to such instruction as I may hereafter to them from time to time give in writing of verbally,

XXXIII. I authorize my Executors and Trustees to cause the establishment of a Library and Free Reading-Room in my native town of New Lebanon in the manner following, that is to say; they shall obtain title to the land on which the building stands which was erected by my brother Henry A. Tilden, and which has been occupied by a school; buying in the mortgage on the same , amounting to Fifteen thousand dollars, and, if necessary, obtaining releases from the heirs of my brother Henry A. Tilden from my sister Mary B. Pelton or her heirs, and from Mrs. Lucy F. Tilden. They shall vest the title in a corporation, if a charter shall be granted on their application to the Legislature, or a corporation can be formed under any general law. My said Executors and Trustees are hereby authorized to require, if needful, proper conveyances to be executed by the heirs of the said Henry A. Tilden or Mary B. Pelton or her heirs and by Lucy F. Tilden as condition precedent to the payment of the legacies herein given to them respectively. They shall also convey to the corporation, if one need be created, any interest which I may have in the said premises. My Executors and Trustees are authorized to expend for the creation and equipment and to invest as a permanent fund to maintain the said Library and Reading-Room the sum of Sixty-five thousand dollars, and any further sum not exceeding Thirty-five thousand dollars which I may in writing instruct my said Executors and Trustees to apply to those objects. They are also authorized to use the said building and endowment hereby provided in part for a school for the training of girls, if they find the same expedient in connection with the Free Library and Reading-Room.

XXXIV.   I hereby authorize my said Executors and Trustees to appropriate out of my estate, in such manner as they may deem most expedient, the sum of Fifty thousand dollars towards the establishment of a Library and Free Reading Room in the city of Yonkers, and such further sum not exceeding Fifty thousand dollars as I may hereafter instruct my said Executors and Trustees to apply to that object. My said Executors and Trustees are requested to apply to the Legislature for a special charter to enable them to carry out this provision or to form a corporation under any general law which in their judgment shall be most desirable.

XXXV.   I request my said Executors and Trustees to obtain as speedily as possible from the Legislator an Act of Incorporation of

an institution to be know as the Tilden Trust, with capacity
to establish and maintain a Free Library and Reading Room
in the city of New York, and to promote such scientific and
educational objects as my said Executors and Trustees may
more particularly designate. Such corporation shall have not
less than five Trustees, with power to fill vacancies in their
number, and in case said institution shall be incorporated
in a form and manner satisfactory to my said Executors and
Trustees during the lifetime of the survivor of the tow lives
in being upon which the Trust of my general estate herein
created is limited to, to wit: the lives of Ruby S. Tilden and
Susan Whittlesey, I hereby authorize my said Executors and
Trustees to organize the said corporation, designate the first
Trustees thereof, and to convey to or apply to the use of the
same, the rest, residue, and remainder of all my real and
personal estate not specifically disposed of by this instrument, or so much thereof as they may deem expedient, but
subject, nevertheless, to the special Trusts herein directed to
be constituted for particular persons, and to the obligations
to make and keep good the said special Trusts, provided that
the said corporation shall be authorized by law to assume
such obligation. But in case such institution shall not be so
incorporated, during the lifetime of the survivor of the said
Ruby S. Tilden and Susan Whittlesey, or if for any cause or
reason my said Executors and Trustees shall deem it inex-
pedient to convey said Rest, residue, and remainder or any
part thereof or to apply the same or any part thereof to the
said institution, I authorize my said Executors and Trustees
to apply the rest , residue, and remainder of my property ,
real and personal, after making good the said special Trusts
herein directed to be constituted, or such portions thereof as
they may not deem it expedient to apply to its use, to such
charitable educational and scientific purposes as in the judgment of my said Executors and Trustees will render the said
rest, residue, and remainder of my property most widely and
substantially beneficial to the interests if mankind.

XXXVI.   I hereby authorize my said Executors and Trustees to reserve
            from any disposition made by this Will such of my books

as they may deem expedient, and to dispose of the same in such manner as in their judgment would have been most agreeable to me; and in such case any of my illustrated books or books of art should be given to or to the care of the institution described in this Will, my said Executors and Trustees shall make suitable regulations to preserve the same from damage and to regulate access thereto. And such disposition shall be subject to such instructions as I may hereinafter in writing give to my said Executors and Trustees.

XXXVII.   In case at any time during the Trust embracing my general estate any interest in any special Trust hereby directed to be constituted shall lapse or no disposition of such interest contained in this instrument shall be effectual to finally dispose of the same, such interest shall go to my said Executors and Trustees to be disposed of under the provisions of this Will, or if the said general Trust shall have ceased, but a corporation designated as the Tilden Trust shall be in operation, such interest shall go to the said corporation.

XXXVIII.   My said Executors and Trustees are hereby invested with the following powers: 1) To manage the funds herein directed to be invested in the Trusts for specific persons until such investments shall have been made, with like authorities as in cases of other portions of my estate. 2) To sell and dispose from time to time, in their discretion, of such parts and parcels of the real estate and other property hereby devised, given, and bequeathed to them as they shall deem advisable, and so sell and dispose of the same at public or private sale, at such price or prices, and upon such terms as to mode, time, and security of payment, as they shall deem proper, and to sign, seal, execute, and deliver all proper and necessary conveyances therefore. 3) From time to time to invest and reinvest all moneys belonging to my estate whether derived form sales of said devised and bequeathed property or otherwise in such manner as they may deem expedient, subject, however, to the same Trusts upon which moneys or property were originally held by my said Executors and Trustees.

XXXIX.   I hereby devise and bequeath to my said Executors and Trustees, and to their successors in the Trust hereby created, and to the survivors and survivor of them. All the rest and residue of all the property, real and personal, or whatever name or nature and wheresesoever situated, if which I may be seized or possessed, or to which I may be entitled at the time of my decease which may remain after instituting the several Trusts for the benefit of specific persons, and after making provisions for the specific bequests and objects as herein directed. To have and to hold the same unto my said Executors and Trustees and to their successors in the Trust hereby created and the survivors and survivor of them in trust to possess, hold, manage, and take care of the same during a period not exceeding tow lives in being, that is to say: the lives of my niece Ruby S. Tilden and my grand-niece Susie Whittlesey, and until the decease of the survivor of the said two persons, and after deducting all necessary and proper expenses, to apply the same and the proceeds thereof to the objects and purposes mentioned in this my Will.

XL.   I hereby authorize my Executors and Trustees to apply Ten Thousand dollars to the creation of a trust, the income of which shall be applied to keeping in repair, improving, and adorning the cemetery in the town of New Lebanon in which the most of my near relatives are buried. I request my Executors and Trustees to make available any lawful power which may exist or can be procured for vesting the said cemetery in a corporation, to the end that the appropriation hereby authorized shall be as permanent as possible.

XLI.   I authorize my said Executors and Trustees to cause to be erected a monument which in their judgment and discretion shall seem suitable to my memory, and to defray the expense thereof from my estate.

XLII.   I also authorize my said Executors and Trustees to collect and publish, in such form as they deem proper, my speeches and public documents, and other such writings and papers as they may think expedient to include with the same, which shall be done under their direction. The expenses thereof shall be paid out of my estate. My Trustees and Executors are authorized and empowered to burn and destroy any of my letters, papers, or other documents, whether printed or in manuscript, which in their judgment will answer no useful purpose to preserve.

XLIII.   Since I have made no disposition of my property according to my best judgment and since as most of the devisees of legatees under it are females, it is impossible to foresee under what influences some one or more of them might possibly come; and since it is desirable to avert unseemly or speculative litigations, I hereby declare it to be my will that in case any person, who if I had died intestate would be entitled to any share in my property or estate shall, under any pretence whatever, institute, take or share in any proceeding to oppose the probate of this my last Will and Testament, or to impeach or impair or to set aside or invalidate any of it provisions, any devise or legacy to or for the benefit of such person or persons under this will is hereby revoked, and such person shall be excluded form any participation in and shall not have any share or portion of my property or estate real or personal, and the portion to which such person might be entitled, if I had died intestate or might otherwise be entitled under the provisions of this instrument, shall be devoted to such charitable purposes as my said Executors and Trustees shall designate.

In witness whereof, I, the said Samuel J. Tilden, the above-nametestator, have herein set my hand and seal this twenty-third day of April in the year one thousand eight hundred and eighty-four.

SAMUEL J. TILDEN (seal)

"OFFICE OF THE TILDEN TRUST—

15 GRAMERCY PARK, NY., OCTOBER 22, 1893"

"To the Mayor, Alderman, and Commonalty of the City of New York:

The trustees of the Tilden Trust, incorporated by chapter 85 of the Laws of the State of New York, passed the 21st of March, 1877, respectfully represent,

That the late Samuel J. Tilden having in his will, a copy of which is hereunto annexed, made provisions for his heirs-at-law and certain legatees, sought, by the thirty-fifth article of said instrument, to consecrate the remainder of his estate to the creation of an institution to be know as the Tilden Trust, with capacity to establish and maintain a free library and reading room in the city of New York, and to 'promote such scientific and educational objects as his executors and trustees might more particularly designate.'

That the validity of the thirty-fifth clause of said will was successfully contested by the heirs-at law of the testator and pronounce invalid. Pending such litigation, and in view of the uncertainties, expense, and delays incident to litigation of this character, the trustees of the Tilden Trust deemed it prudent, prior to the argument of the case in the Court of Appeals, to accept the terms of a settlement proffered by one of the parties contesting said will, in virtue of which the Tilden Trust became possessed of about one third of that part of the estate that had been intended by the testator for such trust, from which they expect to realize from two to two and a quarter million dollars, the annual income form which may be moderately estimated at $80,000.

That the trustees of the Tilden Trust are anxious to apply this fund in the way that shall prove most advantageous to the people of the city of New York, and at the same time most strictly conform to the wishes and expectations of the testator as manifested in his will.

That the income of this trust is insufficient to provide suitable buildings for the accommodation of such a library as was contemplated by the testator, and in addition to equip and operate it if suitable accommodations for its installation are provided from other sources.

In view of these facts, and in view of the fact that the city of New York is not only more destitute of library accommodation than any other city of its size in the world, but more destitute than many cities in our own country of far less wealth and population, the undersigned trustees of the Tilden Trust, respectfully invite your honorable bodies to consider the propriety of availing yourselves of this opportunity of establishing a library commensurate with the magnitude and importance of our commercial metropolis, and taking measure to provide for it the requisite accommodations, with the understanding, to which the trustees of the Tilden Trust hereby avow their readiness to become parties, that they will equip and operate such library so soon as such accommodations can be provided.

By order of the Trustees of the Tilden Trust,
John Bigelow,
President

Oct 22, 1892

On the 2nd of May, 1893, Governor Flower approved an act passed by Legislature authorizing the Commissioners of Public Works, on the request of the Commissioners of Public Buildings, to cause the old city hall 'to be removed, re-erected, furnished, and equipped elsewhere upon the property therein belonging to the Mayor, Aldermen, and Commonality of the city of New York, with the consent of the Department of Public Parks, if such property shall be subject to the jurisdiction of such department. If said building shall be removed and re-erected, the same shall be done in such manner as said Board of Commissioners shall determine, with alterations as may in their judgment be rendered necessary by the site selected and the purpose to which such re-erected

280

building shall be devoted, and as may be in harmony with the present general architectural features of the exterior of said building.

On the same day the Governor approved of an act authorizing the Department of Public Works, with the sanction of the Board of Estimate and Apportionment, to remove the reservoir from Bryant Park.

On the same day the Governor also approved of an act which authorized the Department of Public Parks, to contract with the Tilden Trust for its use and occupation of any building that may be hereafter erected in pursuance of law upon land belonging to the Mayor, Aldermen, and Commonalty of the city of New York between Fortieth and Forty-second streets and between Fifth and Sixth Avenues in said city, and establishing and maintaining therein a free library, and carrying out the objects and purposes of said corporation.

It was hoped and expected that these measures would result in soon giving to the commercial metropolis of the United States a library commensurate with its magnitude, needs and resources, and thus fitly commemorate its obligations to one of its most eminent citizens and generous benefactors. That prospect, unhappily, has been indefinitely postponed by the repeal of the act authorizing the removal of the old city hall. In what way, if any, the municipal government will give effect to the disposition it manifested in 1893 to provide a suitable structure for the Tilden library neither the Trustees nor the public have as yet an intimation.

www.ingramcontent.com/pod-product-compliance
Lightning Source LLC
Chambersburg PA
CBHW031149270326
41931CB00006B/198